"Suzanne F. Stevens takes _____ journey where she shares strategies on ____ to activate your purpose, harness your mission, and lead at home or abroad a social, economic, and environmental initiative. A message for anyone who wants to impact society consciously and sustainably."

Aaron Hurst, Co-Founder & CEO of Imperative, Author of the Purpose Economy and Founder of Taproot Foundation

"Unforgettable true stories and adventures await you on these pages as you learn how conscious-contributions™ can change your organization, and ultimately the world.

The wisdom of African women leaders together with Suzanne's inquisitive, insightful, and meaningful deep dive into how to create a sustainable social impact will motivate you to take action in your own community or business. As an NFP leader you will gain insight into cultivating the opportunities that will lead to the growth of a successful organization.

If you are in the for-profit or not-for-profit world and seeking some inspiration — read this book!"

Susan Slezak Kawa, BScPT, MA
Executive Director of charitable, NFP organization for 20 years

"Make your contribution count for you. me. we" had to be written by a woman. It questions the very foundations upon which we build perceptions of "you" and "me" in a safe and inclusive dialogue that also calls for accountability. In Humility and vulnerability, Suzanne opens up to invite in the wisdom that is gained from diversity. Against the prejudice of prevailing culture, by acknowledging the contributions African women are making to solving the world's common challenges, Suzanne harnesses the power in "you" and "me" to create a courageous new reality of "we," where all things are possible, and nothing can stop us."

Modesta Mahiga-Mbughuni, multi-leadership award recipient, named One of Africa's 'Movers and Shakers', Author, Speaker, and Africa Human Capital Expert

"Now more than ever we need to look to cultures who live connected in communities with a spirit of reciprocity, love and caring. Join Suzanne's storytelling tour to meet inspiring leaders who impart wisdom from the ages. You'll find insights to help you design how you will make your contribution in this one amazing life we are gifted."

Vicki Saunders,
SheEO Founder

Advanced acclaim

"This book is a fantastic read whether you are leading a not-for-profit, social enterprise, or for-profit company. Those of us in the West tend to have the attitude that we need to "teach" others; this book is refreshing in sharing what we can learn.

The inspiring lessons from Suzanne and the accomplished African leaders will ignite your ambition to do good while doing good work to ensure that your contribution counts. As an entrepreneur, I especially valued the messages surrounding conscious leadership and collaboration – that we need to collaborate with a multitude of stakeholders to compete more effectively while not deviating from our mission. You will find yourself energized with a renewed focus on the positive ripple effect that you can create when you work collaboratively with others."

Jennifer Spear, MBA
Founder of Clean Slate Strategies, Keynote Speaker and Facilitator

"Suzanne F Stevens demonstrates the rare ability to see Africa through African eyes, feel with an African heart, and candidly express this without losing her personal Canadian and global perspective.

Suzanne chronicles, in a vivid explosion of prose, the diverse beauty and wealth that is Africa and the immeasurable potential lying in wait when the mother continent comes into maturity. The showcase of rich African culture, norms, and practice, through her powerful women role models, however simple, however accomplished, make this **my** book, about **my** Africa, by **my** friend."

Joanne Mwangi-Yelbert is an award-winning CEO and Founder of top Marketing and PR team, PMS Group Africa Ltd, a Judge and Equity Investor on Kenya's TV show "The Lion's Den" as well as a powerful advocate for women's economic success.

"This powerful book is both timely and engaging for us to embrace and provide opportunities for feminine energy worldwide. Suzanne will take you to unexpected places both geographically and in shifting your contribution perspective. You will discover how to tap into your purpose and exploit it to benefit the community and incorporate a well-aligned mission into your life and career. Her captivating storytelling reminds you about the critical importance of ensuring your legacy lens is holistic, realistic, and consistent so that you will make conscious-contributions™.

This is a must-read book for any organization!"

Cate L, Collins
Powerful Journey Consulting, Leadership Mindset Mastery

Advanced acclaim

"Suzanne has demonstrated that she is courageous, passionate, and determined to provide a fresh look at practical solutions and those that provide them. Through the lens of trailblazing women, she exposes how to provide support to people who are in need. She shares how to help diverse groups of people without making the beneficiaries dependent on a benefactor for their wellbeing. This book is a must-read for women or men alike, who want to uplift the life of someone, or a group, sustainably."

**Diane Tompson, President,
The International Alliance for Women (TIAW)**

"No matter where you are in the world, this book provides insightful tips and firsthand stories, sharing the importance of social enterprises and the power of working alongside communities to create sustainable change."

**Roxanne Joyal
CEO at ME to WE**

"Suzanne captures conscious driven leadership, the importance of human connection, and takes us on a masterfully written journey into the success stories of inspiring African women. Through her writing, Suzanne raises the vibration and provides us with references and an opportunity to reflect on how we can contribute consciously to our teams and our communities. Ways we can be the inspiration, make a difference, and lead with a conscious connection."

Jen Scholte, Real Estate Broker/ Team Leader, NLP Master Coach and Past President of the Rotary Club of Collingwood South Georgian Bay

"Make Your Contribution Count is a unique and inspiring read. We all want to give and make a positive impact with our one life but figuring out just how to do that is not so easy. Through deeply inspiring interviews with female leaders in Africa, Suzanne F. Stevens helps us dig into our purposes and figure out how to put them to work in a useful, meaningful, and sustainable way. She shares our responsibility to each other and our communities, a concept that continues to fade over time in our Western culture. We often don't know how to fulfill that need to contribute, but this book changes that."

Shelby Taylor, Founder and CEO of Chickapea, a Certified B Corporation and Women Owned Enterprise

Advanced acclaim

"Suzanne has demonstrated that she is courageous, passionate, and determined to provide a fresh look at practical solutions and those that provide them. Through the lens of trailblazing women, she exposes how to provide support to people who are in need. She shares how to help diverse groups of people without making the beneficiaries dependent on a benefactor for their wellbeing. This book is a must-read for women or men alike, who want to uplift the life of someone, or a group, sustainably."

Diane Tompson, President,
The International Alliance for Women (TIAW)

"No matter where you are in the world, this book provides insightful tips and firsthand stories, sharing the importance of social enterprises and the power of working alongside communities to create sustainable change."

Roxanne Joyal
CEO at ME to WE

"Suzanne captures conscious driven leadership, the importance of human connection, and takes us on a masterfully written journey into the success stories of inspiring African women. Through her writing, Suzanne raises the vibration and provides us with references and an opportunity to reflect on how we can contribute consciously to our teams and our communities. Ways we can be the inspiration, make a difference, and lead with a conscious connection."

Jen Scholte, Real Estate Broker/ Team Leader, NLP Master Coach and Past President of the Rotary Club of Collingwood South Georgian Bay

"Make Your Contribution Count is a unique and inspiring read. We all want to give and make a positive impact with our one life but figuring out just how to do that is not so easy. Through deeply inspiring interviews with female leaders in Africa, Suzanne F. Stevens helps us dig into our purposes and figure out how to put them to work in a useful, meaningful, and sustainable way. She shares our responsibility to each other and our communities, a concept that continues to fade over time in our Western culture. We often don't know how to fulfill that need to contribute, but this book changes that."

Shelby Taylor, Founder and CEO of Chickapea, a Certified B Corporation and Women Owned Enterprise

make your contribution count

for

you · me · we

An Evolutionary Journey Inspired by the Wisdom of Pioneering African Women

Suzanne F. Stevens

Published by YouMeWe Social Impact Group,
an Ignite Excellence Inc. Company

Collingwood, Ontario, Canada

make your contribution count
for you • me • we
Suzanne F. Stevens

Copyright © 2020 by Suzanne F. Stevens.

Published by YouMeWe Social Impact Group,
an Ignite Excellence Inc. Company
we@YouMeWe.ca
Collingwood, ON, Canada L9Y 5B7

All rights reserved. No portion of this book may be reproduced, stored in a retrieval system, or transmitted in any form or by any means electronic, mechanical, photocopy, recording, scanning, or other except for brief quotations in critical reviews or articles, without the prior written permission of the publisher.

FIRST EDITION, 2020

ISBN book – 978-1-9992612-0-7

This book may be purchased in bulk for a book club, conscious-contribution circle, business or organizational promotional use at
https://youmewe.ca/make-your-contribution-count-book/

Photo credits: Michael K. Gingerich and Suzanne F. Stevens

Printed in Canada on 100% recycled paper.

To the African women who led me to the
mission taken — YouMeWe
To the women who walk alongside me.
And to the man who partnered with me.

*To Cate!
Wishing you joy,
meaning, and impact
on your contribution
journey! Thank you for all your support!
#YourContributionCounts
Suzanne F Stevens
Happy International Women's Day!*

Ubuntu – I am because we are

Table of contents

Introduction: The mission taken i

Part 1: you — make your contribution count — consciously 1

1. Make your contribution conscious 2
2. Infuse the social gap with feminine energy 16
3. Amplify the social impact 28
4. Take small actions to cause big reactions 38
5. Consider the contribution consequences 46
6. Choose a channel of contribution to induce consciousness 56
7. Measure what matters 70

Part 2: me — make your contribution count — maximize your meaning 87

8. Embrace your community responsibility 88
9. Explore your purpose 98
10. Discover your purpose 106
11. Unblock blocks to live your purpose 119
12. Enhance your essence 132
13. Capitalize on your cornerstone to propel meaning 145
14. Volunteering the good, the bad, and the opportunity 155
15. Move from messenger to the mission 167

Photos of journey

Part 3: we — make your contribution count — sustainably 179

16. Generate a ripple effect 180
17. Make your conscious-contributions™ sustainable 193
18. Shift from competition to collaboration 209
19. Develop symbiotic partnerships 219
20. Cultivate your capacity to influence support 231
21. Commit through communications 246
22. Create a conscious culture 256
23. All we need is love 271

24. The time is now	279
Acknowledgments	283
About the author	287
YouMeWe resources	288
Glossary to guide your journey	289
Pioneering African women listing and links	293
Endnotes and references	297
Index	305

Introduction
The mission taken

I want to make a difference. Since I was a little girl, all I wanted was to have an impact on the world. I now know I wasn't alone in this burning desire. But, it wasn't until I stopped focusing on what I wanted that I understood the kind of contribution I could make.

On January 20, 2007, 18 Canadian women, and a couple of young adults, arrived in Kenya. A friend, Ruth Douglas, gathered a group of leaders and entrepreneurs to embark on an adventure. Ruth's sister, Lois Shaw, a missionary and marketer for Africa International University (AIU), had designed our experience after living in Kenya herself for 25 years. Our draw to embark on this customized crusade was a little adventure and to connect with the local Kenyan women and children. We wanted to learn about the culture, provide helping hands, and share insights.

On our first day in Kenya, we attended a welcome ceremony with our host, Lois Shaw, the late Dr. Douglas Carew, the Chairman of AIU, along with a dozen wives of Ph.D. students. We all gathered in the chapel.

The wives were in heels, traditional dress, not a hair out of place. We were in our relaxed Western clothing looking like we'd just spent a month on safari.

They hugged us. We shook their hands. They sang. We listened. They danced. We watched. It wasn't until they grabbed our hands to participate in a traditional dance that the celebration began. This day was the first of many days I would follow the lead of African women.

During Dr. Carew's welcome remarks, he shared what he believed to be the most significant issue in Africa.

> The biggest problem in Africa today is not AIDS, poverty, disease, education, or urbanization; the biggest problem is leadership. When moral leaders with integrity and justice arise, then Africa's problems will be solved.[1]

A message like this can force us to pause and reflect on which direction we will take. Dr. Carew's welcoming words propelled me down a new path. At the time, I did not know how far I would travel or how profound the journey would be.

Within a month after receiving this reflective message, I was training a professor, Ph.D. students, and ambitious women on how to fundraise and communicate as leaders. A few months later, I founded the Ignite Excellence Foundation Fund (renamed in 2016 to YouMeWe Foundation Fund) to raise funds to provide university scholarships for prospective women leaders in Africa. The goal of the investment was to establish more leaders with integrity while addressing injustices suffered by women and children. Higher education would build a bridge to more healthy families and more productive communities.

At the time of writing this book, we have provided university scholarships to 27 women in Kenya, the Democratic Republic of the Congo, and South Africa, making a small stride to crossing a vast chasm to establish more women leaders.

After a couple of trips to Kenya, I returned to my influential communication leadership and sales training organization, Ignite Excellence Inc., back in Toronto. I couldn't kick a nagging feeling. By offering free courses at AIU, was I taking a Kenyan's job? Was there an expert in influential communications that could have been paid to provide training services? If I return, what mission would have the desired impact?

A COUPLE OF YEARS later, I became unsettled. Leading a team of consultants and training corporations whose primary focus was to win business and optimize profits was not filling my soul. I longed to immerse myself into an experience that was more fulfilling than seeking the almighty dollar and more significant than my professional achievements.

On March 17, a day after my 42nd birthday, I was experiencing midlife madness. As I sat on my couch looking around, all I could see was stuff — you know, the things you put on your checklist as signs of success. For me that stuff included a convertible, a two-story loft, paintings, a rooftop hot tub with a view of the city and the water, ... (blah, blah, blah).

Throughout my appraisal of my material accomplishments, questions were blaring in my head: "What contribution am I making? What impact am I creating?" I started to cry. Mike, my dear husband, entered the room. He tried to comfort me. I bet he was trying to figure out what he hadn't done for my birthday.

Through the tears, I asked: "Honey, is this it?"

"Is what it?"

"Is this all the impact we will ever make?"

"What do you propose?"

I anxiously rambled, "I feel it's time to do something more meaningful. Let's take one or two years and go back to Africa. We could create a platform for African women with integrity where they could share their insight to help educate future African women leaders.

"What do you think?"

Mike hesitated, and then smiled.

"You know, you will have to take the lead, but I will follow."

It took time for us to get organized. My husband left his leadership position in sports facility management, and I reorganized my training team. Then we sold almost everything.

The mission taken

In March 2011, we embarked on a new mission: to celebrate, cultivate, and inspire future women leaders in developing countries.

This self-funded adventure took us through 14 African countries. We interviewed 70 pioneering women, representing 17 countries. The goal: to build a bridge between young African women seeking to learn, lead, and succeed in life, business, and community, and to provide easy access to accomplished African women's inspiration and wisdom.

WisdomExchangeTv.com a free website which houses interviews with pioneering African women leaders, was constructed to cross the chasm.

AFTER EACH INTERVIEW I was awed and inspired. Each of these pioneers demonstrated perseverance, tenacity, belief, and unwavering dedication to uplift the lives of others through their contributions to their community, country, and continent. Most came from humble beginnings, and yet they had an impressive ability to address human rights violations or create sustainable opportunities for fellow citizens, all while creating a positive ripple effect. Their aspirations took courage, character, and a choice to serve society. It seemed they all embodied the Mahatma Gandhi creed: *Be the change you wish to see in the world.*

Humbled by the social, economic, and environmental impact of all these leaders, I questioned what had taken me so long to contribute actively to society. All I came up with is that in the West, it's often later in life that we talk about leaving a legacy. African women live their legacy; it is how they live their life. They are on the verge of transforming African societies. Each day they *make their contribution count.*

Here, we tend to think we need to *save* Africans. We need to *teach* them. As we embark on this journey, let's be open to learn from the wisdom of African women pioneers who are conscious-contributors. Let them be our teachers. See how they have contributed to uplifting society in the African context. We can learn how to participate or consciously lead in a worthy cause, not-for-profit or social enterprise at home or abroad.

BEFORE YOUMEWE BECAME OUR ethos, it was a website where Mike and I sporadically shared the experiences of our 20-month journey through Africa. With each interaction, our perspective and beliefs were transformed. Our focus on *me* evolved. *You* and *we* captured our curiosity and took us on a unique adventure, which developed the evolved intention of YouMeWe, from a journal of our journey to a social enterprise and movement.

As a social enterprise, YouMeWe's mandate is to ignite sustainable conscious-contributions™ through what we believe is a receptive entry point to transform society — feminine energy. We aspire to mobilize feminine energy, often found in women-led organizations. Speaking engagements, events, training programs, blogs and vlogs, moderating, facilitating, and curating the best social business practices brought to the YouMeWe community: Women leaders driving social impact. YouMeWe will enhance how we consciously contribute consistently and sustainably.

Through the YouMeWe Movement, we hope to inspire citizens to shift their focus from *me* to *we* and to understand the importance of you in achieving that goal. Consider not only the *helper's high* that satisfies our ego, but also the impact of our generosity. Let us not only concern ourselves with what directly impacts us, but take responsibility for our global community; rely not on what others should do, but what we can do; move away from communicating problems, and move toward sharing solutions; stop amplifying what is wrong with the world, and start celebrating what is right.

The mission of YouMeWe Social Impact Group is to raise consciousness and inspire individuals and organizations to lead or participate in contributions that positively impact their community or beyond. This aspiration will promote more conscious, caring, kinder, and inclusive humanity while making our communities flourish — in effect, *making your contribution count for you, me, and we.*

Context to optimize your reading experience

The YouMeWe ethos is the foundation of the book and divides it naturally into three parts.

Part 1: *you* — make your contribution count — *consciously*

You refers to understanding the needs of the individual or group you would like to contribute to while being conscious of the more significant implications of fulfilling that group's needs.

Part 2: *me* — make your contribution count — *maximize your meaning*

Me refers to the self being a global citizen. We all have a responsibility to contribute to uplift the life of another. We will maximize our meaning when we channel our unique gifts, life purpose, mission, and personal values in the service of others.

Part 3: *we* — make your contribution count — *sustainably*

We is the reality that momentum is not achieved alone. To consistently contribute to an initiative, we need to collaborate with value-aligned people and organizations. We must employ sustainable solutions along with mission and conscious leadership techniques. By harnessing our feminine energy, we will generate a positive ripple effect of our consistent conscious-contributions™.

Throughout this book are stories, examples, considerations, tools, and reflective questions to inspire you to consciously contribute to fill a gap in society, be it social, economic, or environmental; be it in your company, community, country, or beyond.

As a volunteer, philanthropist, small-business owner, entrepreneur, or leader of a not-for-profit or profitable business, you will gain insight and strategies on how to live your most meaningful life and how to lead others to live theirs.

Travel this reading journey with your book club, social club, a group of colleagues, or friends. The questions at the end of each chapter will spark conversation and connect you at a deeper level: the best part, the opportunity to collaborate on a meaningful project or cause. While reading, consider how to make your contribution count collectively by forming a Conscious-Contribution Circle™.

Visit the YouMeWe.ca book community to accesses Conscious-Contribution Circle™ ideas. Share your initiatives at https://youmewe.ca/your-contribution-counts/, and we will celebrate your contribution by investing in a woman's education or business, helping her move from poverty to prosperity.

MANY OF THE STORIES throughout this book are in the African context; however, they address several of the world's shared challenges. Some pioneers transformed policy to advocate for equal rights of women. Others have a voice in the political future of their countries and continent. Several pioneers escalated issues that affect women's health and well-being. Many pioneered social enterprises that lifted thousands of women and their families out of poverty. Courageously, others merged commerce and collaboration to create productivity and peace. All gave hope to those who had little.

Since our interviews, some African pioneers have moved on to new organizations, countries, or careers. When I reference a pioneering woman, it will be in the context of what position she held, where she was living, and the mindset she had when interviewed. Although their situations may have changed, their insights remain very relevant today.

We all need to be more aware of who, how, and when to contribute. By sharing pioneering African women's wisdom, you will have a glimpse into their culture, their courage, and their conscious-contributions while provoking contribution ideas in yourself.

Many of the interviewees mention cultural and national circumstances; such references are from their perspectives, and others are from my own observation and research.

The guidance shared is based on my 20 years of entrepreneurial and leadership experience, years in training and development, the extensive insights from the interviews coupled with research on the evolution of contributing, volunteering, conscious businesses, leadership, and collaboration. The strategies are presented to help equip you with how to *make your contributions count* while creating a sustainable initiative wherever you are on the journey of living your most meaningful life.

In immersing myself in this mission, I have read, listened, observed, and researched. Sometimes it is difficult to know where someone else's ideas end and mine begin. To the best of my ability, I have credited the source that inspired an idea.

Throughout the book, I will share experiences of Mike's and my journey. The stories are from my perspective, and when others were present, they may have a different view of how events unfolded. The intention is to represent the situation to the best of my recollection.

At the end of the book, you will find a link to each of the interviews on WisdomExchangeTv.com. Hear about interviewees' journeys in their words. You can gain further insight into what makes these women unique and inspiring while learning from their *words of wisdom*. In the glossary, you will find the terms I use throughout the book. If you are newer to the world of causes, volunteerism, not-for-profits (being defined as incorporating NGOs, non-profits, charities, and foundations), social enterprises, or conscious social impact, we can stay together on this journey.

There are additional resources to assist you in making your contribution count. You can find them at YouMeWe.ca in the Book Community. With this book you have free access. Here is your community code: **MyContributionCounts**.

WISDOMEXCHANGETV.COM HAS EVOLVED TO include international interviews with conscious-contributors who have a social impact on our communities and beyond. Subscribe to stay abreast of who is transforming our world, many of whom are small business owners. Learn how they are moving the social, economic, and environmental agendas forward to address the United Nations

Sustainable Development Goals. Conscious-contributors will guide you to optimize your impact.

Lastly, the book is targeted to and written about women but can be relevant to anyone. I refer to feminine energy often because I believe we all have feminine energy. I believe it is the power we need to access if we are to experience a profound social or environmental transformation.

If you are looking to maximize your meaning or seeking how your organization can have a social impact sustainably, grab your backpack and join Mike and me on this adventure, on what I hope will be a compass to your *mission taken*.

Part 1: you — make your contribution count — consciously

Chapter 1
Make your contribution conscious

Words of Wisdom
Don't start things for your own fulfillment. Start them to make a difference to uplift the life of someone else.

Katherine Ichoya, executive director of FEMCOM, Malawi, Kenya
Pioneer: co-creator of COMESA gender policy

After experiencing a sense of euphoria with a family of gorillas in the Virunga Mountains, Mike and I were quickly confronted with the reality of being in a rural community in Rwanda.

At the base of the mountain, a young boy greeted us with his drawing of a mama gorilla with a baby on its back. He proceeded to try and sell his one-of-a-kind creation, and we followed our Rwandan guide to his vehicle.

The boy was persistent and ran barefoot alongside our car, while navigating potholes, for what felt like two kilometers. He was waving his drawing in the window.

"Mama, Mama, please, I'm hungry."

His eyes were pleading…my heart was breaking.

I hesitated. Over my three extended trips to several African countries, I had learned and experienced a bit about where and when to give.

However, when the pleading eyes of a hungry child are looking into yours, all sense of the rational escapes. You want to help. You want to save this one child. You convince yourself that the little money you give will somehow make a difference in his life. With love and compassion, you ignore your brain and follow your heart.

I turned to my husband.

"He is entrepreneurial; I like that ... He is persistent, a good characteristic in a young boy. ... It is one-of-a-kind."

My husband listened. So did our guide.

In the rearview mirror, I could see the guide's eyes. I felt I had been caught and was about to be chastised for succumbing to my emotions once again.

"Mama, if you are thinking of buying that drawing, please don't."

"Okay, I won't, but please tell me why."

"If you buy that drawing, the young boy will be here tomorrow, the next day, and the next. Every day he is here is a day he is out of school. Every day he is out of school is a day he limits his opportunities for his future and our community's."

His words reminded me that my desire to give had implications far beyond my emotions and this young boy's wishes. My reflex to give needed to evolve.

When contributing, are you giving a hand out, or hand up?

Are you creating dependency or opportunity?

When giving, are you helping or hurting?

When embarking on our backpacking journey through Africa, our primary mandate was to interview women pioneers for WisdomExchangeTv.com, with the goal of having African women educate and inspire future African women leaders. With every interaction, Mike and I got further glimpses into the culture, circumstances, and social impact of activists, educators, politicians, or social entrepreneurs. We heard perspectives in every conversation that exposed a similar mandate — to amplify women's voices, optimize health, alter biased practices.

The women's graciousness was an ongoing gift. The most valued and unexpected reward we received was the understanding that women don't leave a legacy, but live it. The second most enlightening gift came from a culmination of interview insights and the experience traveling from one African country to another: Giving can hurt and not help.

The interview that most convinced me of the harm giving can cause was with Yetnebersh Nigussie, co-founder of the Ethiopian Centre for Disability and Development. Yetnebersh is a young woman who helped change the perception of disability in Ethiopia. Two of her many accomplishments were the inclusion of people with disabilities into the job market, and founding Yetnebersh Modern Academy, a primary school that educated students — able bodies and disabled — together.

Yetnebersh is a formidable person. It wasn't her beauty, her sparkly jewelry, her poise, or her ability to succinctly communicate the heart of an issue that struck me most. It was her perspective about giving that caused deep reflection. Blind since age five, she sees unsolicited giving to be laced with assumptions. She describes receiving charity as "based on the goodwill of the giver. The receiver has no say. There is an issue of pride and sustainability." Yetnebersh is an advocate for giving opportunities and recognizes that everyone has value to contribute, regardless of their ability.

Assumptions have plagued many givers' decisions. Media, inflamed stories, a celebrity's cause, and social media have shaped our views. But, once you live in the land of perceived receivers, you start to reflect on the motivations and the impact of the giver.

ONE DAY WE WERE walking along a pothole-ridden sidewalk in Kampala, Uganda when we came upon a young man wearing a Toronto area hockey jersey. This was a neat connection with back home, as Mike managed various recreational hockey facilities in Toronto. But there we were, in 31-degree Celsius weather, meeting a young man wearing a hockey jersey. This was the closest Mike had been to his passion for hockey in over a year. It was serendipitous that he met this young man on his birthday. The two had a brief conversation, followed by a photo, never to see each other again.

Where had this hockey jersey come from?

This shirt was probably a sacrifice made during spring-cleaning. Perhaps a wife's attempt to pare down the clothes worn by her husband that were too small, too embarrassing, or just didn't bring out the color of his eyes. To the donation bin it went, in the hope that someone far away would benefit. Now it would be someone else's problem, and a problem it does contribute to indeed.

Once that shirt gets tossed in a donation bin, the container is transported to a warehouse, shipped to Uganda, where someone buys a bale of clothes and then sells a pile to a street merchant who, in turn, sells the shirt for a couple shillings to a mother buying clothes for her son. Presto, the jersey is on a teenage boy in Uganda.

The motivation for this generosity could have been to give affordable clothing to someone in need, or perhaps to save the garment from a landfill. Donating is likely done with the best intentions; however, it doesn't mean that intent is realized.

Exporting our unwanted clothing has had a negative impact on the clothing manufacturing industry in Africa. Some of the women we interviewed suggested it has paralyzed it. African manufactures cannot compete with the low cost of used clothes from developed nations. Westerners don't mean to put people out of work, yet we do. This is one of many examples of Western giving that is wreaking havoc in an industry for a developing nation.

Our clothing donations, however, have created another industry. Unfortunately, it is not in manufacturing, where the export potential and acquisition of foreign currency is highest. Instead, it created clothing distributors and independent clothing retailers who rely on imports and the goodwill of the giver.

Reusing, recycling, and repurposing clothing is increasing in popularity. In the West, second-hand clothing stores are capitalizing on this evolution of society's consciousness. However, don't be fooled. Several charities that encourage you to donate clothes, or thrift shops that can't sell your second-hand items, sell some of the garments to developing countries to help fund their charitable or business endeavors.

Westerners' good nature often comes at a price. Our tendency to respond to a need, often under the banner of *giving*, has a short-term reward but can be riddled with obstacles to achieving long-term sustainability. The Zambian born author Dambisa Moyo, in the book *Dead Aid*, calls this the micro-macro paradox.

> Aid effectiveness should be measured against its contribution to long-term sustainable growth, and whether it moves the greatest number of people out of poverty in a sustainable way. When seen through this lens, aid is found to be wanting.[2]

Assessing whether an initiative is helping or hurting is complex. My intention is not to discourage contributions, but rather to curb the giving reflex, while at the same time promoting a thorough consideration before people and countries attempt to be the white knight in hopes of saving the day.

We interviewed Tereza Mbire, a serial entrepreneur, founder of Uganda Entrepreneurs Women Association Limited, a founding member of Uganda Women Finance Trust and advisor to President Yoweri Museveni. Tereza graciously invited us to have lunch with her and her son at one of the top hotels in Uganda, an experience we couldn't often afford on our affectionately named Mission Africa budget.

Tereza's son, a farmer, shared that local producers are challenged to make adequate margins on their food; many fellow farmers felt that Western food aid was the cause. With food available at low-cost or free, sustaining their farms was almost impossible. "Why would locals pay for what they could receive free?"

How could aid, something intended to lift people out of poverty, in fact, cause it? *Dead Aid* explains that aid does have a place, but knowing that place is paramount. Aid should be given to fix something broken, not to build something that never existed — such as attempting to build an economy in an undeveloped country.

The Western world often operates under the notion that we know what others want. In regard to fundamental human rights, we can be reasonably sure that everyone wants food, clean water, safety, and shelter — long-term. How they receive it and in what variety are considerations of sustainability.

There has been progress in understanding various cultures' and countries' needs in recent history, and developed countries are beginning to realize some of the errors in providing aid. In 2005 at the Food Aid Conference in Kansas City, there was a decision to push aid in a new direction. Instead of Western producers sending food to the African market, they would use aid money to buy from local African farmers and then distribute to citizens in need.

Despite increasing awareness of how to help and not hurt, there are still many opportunities to be more proactive by collaborating with people and organizations to fill social, economic, and environmental gaps. Citizens don't need to depend on how large organizations conduct business locally or internationally, nor rely on government decisions on how they distribute aid. The power is in our hands. Every time we travel, help a local charity, make a purchase, assess how our businesses can contribute to the community, how we select our suppliers, we have the opportunity to make informed decisions on how to uplift the lives of others.

It is from this context, the power of one, as a leader, an entrepreneur, a change-maker, that you can consider individually and collaboratively how to impact the lives of others while you consciously contribute to create opportunity, not dependency. From here, you will perpetuate a positive ripple effect — your micro-movements matter.

Perpetuating mediocrity can create dependency

Since 2007, Mike and I have traveled extensively through 15 African countries. Our 20-month adventure in 2011 and 2012 through the Sub-Saharan region included 610 days of travel through 14 countries, 33 border crossings, 27 flights, and 74,000 kilometers over land, hiking, kayaking and driving.

Traveling over land afforded a unique experience. As we drove through small town after small town, we saw the similarities between the locals' lives whether we were as far north as Axum, Ethiopia or as far south as the southern tip of South Africa, Cape Agulhas. Most buildings were one-story, situated close to the road. A massive telecom sign on a store offered SIM cards for sale, a building supporting the Coca-Cola logo, a small market, a group of men chatting under a tree, and a group of women selling fruit, vegetables or handcrafts.

While crossing the Tanzanian border on a group overland trip to Kenya, a Maasai elder approached me to sell a bracelet. Not liking the design, nor wanting to carry more stuff, I politely declined.

She persisted.

Eventually, she grabbed my arm and forced the bracelet onto my wrist.

"It is a gift." A gift I did not want.

She would not take the bracelet back … an expectation of a further purchase was imminent. To remove my obligation, I immediately regifted the memento to a traveling companion who had not had the opportunity to buy from the Maasai. For her, the gift was obligation-free.

As we started to drive away, the Maasai elder ran after the overland truck, insisting that I had taken her bracelet. I communicated to the driver that she said it was a gift, and he relayed the message. She said in Swahili, "But it was on the condition that she was going to buy other bracelets from me."

The driver translated for me, and I replied, "I clearly said I didn't want the gift, and that I didn't want to buy any bracelets, but she forced it on me. I said thank you."

My translator smiled and told the woman, "You shouldn't force people to take something they don't want," and with that, we departed.

If I had accepted the gift and participated in the law of reciprocity by buying some of the elder's merchandise, the message I would have been sending is, "Your forceful sales techniques worked. If you continue to harass tourists, you will make more money," a message that would have done more harm than good. If people keep buying what they don't want out of force, pity, or guilt, we are perpetuating the use of those tactics. With these tarnished experiences, buyers seek a formal marketplace in hopes of less manipulation.

AT THIS POINT IN our journey, Mike and I thought we had learned enough to know when we were helping or hurting. We agreed to the best of our knowledge and ability, we would not support manipulation, we would not purchase mediocrity, we would not perpetuate dependency, and we would not finance corrupt activities.

Support established social initiatives

Traveling in a country at length exposes one to the underbelly of the society. While observing the negative ramification of local systems, a bleeding-heart tourist can take it upon herself to rectify the situation. With little knowledge, cultural awareness, or local support, a tourist puts on their cape to save the day. Although admirable to want to fill a social gap, leading the charge may not be the best alternative to garner the desired transformation. Many NGOs (non-government organizations), are started by crusaders. Armed with limited knowledge, and a whole lot of emotional zeal, a caring tourist attempts to change a circumstance.

Participating or leading a cause is to be admired; however, if the motivation is to create a sustainable impact, and not just to have your name on a charity, consider joining forces with an already established

NGO that has gained traction. An NGO is any non-profit, voluntary citizens' group organized on a local, national, or international level. It is task-oriented and driven by people with a common social or environmental interest. NGOs perform a variety of service and humanitarian functions, bringing citizen concerns to governments, advocating and monitoring policies and encouraging political participation through delivery of information. NGOs are not limited by short-term financial objectives, and therefore tend to engage in long-term pursuits.[3]

According to The Global Journal, a platform to discuss global governance issues, which ranks the top 100 NGOs, there are an estimated 10 million such organizations worldwide.[4] In South Africa alone, there are 136,453 registered NGOs, and on average, 68 new ones are registered every day.[5] The number does not include those that serve Africans located in other parts of the world. To assess the generosity of Canadians, according to Statistics Canada a total of CA$10.6 billion is donated each year, an average of CA$446 per Canadian.[6]

Westerners' giving and compassion are not enough. Starting another charity can saturate the market with more messages, splitting funding and minimizing impact. To understand all the consequences affiliated with the core issue that tugs at our emotional heartstrings, we must do our due diligence to assess the best approach to having a positive impact or risk making missteps that may cause disruption en route to that discovery.

Setting up an NGO without local strategic partnerships will limit understanding of all the facets of a particular issue. It is complicated to implement a solution that is to be adopted by the intended recipients and sustained over time. Your best course to contribute and make it conscious is to collaborate with a local organization that has an understanding of the culture and can utilize an outsider's expertise, finances, or contacts to expand their impact. As a bonus, it will increase local engagement and employment.

Appeal to cultural nuances to maximize social impact

A Canadian friend who lived in Kenya provided a young woman with a microloan to start a hair salon. It included a five by five-foot area, built with wood, one seat for her customer, a mirror, and hair styling tools. During the year, the new entrepreneur missed many of her loan repayments and would ask again, again, and again, for more investment. The loaner obliged, again, again, and again, as she wanted this woman to move out of poverty.

I introduced my friend to Katherine Ichoya, executive director at FEMCOM, Federation of National Associations of Women in Business in Eastern and Southern Africa, to provide prospective on microloans. Katherine was part of a group of women, along with the National Bank, who assisted Maasai women to sell their beads to tourists, export products, and gain access to loans. The collaboration became the foundation for the Maasai markets that exist all over Kenya today.

As Kenya is a patriarchal society, women often don't have access to collateral, so they need alternative resources to receive seed funding for a business venture. Lending groups, and now more licensed banks, rely on social collateral to secure debts. Social collateral is a form of insurance, in which people are encouraged to create groups to start businesses where each person is responsible to the other members. The groups collectively save the security of the loan, which is only 10 percent of the overall credit. A group member can start their business with as little as US$200. If someone in the group can't afford to pay, the group will assist. As an individual's business grows, she may require more of a loan to expand. The group members share financial risk, but also provide business advice to each other.

A social collateral approach to lending won't work everywhere, or with everyone. In the rural communities in Kenya, women often form groups to execute chores and offer social support. Kenyan women's collaboration makes the extension of being dependent on each other for business and financial support a practice already embedded in their culture.

Utilizing a social collateral approach would undoubtedly assist my friend in receiving timely debt payments. The hitch is that the hairdresser would need to have connections to a group where there is mutual trust; all those reliable women would have to want a loan, ideally be local, and willing to collaborate. Fortunately, there is an increasing number of licensed banks offering microloans throughout Africa.

Gaining a loan through a microfinance lender includes the vulnerability of entrepreneurship. Many rural women do not have the business acumen or education to rely on their marketing prowess. To make enough money to feed their family and pay for their children's school fees, they may depend on a social entrepreneur's business savvy to give them a hand up.

There are many definitions of a social enterprise. Some suggest profits are reinvested to maximize a social mission; however, this structure is quite similar to a non-profit. Without a well-accepted universal definition, it serves, to recognize that most of the African social enterprises described in this book reinvest most of their profits into the mission; however, shareholder gain is acceptable, and YouMeWe avidly encourages it for sustainability.

The multitude of definitions of social enterprise have two elements in common. First, a commitment to social, environmental, or economic impact is central to the mission of the businesses. Secondly, they use commercial strategies to produce a product or provide a service to maximize social return on investment (SROI), with an equal balance of profitability. What differentiates social enterprises is that social mission is the catalyst for its development, and it is as core to success as any potential profit.

If profits are the primary driver for the business, and that business has a program to create awareness, raise funds, or provide a solution to address social or environmental issue, this approach is referred to as corporate social responsibility.

Both social enterprises and corporate social responsibility initiatives are admirable; however, when interviewing African women pioneers, we found the catalyst for their missions was to elevate their community, country, and beyond with whatever means available. It wasn't an initiative, but her way of life.

Janet Nkubana and her sister, Joy Ndungutse, started a social enterprise to help transform their homeland. The sisters were raised in a Ugandan refugee camp. Their parents fled to Uganda in 1959 to escape the ethnic clashes in Rwanda. Both sisters desperately wanted to return to Rwanda after the 1994 civil war. Upon their arrival, the sisters didn't appeal to cultural nuances; they obliterated them. They co-founded Gahaya Links, the producers of Rwanda's one-of-a-kind baskets commonly known as Peace Baskets. The sisters have been celebrated internationally for creating business opportunities for hundreds of women and men in rural Rwanda after a dark point in country's history. They have sold their products internationally through Macy's, Fair Winds Trading, and Oprah Magazine, among many others.

When Janet and Joy created Gahaya Links, they brought women together from both sides of the conflict. This gamble could have created chaos. Instead, women worked alongside each other and communities were woven together. Janet and Joy's vision induced a remarkable connection that has helped transform Rwanda to a much more peaceful nation. Janet reflects:

> I believed women suffered more than everybody. Men were killed, children were killed, and women remained alone. They still needed more peace to settle, to have in their homes, to have in their mind. This business became so successful because, through weaving, women started embracing forgiveness. We had a cooperative where women were friends before the genocide, but families were torn apart. Women started asking forgiveness on behalf of their husbands. During the weaving session, women would find forgiveness, and many would communicate that forgiveness to the seekers. The basket has created a lot of peace in this country. It has brought together both sides of the genocide.

Understanding cultural nuances doesn't transcend economic requirements. Sheila Freemantle moved to The Kingdom of eSwatini (formerly Swaziland) with her husband. She is the founder and managing director of Tintsaba, Master Weavers, located in a remote area along the North Western border. Sheila wasn't just operating a basket weaving company, but a holistic social enterprise that tried to meet the needs of the rural Swazi women weavers. She also initiated an organic gardening program to help fulfill that need. She bought water tanks, provided trees, and other resources to maintain the gardens. Within a week, the tanks were stolen, and the garden ceased to exist. Sheila freely admits, "We have since learned to ask the rural women what they want, rather than thinking we know what they need."

Sadly, Sheila Freemantle passed away October 29, 2012. Her legacy lives on in these pages, and in the hearts of everyone she touched.

How Westerners can make our contribution conscious

We have a saying in the West, *It's better to give than to receive*. The premise of this saying is that we feel better when we give. The real flaw in this adage is giving just because it feels good only satisfies our ego or reduces our feeling of guilt. We need to contribute consciously. We need to ask ourselves, "Will my contribution cultivate the intended behavior? Is the receiver better off because of my giving?"

Giving is handing something over that you may not want; contributing has more emphasis on helping to achieve the desired outcome. Contribution also implies a lifelong pursuit rather than a transaction. YouMeWe Movement uses the word contribution for this reason.

The struggle to consciously contribute is real and is amplified when a situation pulls at our heartstrings. Curtailing our emotions when confronted with the perceived have-nots will continue to be a challenge. Something inside you wants to improve another's lot in life. You're motivated to make a difference, to uplift the life of someone else. An admirable quality; however, to achieve your objective, direct your contributions need to be directed to help, not hurt, to create opportunity, not dependency. The contribution needs to be about *you*, not *me*.

As Katherine Ichoya's words of wisdom say, "Don't start things for your own fulfillment. Start them to make a difference to uplift the life of someone else."

Make your contribution count

When your emotions are affected by a situation, and your reflexes kick in to immediately help, pause to reflect on implications, ask questions about the impact, or conduct research. When we consciously contribute, we are converting an immediate emotional response to rational implementation.

To alter how you give, assess your desired goal by considering — are you hurting or helping? Are you offering a handout or a hand up? Are you perpetuating a dependency or creating opportunity?

To create a flourishing society, we have to consciously contribute. A conscious-contribution is about being more aware. It is assessing the impact of your contribution on the beneficiary and community as a whole.

Reflect on how to make your conscious-contributions™

1. When contributing, is the receiver better off because of your giving? How do you know?
2. What cultural nuances does your contribution need to take into consideration to optimize a positive effect on the receiver?
3. What actions can you take personally and, in your business, to ensure your contributions are conscious?

Chapter 2
Infuse the social gap with feminine energy

Words of Wisdom

Don't fall into the trap of stereotypes. We shouldn't believe that in order for a woman to be successful she must have kids; she must be married; she needs to do certain things or cannot do certain things. We will become whom we want to be.

Maria Sarungi Tsehai, founder, Compass Communications Co. Ltd., Tanzania
Pioneer: producer of Miss Universe Tanzania beauty pageant, recipient of Commonwealth Vision Awards (UK) for excellence in TV production

Since my first trip to Kenya, I've shared the profound insight of the late Dr. Douglas Carew several of times, that Africa's biggest problems lie with leadership. He believed it was when moral leaders with integrity and justice arise, then Africa's problems will be solved.

I couldn't help contemplating that if leadership is, in fact, vital to progressing developing countries, why do so many charities and NGOs focus on children, maternal health, or young girls? Although all commendable contributions, they focus on impacting the life of one, rather than many. Investing in leaders and leadership could transform a nation.

The international community seems to be ignoring the one investment in developing countries that can pay dividends — women's higher education.

It is widely publicized that in developing countries if girls receive a higher education: pregnancy is delayed, she earns 25 percent more income, she is more likely to live longer, child marriage rates decrease, and she has reduced risk of contracting HIV/AIDs.[7] Also, 90 percent of a woman's income goes back to the community as compared to 30-40 percent of man's.[8] University education amplifies these statistics by inducing a ripple effect.

Girls in developing nations want an education. Countless have a strong desire to develop leadership skills that can generate the tides of change. Moreover, many need the means to gain access to higher education to discover their untapped potential.

This gap inspired the YouMeWe Foundation Fund. We generate most of our funding by producing events or donating a percentage of YouMeWe's business earnings. The proceeds, including direct donations, provide scholarships to attend university to vetted prospective women leaders in Africa. Although YouMeWe Foundation Fund is small, the lives of 27 women have changed course due to our investment.

Before pioneering WisdomExchangeTv, I believed that investing in women would change the lives of hundreds. Through our scholarship recipients and interviews, I now know that African women leaders' impact can spread through their communities, and in many cases, affect thousands or even millions of people.

Many people radiate feminine energy. Its essence embraces willpower, nurture, courage, humility, integrity, authenticity, intuition, compassion, and collaboration.

Women have the nurturing instincts to uplift those around them. Our evidence shows that women leaders are the best investment in the future of Africa (and by extension, the world). They are moral leaders with integrity.

THE UNITED NATIONS PROMOTES fundamental human rights for all people. To make that vision a reality, innovative models for healthcare, education, employment, and financing need to be created. Feminine energy gravitates in these directions to offer creative solutions.

When making a conscious-contribution, it is prudent to start with what you know. Mahatma Gandhi suggested, "Try to make a change from the smallest unit from your neighborhood." Vulnerable people often lurk in the shadows. It is not until a compassionate heart hears their silent cries and shines a light on a horrific circumstance that the path to recovery becomes feasible.

Healthcare: empowering the vulnerable

One condition that banishes a woman into the shadows is having a fistula. There are 24,000 women in Tanzania dealing with this disease, and every year, there are 3,000 more. Obstetric fistula is a hole between the vagina and rectum or bladder that is caused by prolonged obstructed labor, leaving a woman incontinent of urine or feces or both.[9] The result is frequent infections and odor. Women are often shunned, abandoned, and pushed out of the village due to the smell. Inadequate access to birthing professionals, childbirth for young girls, or rape can cause a fistula. Unlike many other diseases that leave a woman isolated, a 30-minute surgery can cure fistula — if she can get access to a hospital and the money to pay for it.

Enter fellow Tanzanian, Mwamvita Makamba, corporate affairs lead at Vodacom Tanzania, and trustee at Vodacom Foundation. Mwamvita was instrumental in establishing an innovative solution and proposed it to the foundation. She recommended capitalizing on Vodacom phone technology, collaborating with rural ambassadors, the local hospital, and using M-Pesa cell-phone money transfer system to help women suffering.[10]

The process starts with a local ambassador calling a toll-free number when they find a woman with the disease. Vodacom sends bus fare by cell phone using M-Pesa to be given to the ailing woman. Surgery is arranged at the local hospital. The transaction is completed when Vodacom sends a small financial token to the ambassador, and a cured woman returns to her community. Mwamvita's compassion and ingenuity have been paramount in girls and women with fistula reclaiming their dignity.

With the success of the program, the Vodacom international management team committed to raising US$15 million to embark on a campaign to eradicate fistula in Tanzania altogether.

Mwamvita brought women out from the shadows to find their way to a cure. Vulnerable women need advocates lobbying on their behalf until they can once again campaign for themselves.

Education: providing access to higher learning

TSiBA Education in Cape Town, South Africa is a university founded to educate those who can't afford access. TSiBA was co-founded by Gia Whitehead, along with Adri Marais, Leigh Meinert, and Graham Lashbrooke.

Mike and I had the honor of interviewing Gia, as she was the recipient of Top Women Entrepreneur of the year in 2012. Ten years prior she was acknowledged as one of South Africa's 100 Brightest Young Minds.

TSiBA Education is a non-profit business school that helps youth in underserved communities to transition from unemployable to contributing citizens. Since 2008, South Africa's unemployment rate has fluctuated between 20 and 30 percent.[11] Although youth have been able to acquire temporary jobs as unskilled labor, permanent employment eludes them. Many are excluded from the education system, or it is inaccessible, leaving potential talent underutilized.[12]

TSiBA fills the gap by providing a full tuition scholarship to every student for a business administration program. Although not offering a degree, it does prepare students to either access higher learning, enter the work force, or become an entrepreneur within five to 10 years of graduating. Students do have the opportunity to take a degree program by paying a percentage of the scholarship in the form of a sliding scale tuition fee, which is determined by a family means test.

TSiBA is giving South Africans the opportunity to mold their future by investing in leadership and entrepreneurship, two social gaps needed for a thriving economy and culture. Gia Whitehead shares the ethos of the university.

> We are the only institution that has subjects that focus on entrepreneurship, leadership, and personal self-development as credit bearing subjects. We build it in as a strong focus. It is not only about knowledge but bringing in skills and experiential learning. At the center is an attitude, bringing in values throughout the curriculum that students report, and reflect on, that is just as important as doing the academic subjects.
>
> It is about creating a culture where students think creatively, innovatively and learn how to start a business. It is about growing the students in a supportive model where they are encouraged to fly, strive, and develop what they may have inside them while supporting them to get there.

Gia is a young South African who, along with her co-founders, thought they could make a difference. And they did — from a warehouse with only 80 students into a social enterprise collective. Since 2004, TSiBA has awarded 900 business certificate and degree qualifications to more than 4500 annual tuition scholarship recipients and enabled hundreds of small and emerging business enterprises. This groundwork has resulted in an incredible output, with a 93 percent post-graduate employment rate.

Perhaps the most progressive attribute of the TSiBA University is that it embeds in its culture the expectation of paying-it-forward. The philosophy is not a requirement of graduating; however, it is part of the leadership curriculum, where students must log their leadership hours. Students lecture or mentor on campus, in high schools or a community — a 62 percent statistic that translates into post-grad community participation.

WOMEN ALL OVER AFRICA continue to close the education gap. They are empowering children, youth, and young adults, making what was once inaccessible, accessible. However, it doesn't stop there. It takes visionaries to meet the needs of continued learning in professions, such as Tereza Mbire, from Kampala, Uganda who chartered the first women's association in Uganda, or Joanne Mwangi, from Nairobi, Kenya, who pioneered the Federation of Women Entrepreneur Associations, or Eva Muraya, also from Nairobi, Kenya, who co-founded Kenya Association of Women Business Owners. These pioneers created an opportunity for women to come together, expand their knowledge, network, and collaborate to progress their businesses and society.

Employment: establishing a social enterprise

Rusia Orikiriza Bariho requested to be interviewed at her family compound. She wanted Mike and me to experience all that the Bariho family has achieved under her leadership. Getting a peek into someone's enterprise, family, and way of life was the reason all our interviews had been face-to-face. Rusia and her brother picked us up at our hostel, and we drove an hour outside Kampala Uganda, through the country roads to the Bariho compound. Our three-hour visit did not disappoint.

Rusia Orikiriza Bariho is the founder and managing director of Oribags Innovations Ltd, a social and environmental enterprise that manufactures eco paper bags from agricultural fibers and waste. The enterprise was conceived in 2007 when the Ugandan Government banned the use of plastic bags. Oribags Innovations Ltd. was launched in 2009 when it brought innovative packing and design to the Ugandan packaging industry. The bags were produced near the rural compound, to employ her neighbors. Her customers purchase product online or at the store in Kampala.

When we arrived, we met the compound employees, including Rusia's older brother. As we took a tour, it was apparent that Rusia was the glue, the innovator, and the driver of the family businesses. She shares: "I wanted to create a business where I could apply myself, and that would help me to look after my siblings, as my father and mother have been peasants for years. I wanted to transform the family and create an address for us." That she did.

The compound included a newly built homestay for traveling guests, a farm, and a large hall for community gatherings. It was in that hall that one of my most moving African experiences would take place. Twenty women wearing their gomesis, Ugandan traditional dress, greeted us with open arms and hearts.

Rusia gave a speech of appreciation for Mike's and my interest in her work. She appreciated the creativity of her team and the loyalty of her family. I reciprocated with gratitude for the opportunity to meet the Oribags Innovation production team, the warm welcome, and to learn more about Rusia and the pioneering company. Then we sang, danced and I attempted to follow the traditional Ugandan dance moves while Mike captured it all on video.

A "peasant's daughter" had brought this community together and provided those affectionately called mamas, and their families, an opportunity to earn a living, not only to sustain them but also to help them thrive.

During our interview, Rusia gleamed with pride as she shared her social entrepreneurial success producing an environmentally friendly product that appeals to the Ugandan market and provides income for so many. She sees her young age as being directly associated with her energy and motivation. "By the time I am 40 I will have accomplished so much." No doubt, once there, she will also realize she still has a lot of life to live, and a lot of legacies to leave. But for now, she lets her youth and ambition lead the way for others.

Rusia is an advocate in promoting the spirit of entrepreneurship among youth and women in many associations, including the Uganda Women Entrepreneurs Association. She is using her education, aspiration, and determination to establish an enterprise that will provide for hundreds in rural Uganda while teaching entrepreneurs how they, too, can thrive.

Employment: progressing self-worth

Self-worth is a light that shines from within but can emanate to the masses. Angela Dick, founder and chief executive officer of Transman, the first temporary employment broker in South Africa, took it upon herself to ensure the respect and dignity of marginalized employees. Transitioning from a secure sales job had financial loss implications for her, but Angela was determined to help the thousands of men looking for work every day to give them a hand-up to employment.

> My income went down substantially. Yes, I did take a risk. There were months and months that I couldn't pay the rent, couldn't pay the bond. [My family] lived on brown bread and jam for weeks at a time. We sold all the carpets, the furniture, cars, etc. in order to get this [company] up and running.

Angela's multiracial upbringing, together with her genuine concern for the underprivileged in her country, has given her insight and grasp of South Africa's socio-economic complexities. Transman responds by finding temporary and contract employment daily for 7,000 to 10,000 workers, with a focus on disadvantaged individuals. Being on the frontlines of the unique and often tumultuous job market since 1983 provides a practical vantage point to many South African realities: "I deal with violence on a daily basis. I deal with poverty on a daily basis. You can become very hard if you don't have a strong inner core to deal with it."

Organizations employing temporary or contract workers from Transman, commit to invest in on-the-job training and providing an environment where the worker can develop. Angela hopes that if an employer can observe a worker's ability to learn, and apply that learning, the company will transition the employee from a part-time job to a full-time asset.

Angela inspired a conscious enterprise that frowns on dependency and allows for opportunity while creating self-worth. A citizen need only be willing to work and learn.

Financing: Granting access to the *unbankable*

Granting access to financing to those without collateral has inspired the birth of many institutions all over Sub-Saharan Africa. Over the last 20 years, there has been an extensive movement to provide the *unbankable* with loan solutions, financial literacy, and dignity.

The first microfinancing Trust, and the largest in Kenya today, was originated to exclusively provide for the financial and non-financial needs of the women in Kenya. It proudly carries the slogan, *Banking on Women*. The Kenyan Women Financial Trust, established in 1981, became Kenya Women Finance Trust Microfinance Bank (KWFT bank) in 2010, under the leadership of Dr. Jennifer Riria.

The trust was established by a group of professional women who had the vision to grant financial access to women in rural communities. It was Dr. Jennifer Riria, who led its transformation from a trust of two million in noncollectable loans when she joined the organization in 1991, to the institution being awarded a deposit-taking license by Central Bank of Kenya in April 2010. Eighty percent of KWFT's clients reside in rural communities. The bank has been able to increase access, reduce inequality, and arm women with more control of their assets, including their homes. This privately held institution provides services to over 800,000 clients, employs 2,800 staff, and has branches in 45 of the 47 counties in Kenya.

Access to financing is only half of the equality story. The other half is composed of empowering, positioning, and advocating for women. In the backyard of the recently vacant KHFT building, Dr. Jennifer Riria's shares her vision for her next chapter, leading Kenya Women Holding, now called Echo Network Africa, located in Nairobi. "The biggest issues are beyond finance. Women need skill training, mentorship, leadership creating, and schooling. This is what will really empower women."

A few short years later, Echo Network Africa has over one million members across Kenya. Through collaboration and employing a private sector driven model it enables women, youth, and persons with disabilities to advance their security and prosperity. It is no wonder

Jennifer is a multiple Entrepreneur of the Year Award recipient, including Global Entrepreneur of the Year Award (Ernst & Young), and Most Outstanding Businesswoman of the Year Award (Africa Economy Builders). Dr. Riria is a truly a visionary, who was inspiring, vulnerable, and open. I was humbled to be taken into her world of empowerment with all the highs and lows that entails.

Evolution is inevitable. When there are gaps, and limited access to growth, African women want to fill them and create equality. Granting access to the tools necessary to have some control of their lives, takes vision, action, and perseverance.

WHEN REFLECTING ABOUT WOMEN in business and education and how they demonstrate care determination, empowerment, inclusiveness, consciousness, consistency, and courage to contribute, one can't help considering that if there was more feminine energy in leading government positions, what would that mean for the world?

Advocating for women's rights in Government

I was honored to have the opportunity to interview one of the three women of the six commissioners in the African Union. Bience Gawanas, social affairs commissioner of the African Union, is in her office in Addis Ababa, Ethiopia. Although our meeting was delayed by AU business, she graciously extended our allotted time to ensure the interview was not rushed.

Bience is well known as an advocate for women's equality. As a commissioner, she seeks ways of striking a balance between tradition and progress. She feels that, although equality is part of many constitutions in Africa, many societies remain patriarchal and women are still often excluded or dehumanized. It is up to all of us to contest this disparity, and one of the best ways to *fight for rights* is to first understand them.

With the perception that progression means abandoning African culture, the African Union hosted a conference called *Celebrating*

Courage and Overcoming Harmful Traditional Practices. The purpose of the meeting was to reflect on African culture positively and to deal with the harmful elements. In the conference, Bience asked the question:

> Can we use positive cultural values to overcome the harmful ones? The methods in the West may not be the solution to fight harmful traditional practices.
>
> This is not only about the rights of women, but also about the identity of the African woman. How do we make sure that our cultures are in-line with our rights?

Bience clearly states that African culture promotes sharing, standing together, and caring. "We believe in Ubuntu — I am because we are." Why would Africans want to replace this culture of unity with a Western culture of individuality?

Cultures around the world need to ask tough questions. Feminine energy seeks ways to elevate all voices so that equality can exist not in spite of traditions, but because of them.

Although all over the world there is a call for women to take part in civil society, representation is still falling short. As it stands, Rwanda, Cuba, and Bolivia are the only three countries worldwide with over 50 percent female representation in the Lower or Single House (Rwanda being the highest at 61.3 percent). According to the Inter-Parliamentary Union ranking, no state demonstrates gender parity, and has more than 50 percent representation in the Upper House or Senate. In 1995, the UN Economic and Social Council endorsed a target of women participating at decision-making levels. Although debated, it is believed a shift in policy and practices in government occurs when there is a minimum of 30 percent female representation.[13] As of September 2019, 50 countries of the 193 meet the minimum recommendation, of which only three are part of the G7. As of June 2019, elected women include, 11 women serving as Head of State and 12 serving as Head of Government internationally.[14]

When you assess the rankings of women participating in government throughout Africa, it has steadily increased over the years. As of

September 1, 2019, 11 out of 54 African countries have over 30 percent female representation.[15]

African pioneering women are conscious-contributors, establishing evolutionary futures for their fellow citizens. A pioneer is just someone who is the first. It doesn't mean that what they are first doing can't be done better, differently, be built on, or be executed somewhere else. We don't need to be the first to make our contributions count. We don't need to be the first to change our corner of the world. We need to show up, listen, learn, and be accessible. Opportunities to contribute will find us.

Make your contribution count

We know that women bring unique characteristics to the social, cultural, and environmental issues of our time. We need more of them to raise their hands, and more businesses and governments to make room for them to lead.

Until we incorporate the most valuable resource that society has — feminine energy — we will not be able to turn the tide from violence to reconciliation or from corruption to integrity.

The world needs more feminine energy in leadership positions. Without it, the issues of our time will not be resolved.

Reflect on how to make your conscious-contributions™

1. How do you think feminine energy can address some of the most significant issues in your community?
2. Which organization can you support with your abilities or purchase power to assist your neighbors in regaining their pride and dignity?
3. Is there a role you could play in your local or municipal government? Describe the role that could harness your feminine energy.

Chapter 3
Amplify the social impact

Words of Wisdom

Do every ordinary thing in an extraordinary way, no matter what it is. You will never be mediocre if you strive to be extraordinary.

Mwamvita Makamba, corporate affairs & trustee at Vodafone Foundation, Vodacom Tanzania Limited, **Pioneer:** mobilizing maternal health in Tanzania through Vodafone Foundation

Before meeting my husband in Egypt, I made a detour to Africa International University in Nairobi to provide persuasive presentation training programs for 16 prospective Ph.D. students and faculty. I was honored and welcomed the opportunity to invest in the faculty and future leaders' influence skills. Previous participants said it had been a life-changing experience for them; this time, it was life-changing for me.

In preparation for the program, I scheduled a 20-minute face-to-face discussion with each participant to learn his or her objectives. The insight would help tailor the course. I met with George Ogalo, a man in his mid-thirties, at the time pursuing his Ph.D. His wife, Mary, had been the first YouMeWe Foundation scholarship recipient. I wrongly assumed that George and I would have an instant connection, because of the opportunity that my foundation provided for his wife.

While starting to ask George about his studies and why he wanted to develop his presentation skills, he immediately took the reins. "Why should I attend your program? What is your experience? Why would this program be worth my time?"

It never occurred to me that I had to convince him to attend; after all, my contact had told me that the students and professors had wanted the coaching. It also didn't occur to me that he would challenge the value of a free program. I had misplaced confidence that mentioning my resume of 15 years training Fortune 500 companies, on five continents would suffice.

George, along with 15 others, had to be persuaded to participate. This experience led to two realizations. First, I would never offer a program free again, mainly because of the perception of value by the participants. Second, that just because someone says there is demand, it may be less about what you offer, and more about who is offering it.

However, it was the question the experience raised that changed everything: Why was I here training in the first place? Surely, someone in Kenya could have provided presentation training. Whose job was I taking?

It was time to fuse everything I was passionate about: leadership for women, skill development, providing opportunities, and Africa. I embarked on a new mission — establishing WisdomExchangeTv.com. This website offered a medium to gain access to interview pioneering African women and to educate future African women leaders. I wouldn't be taking a job, rather I would be a conduit to helping others learn from the women in their community who went before them. The bonus, I would learn alongside them.

Becoming a socially conscious enterprise

Starting a business using local resources is not new. However, starting a business that creates superior handcrafts, respects the environment, employs over 750 women artisans, pulls thousands of people out of poverty, has been featured on the runway in the UK, and exports home décor products internationally, well, that enterprise could be considered a little more groundbreaking. Gone Rural, located in The Kingdom of eSwatini (formally Swaziland) is a sustainable company that does just that. Across 53 eSwatini communities, artisans use traditional methods to weave natural fibers, such as lutindzi grass, into contemporary collections. It was started by the late Jenny Thorne, a nurse with a passion for women and humanity who emigrated from England.

In 1970, from a thatched mud hut, Jenny started a sustainable business while fostering a positive economic impact on eSwatini's rural communities by enabling women to earn money while maintaining their customary lifestyle. Providing employment wasn't enough for Jenny Thorne. She immersed herself in the culture and its requirements. As a result, Jenny provided vitamins and health workshops to women, but it was an unstructured initiative.

However, before she had a chance to create a more organized outreach, she passed away. The Gone Rural team and the Thorne family took the reins and founded Gone Rural boMake, a not-for-profit, to support the artisans, their children, and communities. BoMake provides water access, sanitation solutions, pre-school education preparation for children, and health education including HIV/AIDS prognoses and prevention.

Philippa Reiss Thorne, Jenny's daughter-in-law and managing director, who led the organization through major growth years, shares in our interview how boMake builds on the Gone Rural social enterprise to help accelerate opportunities for Swazi women and their families:

> If you don't have food security for the women, or you don't have water, or if your family doesn't have its health, it is very difficult to do anything beyond day-to-day challenges. We focus on income as we realized that it is an important thing for the women. As we evolve, we look more and more at what we can do to address the primary concerns of Swazi women.

With the Gone Rural boMake impact on over 20,000 beneficiaries,[16] it has undoubtedly committed to addressing its purpose as a local economic driver, and as a holistic social, and environmental solution — Jenny's vision realized.

WHETHER AN INITIATIVE IS inspired through enterprise or activism, pioneering African women often seek a sustainable solution that makes them less dependent on the international community, and more reliant on their ingenuity. Samrawit Moges Beyene, founder and managing director of Travel Ethiopia is no exception. Samrawit relies on the international community, not for aid, but for customers.

> I don't believe in aid. I don't want the West to give us wheat and fertilizer. If we keep feeding people all the time, we won't have a productive society. I believe it is through tourism we will be able to reduce poverty and be productive.

Samrawit depends on international visitors to ensure her business flourishes, but it is so much more than that for her. She has great pride in her country and everything it offers. She welcomed Mike and me upon our arrival in Ethiopia. She connected us with Ethiopian women to interview. She took us to dinner with her family to enjoy Ethiopian cuisine and traditional dance and also included us in the celebrations of the annual orthodox religious holiday, Meskel. She taught us the traditional Ethiopian dance called eskista. We never quite mastered the shoulder shaking technique. Still, I only need to move my shoulders to my ears to relieve tension and instantly I am transported back to dancing around the giant bonfire.

In addition to promoting tourism, Samrawit takes guests to the remote corners of the country. Travel Ethiopia owns a lodge in the Afar region. Samrawit invests in women by giving them the training to pursue a career and a platform to demonstrate their talents. One of her employees became a chef, who later became a beacon for many other women in the community to emulate. Investing in the Afar region, and offering employment, provided Samrawit with influence.

> As a result, our voices are also heard. We can go to the elders to discuss important issues such as early marriage. Although not abolished, it is minimized. Negative traditional practices like circumcision (FGM) have also been minimized.

If you ask Samrawit who she is and what business she is in, she may very well tell you she is a woman activist in the business of elevating

Ethiopia out of poverty by creating pride in the country. Oh, and she provides tourism services, too.

Attending to the outliers

When dealing with a social issue, you may choose to focus on a targeted group of people and provides extensive services, as in the case of Gone Rural boMake. Alternatively, you may give all your effort to the issue or cause and provide solutions to a multitude of beneficiaries with the goal of resolving the issue. The latter was the choice of Lydia Muso and Angela Dick.

As we sat in the home of Lydia Muso, the founder of the Lesotho Child Counseling Unit, she discussed a disturbing reality in her society, and in communities all over the world: people are angry. Because Lydia's primary focus is rehabilitating abused children, she advocates for Lesotho citizens to treat children with respect, as human beings. Through her child advocacy, she recognizes that children who have been traumatized through abuse, may display anger. Identifying the source of their anger and working through it is an important step in breaking the cycle of abuse.

Lydia has made it her mission to stop the anger. Lesotho society has started providing counseling for men and women's groups as well as for couples. Lydia's concern, however, is for the people that it may be too late to rehabilitate; the ones who have already landed in prison, driven there by anger. Her concern is that once a man is released from jail, he will still be angry unless he receives the proper therapy.

To address the overflowing prisons, predominantly filled with men, Lydia decided to focus on what she believes is the root issue: anger and understanding of human rights. She has created an initiative that teaches young boys about human rights and how it applies to Lesotho society. By engaging boys, she hopes to circumvent the crime and prison cycle all too common for young men.

Avoiding prison is a worthy goal; however, when someone is released from prison, they need not only rehabilitation but also opportunities to rejoin society. For the benefit of the newly free citizen and society as a whole, companies need to be willing to provide an opportunity for ex-convicts to earn their way to becoming contributors to the community.

The prospect of employment for ex-prisoners is dim. The primary goal of Transman, the temporary recruitment company founded by Angela Dick, is to find jobs for South Africans. But, her company has a problem with securing long-term placement for convicted criminals. Angela's team does try to rehabilitate them or find partnering organizations that will provide an opportunity, but she admits, "Some of our clients are not comfortable hiring them. In my organization, we too have a couple of people who have been convicted." Offering the opportunity for employment will help stop the perpetual dependency on crime to survive.

It is from a place of awareness that new socially conscious initiatives will deliver an extraordinary impact.

Rethinking education

Transforming children to become young adults who live a life of integrity, love, equality, and purpose is a priority for many African women. Ela Gandhi is the founder of Gandhi Development Trust in South Africa and an advocate for instilling the values of her grandfather, Mahatma Gandhi. Ela focuses on teaching children under the age of three. She hopes to prevent the unethical lifestyles that lure young adults.

In Ela's very calm, soothing voice, she explains the need to impart certain fundamental beliefs at a young age, so those values become the foundation of how children live their lives:

> Psychologists say these values will remain within that child, consciously or unconsciously, so we believe that the first three years are essential. After that, it is also very important to provide values education, which should permeate throughout all the different disciplines being taught to the child. When you are learning math, your idea is about mathematics, it is not about values. So how do you bring values into mathematics, health sciences, science and technology, and into every subject? We suggest,

when teaching the alphabet, or counting, we should change our language, instead of saying, 'We consume 10 barrels of rice,' say, 'We conserved ten barrels of water.'

Ela also suggests we need to be mindful of children's natural behaviors and how we can impact those mindsets. For example, if every day a different child hands out biscuits to classmates and some of those biscuits were broken, who would receive the whole biscuits — others or herself? Learning how to share or put someone else's needs before their own needs to be reinforced in early childhood education.

Ela works with childcare centers and the Department of Education to drive more emphasis on early childhood. According to Ela and many other experts, the lack of attention placed on early childhood development is the source of many social problems.

Leah Ngini, founder and director of St. Christopher's Kindergarten and Preparatory Secondary School in Nairobi, designed her schools to address many of those social issues that start at a young age and are amplified as a child progresses through school and life.

I first met Leah Ngini when she came to Toronto as a keynote speaker at the then Ignite Excellence (now YouMeWe) Conference. I was hosting the event to raise funds for the Leah Ngini Community and Women's Center at AIU. Leah was the first woman to serve on their board of governors, and an ambassador for its vision. Her ability to share a Kenyan story, her kind eyes, and insistence that if you "educate a woman, you educate a nation; if you educate a man, you educate a man," makes her a formidable Kenyan.

When Leah started St. Christopher's she observed children and teachers overwhelmed by the syllabus. According to Leah, Kenya's curriculum was too cramped; children had too much work and had little time to enjoy the pleasures of being a child. Leah's school put children and their mental health at the heart of education. In the Kenyan system, if a child doesn't pass their primary school exam, they are not permitted to continue their education — a social failure that makes 13 or 14-year-olds often struggle with the shame, leading to a high rate of suicide.

Leah replaced the intense memorization of the traditional Kenyan system with the British syllabus that encouraged creativity. She also removed the primary school exams and only implemented secondary school testing. By the age of 18, students are better equipped to deal with the stress of exams. Postponing examinations reduced the number of children dropping out early if they didn't pass, as well as giving them a better opportunity to pursue a trade. Leah's philosophies are at the core of her school's operations.

> We love them. We show them that we love them and that they are valued. We show them that each one is special. We talk to them. We smile. We don't beat them. We care for them and, of course, teach them.

Each child is granted respect when they walk through the door in the morning. Teachers are encouraged to love and value the children and to demonstrate that they are invested in their success. Children have a voice at St. Christopher's. If Leah doesn't feel a teacher has the best interest of the children at heart, she will lovingly suggest they work at another institution.

Bringing the message to the masses

Education is the Holy Grail in many African countries. Once you have it, graduates believe doors will open, and nothing will stop them from what they want to achieve. Multi-degreed individuals are starting to realize this is a misconception.

Modesta Lilian Mahiga worked in recruitment in Tanzania for a large corporation. She had the top university graduates coming in for interviews by the hundreds. For every 50 interviews, it seemed only one had the desired acumen. The number of meetings required to hire 200 people was overwhelming. "The question became, everyone has a certificate and so what edge do you have?" Modesta felt, "I had to get out to show them what it takes."

The gap between education and street smarts is what Modesta was determined to fill. She is the founder and managing director for Professional Approach Group. She is also a lawyer, human rights activist, and recognized worldwide as one of Africa's young leaders. When she started to close the gap between graduates' expectations and job realities, her team began to work alongside disenfranchised youth by providing them with interview skills. Every Friday her team went to secondary schools and tertiary institutions to speak with students. Modesta admits, "We were not reaching enough people, so we decided to go to mass media," which inspired the birth of the Maanisha Foundation. The foundation uses national media to empower Tanzanian youth with an objective to bridge the gap between education and the real world. At the core is the mantra: "Only developed people can develop a nation."

Activism can have a profound impact in getting a message out to the masses, but so can the prowess of an enterprise.

When Janet and her sister, Joy Ndungutse, co-founded Gahaya Links, the pressure to conduct international trade was evident. The government wanted businesses to exploit bilateral trade to give more opportunity to Rwandan products. Gahaya Links also saw exporting as an opportunity to expose the fine, unique beauty of Rwandan products while transforming a weaving hobby into long-term employment for rural Rwandan women. With the exporting of 95 percent of Gahaya Links' products, a hobby turned into a livelihood for hundreds of handcrafters.

Gahaya Links brought the outstanding opportunity to meet with a major United States retailer, Macy's, to President Kagame. Because the president realized the international exposure the *peace baskets* were bringing to Rwandans, he agreed to accompany Janet to meet with Macy's. In turn, Macy's felt it was more suitable for the president of the organization to attend rather than a store manager. This meeting forged a long-term partnership with Gahaya Links that has been in place for years. From Macy's shelves to President Clinton's public support, the peace basket awareness was gaining momentum.

A publicity strategy turned the peace baskets into a national icon, a fact that even the hotels in Rwanda could no longer ignore. Gahaya Links confronted the Serena Hotel and advocated that they replace their China-made billfolds with local baskets. Janet's convincing argument was: "If people outside our country are embracing the beauty of our products, why not Rwandans?" That viewpoint, however, was only accepted once the hotel received free breadbaskets and they had the opportunity to examine the quality of the local artisans. Eventually, the astute business gesture translated into changing much of the hotel décor with locally made large baskets. As Janet says: "Now they have pride when someone asks where the baskets came from; they can say, 'from Rwandan women!'"

Make your contribution count

Momentum is not achieved alone; it starts with one person having a vision to consciously contribute and seeking opportunities to expand on an ordinary idea to have an extraordinary impact. Consider which stakeholders could benefit from your contribution. Ask what does a beneficiary need to live their most meaningful life? Staying in tune with the heads and hearts of recipients will ensure that your gifts are empowering, not discouraging.

Reflect on how to make your conscious-contributions™

1. What social initiative can be built on to expand its impact in your community?
2. Are outliers' needs in your community being ignored? What can be done to address the issue?
3. What values do you feel need to be incorporated into the fabric of society? How can you participate in the progress?
4. If you contribute to a cause, what can you or your business do to expand its impact?

Chapter 4
Take small actions to cause big reactions

Words of Wisdom

You need to have the courage to ask questions, and then you need to frame the question. The acceptance of unfairness is the challenge. We need to ask: 'Why does this rule exist?'

Bience Gawanas, commissioner of Social Affairs, African Union (2002 – 2012), Namibia
Pioneer: initiated campaign on Accelerated Reduction of Maternal Mortality in Africa (CARMMA)

I have always wanted to go to Africa. It became evident when I was buying three-foot brass African women in Thailand; even the custom officers found it conspicuous. When the opportunity to go to Kenya came up in my late thirties, I was curious as to what contribution I could make. In 2007, 18 women traveled to Kenya with Women on the Wild (WOW) branded T-shirts. The unfortunate name appeared to suggest to many fellow travelers that we were less on a community development mission and more on a mandate to create havoc. Suffice to say, the future name of the tour changed to Africa By Design — but for now, we are WOW.

The purpose of the trip was to have a little adventure and, more importantly, to connect to and provide advice to African businesswomen, help build and beautify schools, and visit with marginalized girls and women. The latter is where I had one of my most profound experiences.

Our tour was invited to attend a regular support group meeting of women with HIV/AIDS on the perimeter of the Kibera slum, the largest unofficial settlement in Kenya and largest urban slum in Africa. Before visiting, we were brainstorming how we could engage the women in an activity. One of the eighteen WOW women had brought fabric to help a social enterprise with their sewing skills. In our wisdom, we decided each one of us, along with three or four Kenyan women, would use some of the fabric to braid together. Do you have any idea how ridiculous it is for a group of white women to supposedly teach African women how to weave? For centuries, African women braided their hair, baskets, and floor mats. Their stoic facial expressions said it all.

There we were unconsciously demonstrating how to braid together. In our defense, teaching the women how to braid wasn't our objective. We wanted to spend time with them. Let them know we cared.

In smaller weaving groups, I tried to focus on the actual objective of the activity. After my team gathered to braid fabric outside, I started to photograph the women modeling our creations. It was like a cloud lifted. Suddenly we were smiling, laughing, and out-posing each other. This moment of levity was why we were spending time together in the first place. We decided to take our show on the road and join the other women inside, connecting over colored fabrics.

As I walked through the windowless concrete building, I announced, with all the pageantry I could muster, "Put your hands together for the 2007 summer collection." Each woman came in the room and posed for the camera. As I was taking photos, the room erupted in a roar. Within a few moments, the women started incorporating the braided fabric into a vogue pose, hands were in the air, singing filled the hall, everyone was busting a move, and the weight of disease evaporated — for that short time, we were just girlfriends hanging.

We need to show up and treat people like equals — laugh, cry, and celebrate alongside them. People want to be accepted for who they are, and to enjoy what they have — life.

When our group walked into that room, we knew women with HIV/AIDS were often abandoned and left to raise their children alone. All they want is conversation, kindness, and connection.

The best contribution we can make to anyone is to provide our time, energy, and kindness. Spending time with the group of HIV/AIDS women was one of my favorite African experiences because it reminds me that we don't need to do much for people to feel valued. The small actions can cause a big reaction.

When consciously contributing, it doesn't need to be an immense undertaking. Instead, look at what you are doing and consider how to optimize its impact or be conscious of incorporating small acts of kindness in your day. You may never know the difference you made, but the recipient appreciates that you cared.

The power of pride

WOW conducted two school projects, one at a girls' school in Mathare slum and the other at Pistis school, a primary school located on the grounds of AIU. At the girls' school, we offered to paint the interior and exterior. We gave the contact at the school money to purchase all the necessary tools and paint. We anticipated a three-day job.

Our first day, during school breaks, we painted side-by-side with many of the teenage girls. We had the opportunity to have conversations about their education, family, and dreams. As the day progressed, the girls would come and go as our group continued painting. The following day when we arrived, there wasn't much painting left to do. In our absence, a group of men came in to finish the job. Our school contact decided the leftover money from the purchase of paint would be better spent employing Kenyans to do the work.

When we first had the opportunity to contribute to Pistis primary school, we offered finances to build an additional room at the school. We hired Kenyan builders to do what we couldn't. We offered our hands to hammer for posterity, however, we had little effect on the completion of the new school room. We put our energy and time into beautification. We painted the swings and fence and cleaned-up and planted the garden. As more of the WOW group got involved, an intriguing metamorphosis took place. Teachers and the community started to participate. We were once again being squeezed out of the contribution. Our actions planted a seed. Once there was money to fertilize it, Kenyans wanted to own the accomplishment. They weren't asking us to do anything for them; perhaps they just needed the funds to start. Few things can provide more motivation than one's pride. It was a race to complete planting the gardens, painting the swing sets, and building the school. We started it, but the locals finished it.

Pride is a powerful emotion and can motivate people to do many things — even if it isn't their priority.

Influencing mindset through questioning

Bience Gawanas believes that social mindsets can change. It all starts with asking simple questions, such as, "Why does this rule exist?" Bience recognizes she was in a position of authority, but she also advocates that you don't need status to bring about change. Boys and girls should learn at a young age to ask questions about their role in society. A sister asks, "Mom, why does my brother not wash the dishes?" Also, a brother can ask: "Mom, why don't I need to do the dishes?" or, "Why do I get to go to school and my sister has to stay at home?"

Questioning social norms needs to be encouraged. According to Bience, men may feel uncomfortable when women question them. Her perception is that when a woman challenges a man's perspective, she is seen as power-hungry and ambitious and asks, "Is it wrong to be ambitious? Is it wrong to have power? The wrongness of it all is what you use the power for."

Questioning is essential to challenge biases and open minds to new perspectives. Fikile Nkosi, the first female managing director of Nedbank, eSwatini Limited, is a woman who challenges the status quo. In her role, she acts as a self-appointed mentor for all eSwatini women to realize their role in society by taking ownership of their potential. Her mandate is to demonstrate to corporations and her nation that women have power and are capable of operating and contributing at the highest level.

To harness her objective, Nedbank sponsors the country's Businesswomen of the Year Awards, which honors the achievements of women and creates a cadre of women role models. This event endeavors to garner press to amplify the message that women are here to lead.

Fikile Nkosi received feedback that men were not allowing their wives to attend or to be honored for their accomplishments. Having an awards program with none of the recipients in attendance was not going to earn the desired press nor communicate to Swazis that women were open for business. Fikile decided to host another event; the goal was to convince husbands to allow their wives to be recipients of the deserving award.

I had the honor of speaking at this inaugural event. I shared many of the leadership insights gleaned from interviews with Swazi women from WisdomExchangeTv. In addition, I focused on the impact the conscious leadership techniques have had. Then I posed a question, specifically to the 12 men in attendance:

> Of the 48 women interviewed, half the women admitted they achieved their success because they had the support of their husbands. A quarter of the women achieved their success in spite of their husbands, and the other quarter of the women achieved the success because they got rid of their husbands. Which do you want to be?

The audience laughed, but none louder than the deep hearty roars from the two tables of men. They even took notes.

Acts of accountability

Nigest Haile, founder, and executive director of the Centre for African Women Economic Empowerment in Ethiopia, feels that it is not only men who hold women back but also women themselves. Many women entrepreneurs won't invest in their own potential success. Nigest proclaims there is too much donor dependency. There are conferences all over the world with the objective of building business skills for African women entrepreneurs run by well-intentioned NGOs. What began as a gap to address an issue becomes an opportunity to be taken for granted. As she describes:

> Most of the programs have really spoiled our women and really have not encouraged women to cost-share. Women need to put money aside to promote their business and participate in international trade shows. For example, in China last week, 12 applied to be delegates. There was a screening process, to make sure the right buyers and sellers were going to come together. Only four were accepted. International Trade Center was sponsoring the accommodation, and more or less the food. They were asking for the delegates to pay their round-trip ticket. I was the only one who went. I was to be the lead for the delegation.

Nigest feels that if Ethiopian women continue to be provided with opportunities to expand their businesses but don't invest in that privilege, even a small fee, they will continue to do what they did at China trade show — agree to attend, and not show up. Accountability is in the best interest of the host, the buyers, and sellers.

An act of accountability promotes commitment, increases performance, and encourages proactivity. All communities need to enforce responsibility. Gita Goven founding partner and CEO of ARG Design in Cape Town, South Africa, shares her frustration at winning architectural awards on buildings that have never been occupied due to funding for the project drying up. Now when Gita designs a plan for a township, she uses accessible materials, so the project doesn't need to rely on the goodwill of a donor.

The community mindset transformed from building unaffordable buildings with rare resources to affordable, beautiful buildings with easily accessible materials. A shift that gave townships more control and more accountability to maintain what they produced. ARG Design built a community center using tin, demonstrating how local recycled materials could be reclaimed and transformed into beautiful architecture.

Appreciation pays dividends

The lack of appreciation expressed in many organizations and day-to-day life is puzzling. The expression of gratitude is the least expensive gift to give, and yet many people hoard it only to share it when a relationship is experiencing tension. Appreciation should be used to build strong foundations, not withheld to repair fractured friendships.

Sincere acknowledgment can pay dividends. According to the study Workforce MOODTracker 2012, 82 percent of employees indicated that appreciation is one of the critical factors in improving their motivation.[17] Inspired employees benefit customers, the culture, and the bottom line.

We often don't know when or to whom we make a difference unless someone tells us. As citizens of the world, we need to acknowledge more, thank more, and celebrate people more.

The YouMeWe Foundation's first scholarship recipient, Mary Ogalo, upon graduating gave me a note of appreciation and a lovely necklace handcrafted by a local Kenyan social enterprise. I was utterly moved. The card is framed in my office as a symbol of all our scholarship recipients. It is a continuing reminder that each person's contribution counts.

We need to show our appreciation by changing the conversation from who didn't show up, to who did. From who didn't do it, to who did do it. From why we shouldn't, to why we should. From why not, to what if.

I wish I remembered how I thanked the women with HIV/AIDS in that dark room for reminding me that a simple gesture is all it takes to have an impact. I would have also liked to share specifically that I appreciated them humoring us Westerners while we braided fabric, their openness in accepting us, and the willingness to celebrate alongside us. I will forever be in their debt.

Make your contribution count

Our day-to-day actions can have an impact on others. It can be as simple as sharing a kind word with someone or spending time with a neighbor who feels isolated. Perhaps you can encourage a teenager to do something they want to get done or move aside to allow them to make their own decisions. We can celebrate a colleague's success or tell our spouse they make our life better. No matter who you acknowledge, remember it may just be the most notable event to happen in their day.

Reflect on how to make your conscious-contributions™

1. Is there someone, or a group, who is not rising to their potential? How could you assist them in achieving it?
2. Consider who or what your passionate toward, what questions will open people up to a different perspective?
3. How do you show your appreciation?
4. What can you do in your daily or weekly routine to have a positive impact on someone?

Chapter 5
Consider the contribution consequences

Words of Wisdom

As mothers, we need to empower men and teach them to respect girls.

Jennifer Riria, CEO of Echo Network Africa
Pioneer: led in establishing the largest Microfinance trust in Sub-Sarah Africa

One of the toughest decisions I have ever had to make was choosing who would receive one of the five university scholarships. Later, I was to learn Warren Buffet also finds it is a lot easier to make money than it is to give it away (a small similarity I cherish). Aristotle summarizes it best:

> To give away money is an easy matter and in any man's power. But to decide to whom to give it and how large and when, and for what purpose and how, is neither in every man's power nor an easy matter.[18]

To make the selection process less daunting, I solicited help from Lois Shaw and Mary Ogalo. Lois was a missionary who worked at Africa International University as a communications expert, manager of the guest house, and host to guests that traveled to Kenya through her agency, Africa by Design. For 25 years, she and her husband, Mark, and the family went between Virginia and Nairobi, contributing wherever they lived. An advocate and a connector for women in Africa, Lois was my first WisdomExchangeTv interview. Mary Ogalo, a recipient of a scholarship, attended AIU. Because both Lois and Mary worked and lived on the campus, they had insight into the applicants' commitment, knowledge of the courses, costs, and personal situations.

Each candidate had to fill out an extensive application. I was searching for women who were mature and had clear educational goals. Upon graduation, the recipient would want to address a social gap, preferably focused on women or children. With the guidance of Lois and Mary, we established criteria to help us wade through the over 20 applicants.

The scholarship was for tuition; accommodations and transport would have to be paid by the scholarship recipients. At the time, it was important that the scholarship recipient demonstrate she was resourceful, an attribute that upon graduation would serve her vision. The applicant could seek another scholarship through another fund, work part-time, or save money before starting school. Our scholarship team placed a high value on not creating donor dependency, which meant the recipients would not only need to be resourceful, but accountable.

Once the five scholarship recipients were selected, they agreed to post a monthly blog on YouMeWeFoundation.org where each would share her academic progress. Her experiences would give donors a window into her life and education challenges, as well as the potential for her social impact. Postings would provide an update to donors and serve to solicit more donations; a way for the recipients to pay-it-forward so other applicants could benefit from future generosity. The applicants found this request unusual, as they were unaware of other donors requesting similar reporting. Unfortunately, we didn't receive the updates, and I believe it stifled our funding.

When contributing, hindsight reveals the preferred approach and consequences. In retrospect, I would have had the university allocate and manage the scholarships. They have the experience, insight into their students, and are present to enforce accountability. My only requests would be to have awarded them to women seeking university education; who aspired to have a social impact; and, who would provide a quarterly report.

When we interviewed Gia Whitehead, co-founder of TSiBA education institute in South Africa, we were inspired to learn about the thoroughness of their scholarship process. TSiBA provides complete scholarships to people in cities and rural communities, it is a non-denomination school, where accredited academic courses focus on developing entrepreneurship and leadership, and has a pay-it-forward mentality embedded in its culture — we had found another partner.

A child in your wake

Many African women who have the means and the desire to challenge the habitual injustice to women and children throughout the continent seek a university education in Europe or the United States, where the top universities are found.[19]

When Katherine Ichoya, the executive director of FEMCOM, strolled into my makeshift office at AIU, she welcomed me into her world. As we started our conversation, it wasn't long before she admitted her greatest burden. It was as if by sharing her deep-rooted sense of guilt, she would have permission to celebrate her achievements.

Katherine carries the weight of her son's death from an overdose. She believes moving her son, daughter, and husband to the United States to pursue post graduate studies at Harvard was the catalyst.

After she had released the weight on her soul, we settled in like two long lost friends. During the rest of the interview, I couldn't help being affected by her enthusiasm and contagious spirit. She is a woman who has a good grasp of her purpose, abilities, and what it takes to achieve her goals. She is persistent, strategic, and reflective.

Katherine's education helped her to affect gender policy through COMESA (Common Market for Eastern and Southern Africa) promoting regional economic integration through trade and investment. Its membership consists of 19 states. Katherine's contribution was essential as one of the pioneers of the COMESA gender policy, a process and documentation created to make leaders accountable and dictate future decisions concerning gender issues. Katherine had questioned that if she should have just accepted the status quo, perhaps it would have saved her son. Without her commitment to pursue equality and the knowledge to create an opportunity for women businesses to trade, significant advancements may not have been achieved. Katherine was instrumental in leading FEMCOM (Federation of National Associations of Women in Business in Eastern and Southern Africa), which promotes programs that integrate women into trade and development activities in the region, providing a transformational contribution.

An old African proverb states, *it takes a village to raise a child*. African women capitalize on their support systems to afford their children and themselves a better life. Xolile Mkhwanazi, the financial director at Galp in eSwatini and recipient of Corporate Businesswoman of the Year 2012, relied on that village to pursue her ambitions. A single mother, she pursued a career taking her away from her home and her daughter. Being in the oil and gas sector, she was the only woman at the boardroom table; a reality she hoped to see change.

After moving up the corporate ladder, Xolile reveals, "I wonder if I made the right decision. I wonder if I spent enough time with my daughter." I was saddened to hear this pondering since she is a woman who has paved the way for others. Her goal is to help reduce the high unemployment in eSwatini by assisting young women to become entrepreneurs, and yet she feels guilt for pursuing her ambitions. I reminded Xolile that she would be someone her daughter could aspire to be — woman with dreams who is fulfilling them. If she hadn't pursued her aspirations, who would her daughter look up to? Whom would she emulate? Perhaps she would find herself with no ambition at all. Xolile's advice on dealing with fear may have also jarred her from self-questioning:

> Many of us stay stuck because we are afraid of making wrong decisions, but if you are not prepared to make a choice and commit to it, your spirit will stagnate, and we forget there is no such thing as the perfect move. Any

path you choose represents a process of learning. Simply admit you do not know it all. Allow yourself and others to understand that you will be asking questions, observing, and even making mistakes. As a woman, you can be anything you set your mind to.

Listening, then acting on our own advice, could save many visits to therapists, or those very long conversations with gal pals.

Regardless of how profound these women's achievements are, they have one thing in common — a feeling of guilt.

The crusade for equality

Social movements are the catalyst for rapid change, and as they pick up momentum, contributions swing in their direction, giving the perception that the opposing view is no longer viable. Most movements' purpose is to seek equilibrium, not to bring harm to the bystanders — a potential consequence in pursuit of human equality.

When you Google girls' charities, it becomes apparent that the pendulum has swung in favor of supporting young girls' education. In developed countries, we've seen an increase in girls' enrollment in university, often surpassing that of boys. However, there are still corners of the world that make access to primary and secondary school for girls very challenging, including some communities in rural Africa where a girl's place is still in the home.

As attention is focused on girls' education in Sub-Saharan Africa, improving the education of boys is being neglected. As Dr. Jennifer Riria, CEO of Echo Network Africa advises, "As mothers, we need to empower men and teach them to respect girls." Leah Ngini agrees. Her concern is around who will mentor the boys to take a leadership role in the family.

Although an advocate for girls' empowerment, Leah made a conscious decision to make St. Christopher's Schools co-ed. She wanted to ensure girls had someone worthy to marry when they graduate! Leah wanted to replicate the values of equal contribution to the family that she and her husband enjoyed. She believes men are so focused on working that they have forgotten their obligation to mentor their sons. Mothers mentor their girls, but boys fall through the cracks.

Looking at the international stage, we see the consequences of excluding boys' development as part of a productive community. Boys can find other outlets, possibly destructive ones that have massive consequences. Leah's response was to create opportunities in her school to engage fathers and teachers in being a positive influence on young boys, promoting role models for them in the community. Leah shares her message to her students' parents:

> Do not abandon mentoring. Men, mentor your sons and become the examples to be emulated. Women, mentor your daughters. Let every growing boy or girl grow up knowing what is expected of him or her in the home, community, society, nation, and world. The mentees will benefit because someone cares enough to support them, advise them, guide, and encourage them. The joy and fulfillment of passing along hard-learned wisdom as mentors to influence the next generation is appreciated. This used to be done in society before formal education was introduced. Formal education has not met this need, which is sad. Let us retain the things of old which were good.

Leah also fears the increased trend of men and women parting company because a husband doesn't know his role — an unintentional consequence of women as active contributors to the economy.

Socially conscious organizations need to take into consideration the consequences of men standing on the sidelines. Without a husband's support, tension in the family will likely ensue. From the Chilli Producers in Uganda, to Gahaya Links basket weavers in Rwanda, to Gone Rural artisans in eSwatini, all of these organizations have two things in common: they were designed to empower women, and once the initiative became lucrative for the family, men wanted to be involved. Each one of these organizations needed to decide whether to engage men or alienate them. They decided to bring them into the fold.

Each organization approached male participation differently. The Chilli Producers conducted training so husbands and wives could understand their respective gender roles. Traditionally in producing crops, wives would do all the marketing, and husbands would take the money. Sometimes wives would chase a man away so as not to be left with nothing, and he would run right into another woman's arms, leaving his wife alone to take care of their children.

Hellen Acham, executive director of North East Chilli Producers, preferred to bring both husband and wife together to work, side-by-side, to build the family's future. Hellen explains, "They need to understand what they are producing belongs to both men and women in the house. They should work together, not marginalize women." Education increases production, and the collaborative approach seems to work and keeps the family at peace.

Gahaya Links pays their employees per unit, which offers men a production advantage because they are able to weave from morning until night. Women have household obligations, so weaving has to work around their duties. Gahaya Links trained women on how to manage their money so they can hire young girls to do the chores while they increase their basket production. If Gahaya Links was more concerned about their production, and less focused on their purpose, they would have hired more men. Janet Nkubana co-founder explains, "If all men decided to weave, I think we would tell them we would leave it to the women."

That is precisely what Gone Rural did — left the weaving in the hands of women. As managing director Philippa Reiss Thorne explains,

> A chief told us that Gone Rural is the only income provider for his region. They have some men go to the mines, but they may only come back once a year. The rest of the year, women have to provide for themselves.

Gone Rural was seeking other opportunities to engage men, by creating projects using metals to complement their weaving designs.

Lack of equality in the workplace is prevalent in most professions, including aviation. Jane Trembath, an international airline captain out of Johannesburg, South Africa was one of the first female pilots. In 1982, she joined the airline industry when it was still a skeptical male environment. Since then, Jane has become the first female commander of an all-female Boeing crew and the first woman in South Africa to command long-range international flights. Being the first woman to succeed in the industry meant she was also the first woman to fail in navigating the nuances of airline culture.

Jane didn't have a flight plan to success when she started as a pilot, so she decided to create one by spearheading an internship program to help other women navigate the male-dominated industry. Her passion is flying, but her mission is to make it easier for other women to pilot a route through the culture. Closing the gender gap in the airline industry is a work-in-progress, but without pioneers like Jane, the shortfall would be perpetuated indefinitely.

Jane attributes her success to her determination. Sometimes a contribution consequence is our sheer focus doesn't contemplate the broader implications on the culture created due to disparity. During a conversation with a male co-pilot about a particularly rough time Jane was going through, she remarked that she had to hang in there for the girls. He countered, "It is not just for the girls; it is for all of us."

Equality is achieved when you have the participation of all genders.

Make your contribution count

When we set out to have a social impact, consequences are often not visible. To increase your success, consider local experts leading your initiative. Don't ignore your instincts; they are powerful drivers. Listening to them will help you live your potential, making you a role model, not a bystander. Consider how you can engage secondary beneficiaries, but not at the consequence of doing nothing for your primary beneficiary. Moving the primary contribution forward, in time you will be able to examine other inclusive solutions.

Use the **five stages of conscious-contribution™ model** to help guide the process.

You: Are beneficiaries asking for your contribution, or is it assumed?

Personal impact: Is it creating opportunity or dependency for the beneficiary?

Immediate community: Is it in the best interest of the community as a whole?

Larger community: How could repeating the behavior impact the community's future? What opportunities will prevail; what consequences could occur?

Ripple effect: Will this new normal make the community self-sustaining?

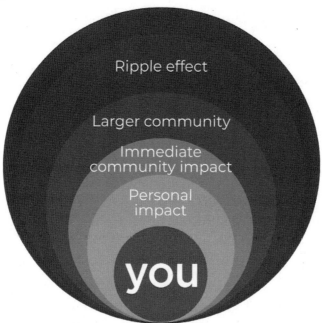

The reality is that we only have limited visibility when we start contributing, so we must be prepared to adapt to the new information in order for it to be a conscious-contribution.

After due diligence, the best thing to do is start.

Reflect on how to make your conscious-contributions™

1. Have you contributed and felt it didn't have the desired impact? What would you do differently?

2. If you are a parent, how have your choices impacted who your child/ren are today?

3. What biases do you have? How do your preferences reveal themselves in your personal and professional life, and while contributing? What can you do to address them?

Chapter 6
Choose a channel of contribution to induce consciousness

Words of Wisdom
Work hard and network. As an individual, we cannot do it ourselves. Have patience and be trustworthy, as you cannot buy either of those characteristics.

Rusia Orikiriza Bariho, founder and managing director, Oribags Innovations Ltd, Uganda
Pioneer: environmentalist, under 25 entrepreneurial award

Mozambique is a beautiful country located on the east coast of Africa, renowned for beaches and police bribery. Before our drive to a small town in southeastern Mozambique, friends cautioned us, "Make sure you have an emergency triangle and a reflector vest. Put the reflector vest right on the back of the driver's seat — that way the police will leave you alone."

Following this local advice seemed to be satisfactory as we were waved through six checkpoints. On our return to the capital, however, the reflective vest wasn't enough. When the police pulled us over, they asked for all the expected safety items, including a flare. "A flare?" None of the advice we had received indicated the need to carry a flare. The police officer told Mike to follow him and for me to stay in the car.

Mike and two officers proceeded to a small building. Locals had warned us not to trust the police, so after 11 minutes and 15 seconds had passed with no sign of Mike I was starting to get concerned.

My internal voice started up, questioning, "Is Mike okay?" Then my internal voice started to have some bravado: "They better not put a hand on him! I'm going in there in three minutes if he is not back." At exactly fourteen minutes I saw Mike crossing the street back to me.

Mike climbed into the car and started to drive as if nothing had happened. Anxiously, I demanded an explanation about his treatment. While my heart was still palpitating, he casually reported,

> After sitting awhile, they told me I had to pay a fine for not having a flare. I asked if they took Visa. And they told me I could pay cash. I told them I didn't have any cash. The officer conferred with the big boss, and then I was allowed to go without paying a fine. They were friendly enough.

Offering to pay by Visa protected us from fines on two other occasions.

Paying a fine is not a contribution to society in the context of this book, but what it does emphasize is becoming aware of formal local systems and practices, so that you can navigate unethical processes and advocate moral ones. For example, if you give a pencil to a child, your intent is likely for the child to use it for school. In actuality, he probability will sell it. There are channels of contribution that will increase the likelihood that your finances and efforts are directed to the betterment of the individual and society.

Immerse into a culture

The most effective way to contribute is to gain in-depth knowledge of a beneficiary's culture. By immersing yourself where they live, you learn to navigate the nuances, customs, and communications.

Her Excellency Nouzha Chekrouni, the first Moroccan woman minister and the ambassador of the Kingdom of Morocco to Canada did just that. For an ambassador to be effective, she needs the political and economic understanding of her country, and contacts both locally and in the state she represents. Nouzha says that the culture and the human dimension are just as important, if not more so. "You cannot succeed in business if you don't know the culture of the country you will be working with. You should know how various cultures conduct business, think, and behave." This philosophy would also benefit how we contribute locally to ensure progress.

On my first visit to Kenya, many of our WOW group went to North Eastern Kenya to meet the Rendille tribe, who live in an arid semi-desert area. The Rendilles previously lived a nomadic life, but due to the war near the northern borders, their travel has been limited. The heat, aridity, and the scarcity of water sources make growing plants next to impossible. They cling to herding cattle, goats, and camels for survival. They drink camel milk, as it is an easily accessible source of nutrition.

Our hosts here were an Australian evangelical Christian couple who elected to travel to the county to transcribe the Bible into the native tongue. While introducing our group to the history and culture of the area, our hosts explained the various challenges of the community, predominantly the struggle to acquire food sources to survive.

One of my fellow travelers was curious. "How is the Bible translation going?"

With a hint of embarrassment, our host replied, "Well, it has been 20 years, and we are halfway through."

The missionaries, like so many well-intentioned individuals, realized once they had arrived to implement their mandate that it was futile. The Rendille tribe was more concerned about how to maneuver through their food scarcity situation. They also didn't know how to read. The evangelical Christians had a new mission, to teach Rendilles how to read, then they could return to translating the Bible.

On our flight back to Kenya, many of our group questioned why the missionaries were spending so much time educating Rendilles to read when it was clear they had food and safety needs. I suspect it was because the missionaries could have little impact on food availability and the reduction of conflict. They could, however, develop an education system to assist future generations to navigate through the region's circumstances.

It was difficult to leave a community where people are starving, but it became apparent that education was the best way to open doors to new possibilities. Years later, the missionaries completed the Bible translation, and the Rendilles were better off because they immersed themselves in the community and helped build a way out of poverty.

Four years after our visit, the YouMeWe Foundation provided a scholarship to the second Rendille woman to receive a university education. An achievement that was possible because she started her schooling close to home.

Upon graduating in psychology and counseling, the scholarship recipient hopes to return to her tribe with her husband and child. Traditions have suppressed many women in the Rendille community. Her ambition is to empower these women by having conversations about female genital mutilation and teaching them about their rights, family planning, and HIV/AIDs. She hopes her education will in-turn help her advance her society and eliminate the injustices done to women.

Consult with local experts

No matter which community, or country you want to have a social impact in, experts can provide direction to ensure your investment of time, money, and energy is optimized. The authorities include local NGOs, consultants, traditional healers, community leaders, private businesses, government institutions, and residents of the community.

Marsha Gabriel is a consultant, as well as the founder and president of the CSI Business Congress, in South Africa. Her organization leads research, advocacy, and capacity building on sustainability matters contributing to social reform. A primary focus of the social enterprise is to create programs for artisans and NGOs to facilitate their sustainability.

Marsha works with 102 NGOs; she helps "change their mentality and change their thinking capacity. There is more to life than just maintenance. We share with them what you can do to instill growth in your institution." As an advocate for learning and development, Marsha believes if you keep giving, people will keep taking.

NGOs have the best intentions, but that doesn't necessarily mean they have the best execution. In contributing one's finances or time, consider Marsha's advice to assess an NGO's impact:

1. They have to be selfless.
2. They have to create a sustainable project.
3. Their plan has to be income-generating.
4. The project has to affect the people that the NGO was designed to serve.

Marsha advises:

> You can be passionate about what you do, but passion does not pay the bills. I have developed three projects that are income-generating, sustainable, but at the same time, very attractive to corporate and government. A government in and of itself cannot make all the changes we need in our country. They need people on the field that understand the hearts of the people.

Any initiative's success is directly related to whether the beneficiaries of the project are consulted before its implementation and engaged throughout the process. Tisha Greyling founded the first company that focuses on public participation and engagement of stakeholders in South Africa. She acts as project director, strategic advisor, reviewer, and mentor for social and environmental assessment on large international projects in various sectors, particularly in infrastructure, mining, or gas.

Tisha advises firms to alter their perspective of how they perceive public participation:

> [Change it from] something we have to do to something we want to do, because all stakeholders, which could include NGOs, housewives, or communities, are all like free consultants that help design your project for sustainability.

Tisha also advises that when an organization is executing a local project, it should also apply a program to uplift the community. For the project to be sustained, the community needs to decide on which project to implement. "We see very well-meaning projects vandalized because people [in the community] say, 'You never bothered to ask us.'"

Engage a cultural influencer

Providing healthcare to people in rural communities in South Africa is complex. There are many obstacles in the way of proper care for residents. One at the root of it all is the community's belief in, and comfort with, their local healer.

Dr. Thandeka Mazibuko is the founder, of SinomusaNothando Community Development in Kwa-Zulu Natal, South Africa. As a medical professional who specializes in radiation oncology, she uses her government salary to offer free cancer screening in rural communities. Although the testing can provide a reasonably accurate diagnosis, the locals believe the technology is no match for the advice of a traditional healer.

> Our patients would go to a traditional healer rather than go to a doctor. They would rather believe the mechanism of disease is a spell because the healer is visible in the community. They eat their food; they walk their walk; they talk their talk. Their books they understand. I tend to see patients, and even though I speak good Zulu, they will still go to a traditional healer, saying health issues are a spell. 'It's my neighbor's spell,' or 'it is my husband's girlfriend putting a spell on me, that is why I have vaginal discharge. It's not cancer.'
>
> It is because the person who tells them the genesis of disease speaks their language. So, doctors need to go to the communities and speak the local language. We need to learn the patient's culture.

Perhaps a more efficient channel to penetrate the community is demonstrating to the influencer, in this case the community healer, that by expediting a diagnosis, healing can commence at a more rapid pace in conjunction with traditional approaches. Gaining the support of the healer could facilitate community acceptance of medical solutions. Having the healer participate in the screening process would garner the most confidence.

The healer is such an important channel to infiltrate; without early diagnosis, the consequences can be fatal. Thandeka said she was the only doctor in her province bringing screening to a rural community. So many people with cancer go undetected. When they are diagnosed, it can take years to be treated. She describes, "By the time the patient sees the oncologist in a tertiary hospital, the patient has been walking this path for sometimes two years. What is happening to that cancer? It is growing."

To increase access to rural screening, Dr. Mazibuko needs the support of the department of health and community leaders to create an integrated system. If public and private partnerships were to form, funding could flow to assist in decentralized screening. Doctors would screen in rural communities where patients could walk to them instead of attempting to hitch a ride from a willing passerby.

In many African cultures, having a father's support can elevate a person out of the oppressive belief systems common in so many communities. In a patriarchal society, the leader of the family has the final word. When that word challenges traditional norms, society is more likely to listen. Gaining a father's buy-in can be a powerful channel of influence to move social agendas forward, particularly if he created the platform in the first place.

Hilina Enriched Food Processing in Addis Ababa, Ethiopia was established in 1998. The founder, Beyene Belete responded to a dire need. The company manufactures and processes a range of food products specifically designed to combat the various forms of malnutrition and other micronutrient deficiencies affecting children and other vulnerable groups. We interviewed Beyene's daughter, Hilina Belete the deputy general manager.

Hilina is in her early twenties, and eager to learn and lead. Because 70 percent of the ingredients in the products are locally produced, Hilina often found herself negotiating with older male farm owners. During the dialogue, she was frequently asked, "Who is the manager?" She would reply, "I am." She admits that she felt a sense of pride especially when a girl child was listening in on the conversation.

When Hilina's father started the business, he had every intention of his daughter taking a lead role in the organization; after all, he did name it after her. The career, and consequently the confidence Hilina had stem from her father's belief in her. To gain support for contributing to girls or women in patriarchal societies, engaging fathers in the dialogue can expedite any conscious-contribution.

From the head of the home to the head of the state, this is another channel of power that can institute social transformation. Altering embedded cultural perceptions takes years of dedication and collaboration with influential leaders. Without the support of respected individuals, the uphill battle to be heard and progress deep-rooted cultural norms may never be realized.

In Morocco, it was the commitment of King Mohammed VI to examine the Koran and demonstrate through its teachings that democracy, and therefore equality of all people, men and women, was possible. Nouzha Chekrouni, explains how Moroccans were able to reconcile the Koran and democracy through the highest channel of power.

> The political will was there to change society. His Majesty set up a multi-task and multi-dimensional commission with men and women from the religious side, political side, and civil society. All these people started to examine how we can understand Islam and at the same time achieve democracy. When you make an effort to contextualize Islamic principles, they are not contradictory to democracy and equality.
>
> The essence of religion is to make people live well and have their rights. So how can we interpret those principles and put them into a new context to communicate that Islam is alive and not contradictory to universal values? This is the work we achieved in Morocco, thanks to the vision of His Majesty.

We also achieved this because society wanted this change and women wanted their voices to be heard by everyone. We sent a very strong signal to other societies that we could keep our religion, as we are deeply Muslim, but also open to modernity, equality, and democracy.

To have access to the most influential voices takes years of education and demonstrating your value and ability at the highest level. Nouzha was able to achieve such power because at an early age, she, like so many of her fellow students, was swept up in the crusade to improve society. Communicating to local government or being active politically can provide you with access to the people who can make change, and the voice to make them accountable.

Connect with a charity or learning institution

There are many options to donate and collaborate with a charity or institute of learning. When the not-for-profit of choice is local, it makes it easier to attend a local function to assess if values align. If they are national, there may be a charity evaluation tool available to determine their financial health, transparency, and accountability. Where the charity is registered will dictate which tool or resource to utilize. For example, Charity Navigator website is used in the U.S; and Charity Intelligence website is used in Canada. Contributing becomes more complicated when you want to invest time, money, or expertise in another country, especially when you don't have a network to connect you. A good place to start is through a local charity that supports your desired cause in your preferred community.

Another point of consideration is that there are rules and regulations (e.g., Canadian Revenue Agency) in place when you funnel money to a cause. Tides Canada, a registered charity, manages the YouMeWe Foundation Fund. Scholarship applicants will reach out to our fund directly to ask for support; however, the regulations preclude giving money directly to an individual. Canadian charities can only donate to another registered Canadian charity. Although Canadian Charities can conduct their activities in other countries, foreign charities and NGOs are rarely qualified donees.[20]

There are 85,000 charities in Canada.[21] Therefore, many of them will have established networks to funnel donations. Similarly, many African businesses will be seeking organizations to expand awareness, gain funding, or diversify their education. When selecting whom you want to contribute to, it is essential to consider whether they have an established local network that understands the culture, issues, and local processes. Again, this will reinforce a conscious-contribution, and enforce following rational discourse.

Join a service club

Service organizations globally can provide grassroots insights into the needs of a community and country; as a result, they move social issues into the light, where local and international partners can implement conscious and holistic solutions.

To have various volunteer experiences, join an organization and test out different roles to assess where to best utilize your talents. Three international service organizations likely to be conveniently located are Rotary, Lions Club, and Soroptimist. Both Rotary and Lions Club started as men's service clubs and have transitioned to open their doors to women. Both conduct local and international projects for the betterment of communities and the world.[22]

Soroptimist started in 1921, within 20 years of Rotary, the oldest service club. Because Rotary and Lion's club didn't welcome women, Soroptimist made way for women who wanted to give. Over time, their mission became to improve the lives of women and girls through programs leading to social and economic empowerment. Although other service clubs opened their doors to women, Soroptimist has stayed with the core intention: "Women at their best, working to help other women to be their best."[23] Beyond giving to the community, service clubs have other social benefits and sustainability obligations.

Rotary International has one of the most established networks and holds the highest consultative status offered to a nongovernmental organization in the United Nations. There are over 1.2 million members in 35,000 clubs on five continents, with one goal — to take action to change the world. Having a global network of clubs provides access to humanitarian needs, an understanding of the culture, and collaborative opportunities with people who have subscribed to similar values.[24]

In 2018, I attended the Rotary International Conference in Toronto. The sheer number of delegates, the multi-cultures represented, the diverse projects supported internationally, overwhelmed me. One talk had the most profound impact on me. It was a panel of five Rotarians speaking about changing the nature of volunteering — each panel member came from different country and gave distinct cultural context to how volunteerism is perceived locally.

Joe Otin was the speaker from Kenya. He is the Chief Executive Officer at The Collective - Interactive Ad Agency and a Rotarian. With all his charisma, he placed context around the power of community, regardless of financial means. Africa has fewer Rotarians than anywhere else in the world, but its culture is woven together through the belief in unity, and communal living. Joe shares that many Kenyans don't understand Rotary. He would be asked, "Why do you need to join a club to contribute to others? We do it every day." As Joe says, Kenyans give a lot to family, friends, and neighbors.

Kenya's giving was never more evident than in 2011 when Marsabit, the county in Northern Kenya where the Randille tribe lives, and other surrounding counties were suffering the worst famine in 60 years. The Government and the international donor community were slow to respond. Kenyan's had to take matters into its own hands. Lead by Kenya Red Cross, they organized a campaign called *Kenyans 4 Kenya.*

The Kenyan Red Cross is part of an extensive international humanitarian network.[25] As a trusted organization, they were able to leverage the brand amongst Kenyans. A coalition in the private sector and citizens raised over US$11 million in three weeks to contend with the drought, of which 5.5 million were donations of US$1 or less.[26]

The people had the power, and they used it. Kenyans rose to the occasion to contribute financially; they demonstrated Kenyan pride, and their actions announced to the world: do not dismiss us when it comes to offering a viable solution that affects the future of our nation.

More African Rotary clubs are emerging, and there are more opportunities for local clubs to collaborate with other clubs internationally. Many of the women we interviewed for WisdomExchangeTv have joined Rotary as a way to engage their children in volunteerism, to connect to people globally, and to continue to embed the Rotary ethos of *service above self*.

Volunteer with an established organization

Volunteering for an organization is one of the most efficient ways to assess if you want to make a longer-term commitment. There are endless possibilities when it comes to where to volunteer — from a retirement facility, hospital, animal shelter, association, soup kitchen, to schools — the needs are truly endless. Although some volunteer options may require a police check, it is relatively easy to find one that can use a willing heart and able hands.

Some people don't have time to contribute beyond their family, but the best contribution a parent can make is to rear their children to be actively contributing citizens. If time is the only restriction, and you want to give to several initiatives, consider the 100 Who Care Alliance. This program offers a unique opportunity to gather with 99 others and listen to three short presentations on local charities that a member wants to support. Within an hour, each member has an opportunity to vote. The local charity with the most votes receives the members' collective donation, totaling a minimum of $10,000 ($100 per member). Meetings take place each quarter with three new presentations, and three new recipients — an innovative way to be connected to like-minded people and contribute to the local community needs when your time is tight.[27]

Establish trust — a channel not to be missed

Regardless of the channel you choose to explore when consciously contributing, either going through a third party or directly to the source, establishing trust is essential. As Rusia Orikiriza Bariho says, "Work hard and network. As an individual, we cannot do it ourselves. Have patience and be trustworthy, as you cannot buy either of those characteristics."

In this trifecta relationship between the beneficiary, benefactor, and yourself — trust will be the conduit to accomplish the desired goals. The congruence of words and actions will be conducive to assessing the others' integrity, competency, consistency, loyalty, and openness — all qualities that nurture trust.

Regardless of which stakeholder is a conduit for your contribution, ask questions about their mission, goals, measures, progress, and finances. Visit YouMeWe.ca book community to download questions that help you elicit if an organization aligns with your intentions and is your best channel of contribution.

Regardless of the contribution channel and the trust you've established, you will need perseverance and patience. Meaza Ashenafi a co-founder and the chairperson of Enat bank, lawyer, and women's activist from Ethiopia, advises people to control their expectations when they want to make a change:

> When you are an activist, you know it will take time. You learn from the experience of others; you build on what has been done before you. You just continue to fight. There is no other way. It is important for you to control your own expectations.

Make your contribution count

Infiltrating a culture or collaborating with organizations that are trusted and connected within a community will expedite your mission. However, we don't need to lead an initiative. Joining an established organization will provide you with access to causes you care about and systems that are tested.

We all have something to contribute; we need to assess who, what, where, when and why, all of which will be address in Part 2.

Research, collaborate, and ask questions in order to prepare a well thought out plan to execute your social impact priorities.

If patience isn't your virtue, and time is not on your side, but you want to contribute to a cause in Africa, perhaps your best course is to invest in a woman who is already making her contribution count. They understand the culture, they have integrity, and they have the perseverance to see it through. You can invest in a person in any country who has a healthy dose of feminine energy that you trust and who has shown similar characteristics to the pioneering African women, and your investment will likely pay dividends.

Reflect on how to make your conscious-contributions™

1. Which group (or individual) has the most influence with your chosen beneficiary?
2. Which not-for-profit, organization, service club, or institution serves your chosen beneficiary?
3. How trustworthy is the organization you want to contribute to? How do you know?

Chapter 7
Measure what matters

Words of Wisdom

The biggest rules of the game I have influenced is about making women equal. Not equal to men, because there is no men's standard that I want to be equal to. It is about women and men being equal to each other, and the standard that we use to measure that equality is the human standard.

Bience Gawanas, commissioner of Social Affairs, African Union (2002- 2012), Namibia
Pioneer: established the Campaign on Accelerated Reduction of Maternal Mortality in Africa (CARMMA).

When I returned to Kenya in 2011, Mary Ogalo, was leading the Global Bag Project out of a classroom at AIU in Nairobi. The Global Bag Project is a US-based non-profit social enterprise that donates the proceeds from the sales of reusable shopping bags in the developed world to microcredit ventures in the developing world.

Mary employed a group of women from Kibera slum to produce the bags. The opportunity provided them with a stable job and income, both difficult to find with little education. Many of the residents of the urban slum live on less than a dollar a day.

As Mary was part of the YouMeWe Foundation scholarship selection committee, and its first recipient, she was aware of the mission we had when we returned to Africa: to provide scholarships to prospective women leaders. Mary seemed motivated by our second mandate, to celebrate, inspire, and develop future women leaders by interviewing pioneering African women for WisdomExchangeTv.

One afternoon, while wandering through the AIU campus, I came upon an intent Mary on her way to a workshop. After sharing pleasantries, she made a proclamation. "You will want to interview me for WisdomExchangeTv someday, someday soon."

Mary bonded with the seamstresses of the Global Bag Project. Because she was trusted, the women shared their lack of readiness to move from rural Kenya to the slum's deplorable conditions. Mary listened and learned what they wished they had known before embarking on the journey. Their responses inspired the launch of the *County Girls Caucus*, a series of training programs deployed in Kenyan rural schools.

The Caucus's primary mission is to mitigate the vulnerabilities women encounter later in life by intervening earlier. To meet the mandate, they instituted life skills training and leadership programs addressing a variety of issues not taught in African schools, such as human rights, building self-confidence, communication skills, personal hygiene, academic success, women's sexuality, and how to develop a strategic life plan.

The County Girls Caucus, in collaboration with the Kenyan Ministry of Education, has reached 2,550 girls in 123 schools, and trained 134 teachers as coaches. Over 114 girls' clubs have formed in schools and are using a discussion booklet developed by Mary to initiate conversation.[28]

Many girls are forced to drop out of school due to poverty, early pregnancy, early marriage, or a combination. In 2016, the County Girls Caucus reported that girls aged 10 - 20 dropout rate from school was down by 88 percent. A high percentage of respondents said it was due to the program — a key performance indicator of the caucus achieving its mission.[29]

With Mary's understanding of the culture and social issues, and her ability to navigate the school system, she was able to fill a social gap and initiate a program that will have a huge ripple effect across Kenya — a key performance indicator that the YouMeWe Foundation measures. Mary is right: I would be honored to interview her for WisdomExchangeTv.com!

Measure the mission's metrics

Four performance metrics every organization should measure are: success in mobilizing resources, employees' effectiveness on the job, financial growth, and progress in fulfilling the mission. When working with not-for-profits, economic growth is not a measure, but reporting finances is a requirement to meet regulations. Here we will focus on progressing the mission, as it is the driving force in influencing a decision about where to *make your contribution count*.

Measuring the success of an organization's mission can be challenging, particularly when there are no metrics for its achievement. Often not-for-profits or social enterprises use overarching missions that are intangible, as a result, when assessing what sort of relationship you may want to establish, it may be difficult to quantify the impact of your contribution. For example, Gandhi Development Trust is a non-profit organization out of South Africa whose mission is, "The promotion of a culture of peace, justice, non-violence and ubuntu." To assess if the mission achieves the objective, they could evaluate the violence in schools or monitor the number of convicted criminals. However, the achievement of ubuntu, I am because we are, a philosophy that espouses the universal bond of sharing that connects all humanity would be much more challenging to affirm. A not-for-profit can make its mission more measurable by narrowing its focus or breaking the mission down into micro-level goals that, if achieved, would imply success on a bigger scale. As the tenet says, *what gets measured gets done*.

To ensure there is consciousness of a contribution's impact, understanding how a not-for-profit or social enterprise measures its mission is a great place to start. All organizations should have specific metrics in place, to evaluate themselves and identify key performance indicators.

A *measure* is a value that can be summed or averaged. A *metric* is one or more measures that are used to track and assess a specific process, and they are different for every organization. Although all metrics may be valuable, specific ones demonstrate if a mandate is being achieved within a specified time; these are key performance indicators. For example, Mary Ogalo had a target of the number of girls (measure) she wanted to go through the County Girls Caucus program; a metric to evaluate the program is the reduction of child pregnancy; one of the key performance indicators is the number of girls who stayed in school.

As mentioned, the Caucus's mission is to mitigate vulnerabilities of women later in life. By providing girls with sex education, the hope is to reduce pregnancy. As a result, more girls will stay in school, which will provide them with more learning about their options and control they have in their life — the mission.

To evaluate if an organization is meeting its mission, ask, "What would need to happen for your organization to be made obsolete?" The question will expose the metrics that they should appraise. To isolate key performance indicators, ask: "What would the desired situation be if the organization met its mandate?" To garner insight into your role, ask: "How do you see my involvement impacting the mandate?" If you want to initiate a project that helps address a cause, the same questions will help decide on the measures to monitor.

Starting an initiative with the impact in mind is not revolutionary; however, when a person's heartstrings are pulled, vision can become blurred. We see the need to help, often disregarding whether that help will produce the desired effect. Conversely, we may think of the implications of our support in our own familiar environment without considering unfamiliar community response to that aid; or if the individuals receiving it will desire it, or if it is in their best interest.

If you are directly contributing to beneficiaries, you will increase the likelihood of achieving your contribution mandate by discussing all possible issues with them before you begin. Preparation reduces dithering and cultivates perseverance, especially when the obstacles pile up. Transforming any situation takes time, particularly in philanthropy.

Marsha Gabriel, founder, and president of CSI Business Congress, who works with 102 not-for-profits in South Africa, advises:

> A philanthropist must have staying power. They cannot get tired of what they are doing. If you are concerned with the wellbeing of others, you should stay until that situation is rectified and you can see success with what you are doing.

By thinking of potential obstacles, you also come up with possible solutions, which will promote buy-in and increase the commitment of your co-contributors and the beneficiaries.

We have a business plan, a life plan, and a financial plan. How about a contribution plan? Communicate the strategy to all the stakeholders so they will appreciate the commitment from the onset. A clear plan with specific measures, metrics, and key performance indicators will increase transparency and make it easier to identify when the mandate is met.

Mission: beneficiary impact

Sitting in the dining hall at AIU, the WOW group had a guest speaker, Oscar Muriu, bishop, and senior pastor at Nairobi Chapel. He shared his experience of walking into a Walmart in the United States and picking up mosquito repellent that had a plastic straw attached to it. He questioned its use then realized that it was to stop the spray from dripping down your arm. He proclaimed, "Everything in the West is about making what is working better or fixing what isn't broken."

We all laughed because it is true. You need only walk down the clothing detergent aisle and look at one brand and see how each one is fresher, whiter, gentler, or more efficient. Western instincts are to want more, better, faster.

Oscar continued, "Not everything can be fixed, and not everything needs to be, at least not to the *standard* of the West."

He shared a story about one of the hundreds of investments gone wrong in *the continent of need*, a project called the Lake Turkana Fish Processing Plant, which was initiated by the Norwegian government and executed in Northern Kenya. In 1971, US$22 million was invested to provide jobs to the Turkana people through fishing and fish processing for export. However, the Turkana are nomads. To survive, nomads live off the land, so they move from place to place. One might think, "They wouldn't have to move if they could live on fish."

Turkana people had no history of fishing or eating fish, and some clans believed fish are a curse. Once the processing plant was completed, it was quickly shut down. The cost to operate the freezers to prepare the fish for export and the requirement for clean water in the desert was too high. The plant remains a white elephant in Kenya's arid northwest.[30] Although this wasted investment took place years ago, limited due diligence is still prevalent today.

The critical mandate for any organization is to ensure it meets the beneficiaries' needs. The recipients are advocates for their cause and must be consulted before a not-for-profit tackles a solution, or its effort will be futile. To measure a not-for-profit's impact, ask about their social return on investment (SROI). "For every dollar received, how many dollars' worth of social value is being created?"

Like any profitable business, not-for-profit, social enterprise, personal contribution, or corporate social responsibility initiative, it needs ongoing evaluation to assess if the impact intended is being achieved. Bi-yearly strategic assessment of the progression of community impact can expose unproductive partnerships.

The Kingdom of eSwatini is a small, struggling economy. Poverty is high, literacy is low, and HIV/AIDS infection is highest per capita worldwide, leaving children without parents.[31] Nedbank wanted to contribute financially to help fill these three social issues. Fikile Nkose, shared their corporate social responsibility strategy and how it missed the mark.

We had an agreement with the organization that did not specify terms of outputs. It is not giving us what we want out of that partnership. This is a long-term arrangement. For me, that is the biggest regret I have at Nedbank. Now, we have looked at all our partners and stakeholders when it comes to corporate social responsibility. We ensure we have a memorandum of understanding that is targeted at initiatives. We outline the deliverables.

What is measured will provide insight into how a project is progressing toward objectives, but quantitative data only tells part of a story. The beneficiaries and their perceptions will provide qualitative insight that numbers can't convey. Gone Rural's foundation, boMake, prides itself on staying abreast of its artisans' future needs. They conduct regular surveys to assess metrics such as the beneficiary needs and satisfaction, both quantitatively and qualitatively. Philippa Reiss Thorne, managing director explains,

> We are now embarking on a benchmark survey. We have done one previously, and now we are comparing. In terms of educating children, the impact has been huge because we pay for 340 orphaned and vulnerable children to go to school through our scholarship program. It takes a lot of weight off their mothers. Based on our last survey, and in terms of the family, Gone Rural is the only source of income.

Focusing attention on a mission, setting goals, and measuring progress are vital to ensure your impact is conscious, and your stakeholders are fulfilled. However, when we are so focused on the objectives to achieve the mission, we can miss the more immediate need to help a community. When contributing, adapting to the pressing needs of the beneficiary will secure their continued support, as in the case of the missionaries recognizing Rendille tribe's need for literacy when they balanced teaching the children and developing a school system. Measuring is important, but sometimes not as life-altering to the recipient as your accomplishments.

Mission: global development

It has been well-documented that aid has had little effect, or arguably an adverse one, on the economic development or poverty reduction in

Africa. Over US$2 trillion of foreign aid has been transferred from rich countries to poor over the past fifty years, and US$300 billion in aid has gone to Africa since 1970. Rwandan President Paul Kagame explains the period post-second world war when geopolitical, strategic rivalries and economic interest were at their height: "Much of the aid was spent on creating and sustaining client regimes of one type or another, with minimal regard to developmental outcomes on our continent." Dambisa Moya, in *Dead Aid*, exclaims that although it is well known that aid has failed, policymakers continue to endow Africa with aid.[32]

It would appear that aid hasn't had the right metrics in place to provide positive, measurable change. However, that is not meant to disqualify the international communities' ability to help developing countries. The United Nations claims that global development assistance along with regional, national, and local efforts have moved economic growth and poverty reduction. In 2000, the United Nations created the Millennium Development Goals (MDGs), which were to be realized by 2015. World leaders committed to an objective to "spare no effort to free our fellow men, women, and children from the abject and dehumanizing conditions of extreme poverty."[33] MDGs consisted of eight goals and were the catalyst to facilitate the most successful anti-poverty movement in history. The then Secretary-General of the United Nations, Ban Ki Moon states:

> The MDGs helped to lift more than one billion people out of extreme poverty, to make inroads against hunger, to enable more girls to attend school than ever before, and to protect our planet.[34]

These goals not only measured money going to developing countries, but also many other initiatives, such as manufacturing and exports. For example, 79 percent of imports from developing to developed countries were admitted duty-free in 2014, up from 65 percent in 2000.[35]

Despite over 15 years of tremendous progress, there is a long way to go to meet the objectives. In Sub-Saharan Africa, where poverty is most severe, 61 percent of the countries don't have adequate data to monitor poverty trends, often leaving huge data gaps and leaving the poorest invisible.[36]

The United Nations took the lessons learned and over three years all the countries in the U.N. General Assembly underwent one of the most extensive consultation processes ever taken. A global survey was launched, MyWorld2015, and completed by 9.5 million people giving them the opportunity to share what issues matter most. Citizens all over the world had a voice, which contributed to the 2030 Sustainable Development Goals — 17 goals and 169 associated targets that are integrated and inseparable.[37] I prefer to use the more accountable term inspired by a women entrepreneurial investment organization, SheEO, to describe the goals, *The World's To-do List*.[38]

The goals and targets will stimulate action in five critical areas: people, planet, prosperity, peace, and partnership.

The World's To-do List addresses issues common in all countries. There is no arguing that developing countries are more vulnerable concerning each of the 17 overarching goals, and attention needs to be brisk. However, the wealthiest nations have to be more conscious of preserving and replenishing our environment. In the West we still strive for equal pay for women, many children do not have breakfast before they go to school, many are homeless, and mental health and well-being is a huge consideration.

Never before have world leaders pledged common action and endeavor across such a broad and universal policy agenda. The goals are composed of key performance indicators with time-bound targets; each has aligning metrics whereby countries can measure their contribution and progress, encouraging transparency and accountability. The historically significant goals and targets came into effect on January 1, 2016 and will guide the decisions of the United Nations. One of the many highlights is the goal to end poverty by 2030. In partnership, the United Nations committed to "Build a better future for all people, including the millions who have been denied the chance to lead decent, dignified and rewarding lives and to achieve their full human potential."[39]

Organizations, small or large, are in a position to gravitate to one or a few of the development goals. They can structure their businesses to address a passionate issue. In the process, they will attract, engage, and retain customers, colleagues, and collaborators who hold the same values and interest while conquering the concerns that stifle society's sustainable development. It is up to governments, businesses, civil society, and citizens, to collaborate, coordinate, and financially contribute to help turn the tide on the critical issues of our time.

Mission: human rights

Although many human rights violations are highly visible in developing countries, they also lurk in developed countries to various degrees.

According to the United Nations Human Rights Office of the High Commissioner, human rights are rights inherent to all human beings, whatever our nationality, place of residence, sex, national, or ethnic origin, color, religion, language, or any other status. We are all equally entitled by laws, treaties, or general principle, to our human rights without discrimination. These rights are all interrelated, interdependent, and indivisible. [40]

Ninety-nine percent of the women we interviewed from 17 countries had the goal of empowering women. They measure their success against how much they can move either toward equality, optimal health, or economic well-being, with the inspiration to optimizing women's human rights. There are 30 rights and freedoms that belong to all of us. The first Universal Human Right states, "All human beings are born free and equal in dignity and rights."[41] A pursuit many African women will not ignore.

Bience Gawanas grew up under apartheid in colonized Namibia. After serving as a commissioner to the African Union, she went back to Namibia where her pursuit for equality begun.

> As a black person, you were nothing. You had no rights. You did not exist apart from providing the labor. I decided to study law after my

youngest brother was murdered in Namibia. A white man told me that my intelligence as a black person is much lower than a white person, and therefore I will never be able to study law. Then I became a lawyer.

For me to become a lawyer was a passion, to seek justice and fairness. The motivator was the death of my brother, but more importantly, I wanted to prove apartheid wrong. I wanted to prove men wrong. It has got nothing to do with the fact that I am black or that I am a woman to want to achieve and also to contribute and make a difference.

Bience fought for dignity and for equality. As a black person, as a woman, and as a citizen she expresses what justice means to her and how she measures it.

The biggest 'rules of the game' I have influenced is about making women equal. Not equal to men because there is no men's standard that I want to be equal to. It is about women and men being equal to each other. And the standard that we use to measure that equality is the human standard.

In 2018, Bience received a new role as the under secretary general and special advisor on Africa at the U. N. — a institution in pursuit of peace, security and stability.[42]

Endless research suggests that women internationally are not treated equally to men, that they need more representation, and they need to occupy more leadership positions, including in not-for-profits and NGOs. According to a report by the HR Council, for every four employees in an NGO, three are women; however, few are leading them.[43] In government, on boards, as executives, women are left wanting. The goal is not to occupy more positions than men, but to have access to positions to occupy.

A lawyer by profession, Meaza Ashenafi established and managed the most successful national women's rights advocacy organization, the Ethiopian Women Lawyers Association. She was instrumental in working on reforms, amendments, and additions to existing laws affecting women's rights. She found herself in the position of adopting the Ethiopian constitution in 1995 and included the rights of children and women. Meaza continues her fight for women's rights. Admittedly, she didn't think she would ever live to experience her vision of equality realized, but that did not stop her from taking action.

> You don't see transformation quickly. The issues I have been fighting for the last 15 years are still there. They manifest in a different form, but they persist. Sometimes working for social transformation is not easy. It takes time. You need different input to make it work, and all of that takes patience.

Meaza's key performance indicators are clear. Ethiopia will experience equality when: more women are empowered economically; more women are involved in decision-making in the public and private sector; more women are included in the private sector; more women speak up against abuse and violations of their rights; there are more women's agencies to speak up; more recognition of women; and more distribution of power.

Although Meaza doesn't put a measure in front of any of these goals, she knows movement happens in degrees, and progress is palatable. Meaza is a torchbearer when it comes to equality. In November 2018, she was appointed by the Federal Parliamentary Assembly as president of the Federal Supreme Court, which is one of the most powerful positions in the country, and the first time to be occupied by a woman.[44]

Equality is everyone's responsibility. If only one cohort in society is attempting to move an agenda forward, the transformation will be slow. Everyone benefits from equal representation. To establish a *we* society, it takes *you* and *me* to become aware of our bias filters. Being conscious of biases gives us the ability to remove them. Meaza advises, "When you see something that is not right, don't feel sorry for someone — do something about it."

Doo Aphane is a woman who *does something about it*. She is an activist, lawyer, human rights and gender specialist, and director of Women for Women Development Consultancy in The Kingdom of eSwatini. As the first woman to win the right to own land in eSwatini, she is considered a force, even for King Mswati III Dlamini, who consults with Doo on gender issues and will ask advisors if a proposal is "Aphane compliant."

While Mike and I traveled through eSwatini, citizens didn't mention inequality. I found this peculiar, as in every other country many conversations led with the lack of parity. Doo declares it is cultural, "We do have a problem. We call it *do not hang your dirty laundry in public*. It is very strong. You are a true [eSwatini] woman if you don't talk about your challenges." The silence is behind Doo's often battling equality alone. She dedicates her life to elevating women's voice, and it starts with challenging their right to ownership.

> Up to today, women are disinherited in their families. When you look at the livestock in the communities, it belongs to future generations, but what they mean by future generations is the males in the family.

> We should be holding hands in groups of women in whatever space we are in and then we should come together with another layer, another layer. We need agency. We women need to help that agency to act. Each one of us has the potential to be the agent of change.

When Doo Aphane fought for her right to own land, she was fighting for her dignity. In the constitution, it states that both men and women should have access to communal land. However, only her husband could acquire it. A chief approves access to community land, and very few will provide it without a male initiating the request. That male could be a three-year-old grandson. It is degrading for a grown woman to ask a child to be their voice and advocate. As a second-class citizen, Doo explains the plight of women:

> I know too many who lost their homes, lost their funds because their homes were sold behind their backs without their knowledge. Sometimes the house was sold with knowledge but without their consent.

Because Doo went to court and fought for her human right, women are finally entitled to register by law to own land, a vital step in restoring pride in the pursuit of equality.

Mission: sustainability

Hellen Acham's decision to grow chilies in the fertile ground of Northern Uganda makes North East Chilli Producers one of the biggest in Eastern Africa. With over 1,000 women contributing economically to the family and the community, Hellen has achieved her key performance indicator. She surpassed her goal after she made a significant shift in her business operations.

Traditionally, Hellen gave away chili seedlings to farmers. She was encouraged, and then instructed to alter her approach by her Dutch partner, ECHO, an NGO whose mission is to provide sustainable farming solutions to stop hand-outs and start hand-ups. With funding on the line, she had little choice but to start charging for the seedlings. She wasn't sure how the Northern Uganda people would cope as they were already financially challenged.

What Hellen experienced was a considerable behavior shift.

> Traditionally when we give the seed for chili, they would say, 'That is Hellen's chili.' Now they have ownership themselves. They take very good care of what they are doing; they produce good quality.

> Initially, there was high resistance to paying, but people who were contributing were becoming more successful.

The business adjustment increased the ECHO Funding impact. Over 10,000 households are now in the chili production business across Northern Uganda, producing over 500 metric tons. The seedling ownership approach has increased the farmers' power, pride, productivity, and sustainability.

Benefactors' fulfillment

Without the continued support of benefactors (donors, volunteers, employees, customers, suppliers), a mission can be short-lived. Understanding what a benefactor cares about, why they have joined your crusade, and how they want to be acknowledged will assist in designing how you execute your mission. The more conscious you are of each benefactor's desires, the better you will be able to align with their values and measure your impact against what matters. A tailored report with access to the detail will increase relevance, transparency, and engagement.

With the launch of B Corporation certification, for-profit companies' measurement has been made easier. Companies receive a score through an audited assessment on their impact on employees, customers, community, and the environment. To become certified, the company's board of directors is required to amend the governing document to balance profit and purpose. The combination of third-party validation, public transparency, and legal accountability has helped these organizations build trust and value for all stakeholders.

Make your contribution count

Being compassionate and passionate can inspire action; however, if that action doesn't take into consideration the beneficiary, the global development goals (*The World's To-do List*), human rights, and sustainability, then it becomes about the benefactor's ego and not social, economic, cultural, or environmental improvement.

Progress can be measured, so having metrics in place will ultimately help create more awareness, support, and impact. Establishing parameters will help get rid of what isn't working, adjust what isn't growing, and stay the course with what is performing.

There is nothing more rewarding than addressing a social issue and experiencing transformation. As citizens we have the power; now we need to ensure we have the know-how to make the most of our community contributions. It begins with assessing what will provide you with the most meaning — a key to sustainability.

It is time to explore and embrace your feminine energy to *make your contributions count*, be it through politics, activism, education, commerce, or philanthropy — your time has come.

Reflect on how to make your conscious-contributions™

1. What key performance indicators are most valuable to you when assessing a cause's impact?
2. How often will you evaluate your contribution impact?
3. What metrics will you consider when determining if an initiative is sustainable?

Part 2: me — make your contribution count — maximize your meaning

Chapter 8
Embrace your community responsibility

Words of Wisdom
We don't need other people to donate to us. I am here. I am working. I am capable to establish what we need in my country along with other women. You just need to be willing to work.

Nigest Haile, founder and executive director, Centre for African Women Economic Empowerment
Pioneer: founder of the first NGO and co-founder of Enat Bank, first women's bank in Ethiopia

Nigest Haile, founder and executive director of the Centre for African Women Economic Empowerment (CAWEE) in Ethiopia and I were driving to the African Union to propose an international trade initiative — a project I was collaborating on to promote increasing exports.

During our drive, Nigest pointed out several of her clients' large beautiful homes. She shared that when showing her daughters her clients' homes, they would asked "Mom, why are your clients' homes so big, and ours is so small?" She explained, that her purpose is to help build women's success; everything is not about making money.

Nigest is passionate about the responsibility of citizens to invest their time and energy for the betterment of the community. Although everything isn't about money, she feels that citizens have a responsibility to expand, particularly in poorer nations. "If entrepreneurs don't aspire to grow, they are just serving themselves and not the country. They have an obligation to grow, export, and capitalize on obtaining foreign currency — this is critical for Ethiopia." Nigest owns her responsibility to help Ethiopians flourish.

Claiming your duty

Nigest, along with the other women interviewed, all have one thing in common: a sense of responsibility to take the lead and consciously contribute to society. We spoke to women who were pioneers in politics, education, activism, and business. Some had been beaten, raped, and kidnapped. Some had fewer rights than a two-year-old boy; some had no rights at all. Some were discriminated against from the time they were born, while others had a front row seat to prejudices and saw people they loved killed before them. Conversely, others were not in their country of birth during civil conflicts, but they felt the need to return and rebuild.

These conscious-contributors realized their aspirations because of their courage, their character, and their choices. Pioneering African women feel a broad sense of responsibility to contribute to their community, country, or continent. Their motivation isn't fame or fortune, but rather freedom: the liberty to mold a society rich with tradition and culture that will adhere to human rights and capitalize on opportunities.

As the managing director of the Tanzania Women's Bank Ltd., Margareth Chacha took a salary cut to fulfill her sense of obligation to uplift society. She harnessed her courage and her *can-do* attitude to lead an essential change. Tanzanians didn't need to look outside their country for talent to open a bank to meet the requirements of local women. Margareth admits her hesitation to take on the challenge, but she eventually came to a realization:

> I needed to leave something to my society. I left my big salary, which was double what I am making now, but I decided to leave it as the country has been paying for us to get here [to democracy]. I believe the skills we have are the same as international candidates, as many of us have been educated internationally, but we just don't have the confidence in ourselves. I wanted

to show that I had the confidence to take this on for all other women. I feel I will inspire a lot of other women.

As a woman who has a front-row seat to the complexities of Tanzanian culture and women's funding limitations, Margareth is an ideal leader for a bank that provides access to financing for women.

Beti Olive Kamya echoes this sense of responsibility in her pursuit of the highest office in Uganda. She was the only woman vying for the presidency in the 2011 election. Beti didn't win, but this was not failure. Her aspiration wasn't to become president, but to have her message heard by her fellow citizens. Beti believes the political system needs to change, so she became the first woman to form a political party, The Uganda Federal Alliance. Beti describes its goal:

> Most people who were running were arguing about the chair [presidency]. Who will sit in that chair, and when they sit there what will they do? For me, it was a different argument: was the chair properly designed for the job? I decided since no one running for president was raising this argument, I felt very passionate that this perspective needed to be discussed. If we just continued to argue about the chair, then we were driving the wrong course.

By pursuing the presidency, Beti was able to utilize media to amplify her mission and challenge how the government is structured, a message ignored when she spoke from the lower levels of government. Beti took the opportunity to start and continue the conversation. She believed someone had to.

Some women feel their duty to their country, so they take on the role of crusader. Others see their responsibility as innate. Ela Gandhi started the Gandhi Development Trust in South Africa in 2002. The aim was to manifest the values Mahatma Gandhi started in South Africa and promoted over his life — a spirit of reconciliation and a culture of peace and non-violence locally and internationally. Ela continues to spread Mahatma Gandhi's values, which include having true integrity, living a selfless life, living in a communal situation, giving more attention to what we do and how it affects the community rather than how the community benefits us personally.

As Gandhi's granddaughter, Ela was schooled in selflessly contributing to others, without expectation. This life, as Ela describes it, is not for the easily swayed.

> [Our religious practice is] looking at how we can improve the lives of others rather than ourselves. It is looking at the right thing to do. It sounds simple, but as soon as we get up in the morning, we have challenges, and you have to decide what is right and what is wrong.

Those who were not born into the values of selflessness or immersed in a culture where complacency is not an option, may become numb to the inequalities of society, such as the discrepancy between rich and poor. Complacency has never been so evident as with the realization that women have either accepted status quo or have felt their abuses will not garner the attention they deserve in the court of public opinion, or for that matter, a court of law.

Although the perception that women's rights have recently progressed in the West, violence against women is rampant. In Canada alone, every two and a half days, a woman is killed.[45] Abuse knows no boundaries; it affects all cultures, races, and economic circumstances. Violence against women occurs daily, and it is impossible to track the emotionally or physically damage due to a lack of reporting. Peel another layer of the onion, and it is evident inequality persists due to the lack of equal pay and fair and respectful treatment in the workplace.

The #TimesUp, and #MeToo movements have demonstrated that society was apathetic and tolerated inappropriate behavior for too long. Not only did we think no one cared, but we didn't want to rock that proverbial boat. As the ninth UN Secretary-General, António Guterres says: "Achieving gender equality and empowering women and girls is the unfinished business of our time, and the greatest human rights challenge in our world."[46]

More than one's circumstance, a belief or observing an injustice is often the inspiration for dedication to a cause. It is also motivated by a personal sense of duty, intolerance for the status quo, and a craving to make a difference in the world — ultimately providing us with a sense of meaning. Meaning starts with living our purpose. Our purpose gives us a reason to wake up in the morning and live each day with intention, knowing every action we take is motivated to *make our contribution count*.

As Dr. Martin Luther King Jr. said during the speech in Selma, Alabama on March 8, 1965, "A man dies when he refuses to stand up for that which is right. A man dies when he refuses to stand up for justice. A man dies when he refuses to take a stand for that which is true."[47]

The Milieu Reality

As cultures continue to cross borders, citizens have the opportunity to become more socially aware. Amalgamating cultures exposes citizens to new perspectives that can enhance their own. Through migration, society's preferences and priorities change. Increasingly, all citizens must demonstrate tolerance, or they will find themselves trying to impose conflicting values with a lot of resistance. If society stops embracing new perspectives from different cultures, it will isolate itself and its ability to adapt to what is inevitable — change.

By digging into African history, you can understand why there are so many activists today trying to move societies forward. All African countries, except Ethiopia, were colonized. After 1955, most acquired their independence and since then have been trying to regain the values that serve their society while transforming the ones that don't. Through revolutions, civil wars, and activism, Africans are drawing attention to social injustice.

Because many African countries' independence occurred in recent history, women now in their fifties were pioneers in helping to forge the way forward at the grassroots. Her Excellency, Nouzha Chekrouni, the ambassador of the Kingdom of Morocco to Canada, shares how her generation was involved in politics and believed in making a change.

We were fighting for democracy. We were part of this evolution of our society. You couldn't be a student without being active in society. It was like a trend. It was part of the philosophy in my country, and part of our strength. This belief brought me to politics.

When I was a student, I was part of the union of students, fighting for our rights as students. When I finished my studies in Paris and returned home, I was aware that I couldn't stay out of politics, because that is what I felt was the best way to stay active in our society, to make the changes that we dreamed of.

Generally, people in Western society have forgotten the desperation required to be part of a movement. We talk about *leaving a legacy* as if is something to do at a point later in our lives, rather than a way to live our lives.

Westerners generally perceive their obligation to society as being quite minimal. We tend to identify with the *me* mentality rather than the *we* society. We ask ourselves, what can *I* get, rather than what would benefit the welfare of all. We gage our social-wellbeing by our individual progression and not the advancement of all. The political economist Adam Smith has influenced this perception with his notion of the *invisible hand*, which suggests the realizing of unintentional social and economic benefits for all with the pursuit of self-interested profit-seeking individuals.

In many cases, he is right. With this pursuit, however, Westerners' sphere of influence is minimized. There is no obligation to the greater good. There is a limited responsibility to our fellow citizens and no accountability for their progression. We are, however, not completely void of our civic duty. Some citizens vote, abide by laws, volunteer, serve in the military or government, and most pay taxes (grudgingly). What we don't have is a collective belief that we have a responsibility to serve society. In the book *Social Entrepreneurship*, by David Bornstein and Susan Davis, the authors describe the disconnect between democracy's pursuit and the co-dependence required to thrive.

It's worth asking how modern democracies have evolved to accept individualistic social norms that would cause tribal societies, military units, and sports teams to collapse.[48]

At humanity's core is the need to feel connected to others. If we are a passive citizen, we relinquish our claim on society's performance and become a bystander to the ecosystem that influences our lives and connects us to the broader community.

At the start of the new millennium, it appeared there was progression in our evolution of humanity to take care of others; however, more recently it seems to have taken a few steps backward under the current leadership in several countries. Society can choose to diverge, like those led by political leaders who are moving toward a polarizing mentality of protectionism, individualism, and consequently racism. Alternatively, they can converge toward a *we* reality where organizations, including the private sector, are promoting social contribution, consciousness, and collaboration.

Despite some political leadership recoiling, more business leaders are becoming inclusive and are making progressive decisions that are evolving society and the environment. As more citizens become intolerant of self-serving leaders, and silo nations, there is no doubt that we are on the cusp of a profound movement.

The private sector taking the lead to social change

Internationally, more organizations are seeking to operate their businesses consciously. Conferences are promoting pursuing purpose, consciousness, and social innovation. Companies have new metrics to measure their impact on all stakeholders through the B Corporation initiative. Many leaders and entrepreneurs realize that by placing a social issue or the environment first, not only can they have a positive impact on society, but in the long-term their companies can reap greater profits. Perhaps over time, companies will recognize a social shift in which uplifting the lives of others is a common cultural practice — one where everyone capitalizes.

The private sector must not sit idly by and allow any government's mandate to dictate their own values and actions. Each of us has the power to take responsibility and *make our contribution count*.

A demographic shift is upon us, and with the transition comes a change in how the workforce operates, what they value, and how they contribute. In Canada, in 2020, 50 percent of the workforce will be millennials and by 2028, 75 percent. The cohort will have amplified purchasing power, donor dollars, and investment influence. Millennials want to have an impact, and 76 percent consider a company's social or environmental contribution before joining an organization. Nine out of 10 would switch the brand they buy to support a particular cause.[49] In addition, 40 to 55 percent of buyers in 60 countries, across generations, will pay more for a product or service if they know it is having a positive social or environmental impact.[50]

So being better or different than competitors is not enough anymore. Being a mission-focused organization will attract, engage, and retain well-aligned customers, colleagues, and collaborators. Businesses need to meet the call. There is an upsurge of social enterprises and socially conscious organizations. We need a grassroots uprising of businesses deciding how they will meet the conscious demands of their employees, customers and society. Millennials' voices are growing louder, and the trend toward their desire to be employed by conscious organizations is becoming inevitable. Companies have an opportunity to be on the right side of addressing *The World's To-do List*.

There are many gaps in communities that the government can't fill, or don't feel are a priority. With the U.N.'s Sustainable Development Goals, the need, and the demand, is now. This is where you can assist, with your buying decisions, donations, wisdom, and time.

Each of us has the power to decide where, or how we choose to contribute. As a citizen, don't only look to NGOs, charities, governments, the wealthy, businesses, or others to provide. We all have a role to play; the question becomes how big a part will you seize?

How big is your backyard?

Once one decides to contribute, it becomes a question of why, who, how, when, and where. For now, let's focus on the where.

During the Syrian refugee crisis, I posted on my Facebook page asking if anyone would like to join me and donate money to help a refugee family relocate to Canada. Living in Canada, a country built by immigrants, I and many others, couldn't ignore this horrific situation. Unfortunately, it did not elicit the response I had hoped for.

One particular rebuttal post could be summarized by, "Why don't we give our attention to those in our backyard first?" And in fact, this is reflected in a lot of current debate.

Experience shapes our perspective. Some of use focus on our tribe, our community, or our nation. While discussing a disaster on a different continent, the media will often say, "There were *x* number of Canadians, injured or killed." This is evidence of the proximity paradigm — we care if an incident directly impacts our community, city, or country, which is why the media reports information in the context of the listener.

The expression, *take care of the people in your backyard first*, suggests taking care of our own. Who is that? Who are our own?

Is that to say we can ignore injustices to people who are not of our race, culture, or gender?

Dr. Martin Luther King Jr. didn't ask the white people who walked hand-in-hand with the black people across the bridge in Selma to go home.

An us versus them mentality is the cause of wars, terrorism, gangs, and hatred in general.

To make real change, we need the participation of all people, those in the direct line of fire, and those citizens who realize it is unjust not to honor human rights. Appreciate that there is only one race — the human race.

The size of your backyard is relative to your view of the world. If you have a *take care of your own* philosophy, your picture may be smaller. If your contributions are far-reaching, your view is likely larger. We must not condemn people for their view, but rather celebrate that they are embracing their responsibility to society, wherever that may be.

Make your contribution count

We would be wise to take a lesson from leading African pioneers and their demonstration of the *we* ethos, engulfed in their feminine energy. Life is not just for living but also for serving the living. Legacy is not a stage in life — it's a way of life.

Where you decide to consciously contribute your time, energy, or money is dictated by your viewpoint, your values, your passion, and your purpose, all of which we will explore in the next chapters.

Reflect on how to make your conscious-contributions™

1. Are you content with your contribution to society? Why is that?
2. How, if at all, have changing universal values impacted your decisions?
3. How does where you work or where you make purchase decisions contribute to *The World's To-do List*?
4. What is happening in your backyard that you have been waiting to do something about? Under what circumstances would you help address the issue?

Chapter 9
Explore your purpose

Words of Wisdom

You were created for a purpose. You didn't come to the world to start building yourself up through school and through work, to find significance. You are significant already. Listen inside. You are not created to fit in, but to stand out and attract.

Modesta Lilian Mahiga, founder and managing director, Professional Approach Group
Pioneer: recognized worldwide as one of Africa's young leaders

Personal purpose. It has so much pressure associated with it. I recall trying to find mine in my late twenties and being in the Rocky Mountains hoping to be inspired. In the copious amount of journal entries, I brainstormed my strengths, weakness, barriers, and aspiration. I hoped my fate would jump off the page, and I would follow it to eternal happiness. What did spring off the page was my deep desire to dive into the hearts and minds of pioneering women — a purpose short lived. There were too many obstacles to sustainability. Years later, after addressing many of the barriers, I was in pursuit of my purpose again. I collided with another block. The realization that finding a *purpose* is not a destination but rather a direction of how to live our lives.

A purpose is not a cause, such as civil rights, education, or fighting disease. You can have a sense of purpose without contributing to a cause, and you can contribute to a cause while you explore your purpose. In his book Purpose Economy, Aaron Hurst describes a cause as a noun, something you support and a purpose as a verb, it's not only what you are doing, but how you do it and thereby relate to the world.[51]

Each woman interviewed for WisdomExchangeTv seemed to have an aura composed of self-confidence, determination, faith, and calmness. She had confidence that she was where she was meant to be, doing what she was meant to do. She was determined in her chosen mission, no matter what obstacle confronted her. She had faith that she wasn't alone on the journey, and that she was serving something more significant than herself. She exuded calmness — not to suggest she hadn't fought, but rather that the fight was hers to have.

This force was prevalent, no doubt, because each pioneer was living her own purpose — not her mother's, father's, or society's. Purpose is explored by you. Determined by you. Lived by you.

We all have a unique path on which we can explore our *why*. While it may take some time to discover as it can be ever changing, once you are conscious of your purpose, you find a renewed motivation and a deeper sense of your authentic self.

You may not know your purpose, perhaps because you haven't consciously thought about it, or you don't have the roadmap to understand how to pursue such a meaningful course.

Why explore your purpose?

Purpose is our driving force. Purpose is where we utilize our talents and realize our potential. It is the drive that motivates us to explore and the need for us to be exalted. Purpose is constant and contributes to our overall well-being, unlike happiness which is a mood and can be fleeting. There will be moments of both elation and struggle all of which are part of our purpose realized. Believing that our talents and potential are respected will be enough to persevere through obstacles that present themselves as we self-actualize.

According to the book *Purpose Economy* and its extensive research, people live their purpose in three ways: they seek a sense of community,

Part 2: me — make your contribution count — maximize your meaning

an opportunity for self-expression and personal growth; and the ability to serve others and the planet. Thereby, personal, social, and societal purpose are accomplished.[52] Here we will focus on societal purpose where your meaning is maximized.

Four avenues where you can explore your purpose

There are four distinct avenues where purpose can be explored, some more organic than others. All four require you to relinquish control, connect to your deep desires, listen to your instincts, be conscious of your circumstances and dare to surrender to the universal signs guiding you. Your purpose is exposed through a calling, circumstance, evolution, or conscious quest.

Calling — called to your purpose

A calling is an urge by an internal or external force to do something specific with your life. To hear a calling, requires a very conscious life in which you are aware of your true self, your authentic being. The ego has been neutralized, allowing you to live the way you are meant to live, to be whom you are meant to be — unapologetically just you.

Jane Wathome's calling came through self-questioning. Jane was volunteering at her church in Kenya while she was working in sales and marketing. During that time, she decided to get her degree in counseling, which led her to the decision to focus on vulnerable women with HIV/AIDs. As Jane shares:

> I looked at my long-term vision and I asked myself, what I wanted to spend the rest of my life doing. I knew I didn't want to go back to the corporate world, but I have gifts in business, marketing, counseling, and evangelism. My goal was to take a holistic approach to HIV/AIDS.

Jane would bring food to women with HIV/AIDS and provide them with an education. When she returned to her comfortable home, she had an overwhelming feeling that she needed to do more.

> April 2002, I remember the conversation with God, and he was asking me, 'How far are you going to go with this? Is it a hobby?' I knew I was ready

to donate my life. Then the next question came: 'If you need to wash them [a woman with HIV/AIDS], will you wash them?' I believed I would.

Two days later Jane was tested. Others would not help a woman with HIV/AIDS who needed bathing, so Jane did. She proclaims this was her calling to continue to serve the vulnerable, not as a hobby, but as a life purpose. She founded an institution where women who lacked medical care could visit, feel safe, and rediscover independence or find it for the first time. Beacon of Hope was born. Jane integrated her holistic strengths to create a faith-based and community NGO to address the HIV/AIDS pandemic among poor women.

Jane believed God called her to her life purpose. She followed the call. No doubt, the hundreds of women to whom she provides skill development, health care, and hope, appreciated her listening so they could reclaim their lives.

Circumstance — led to your purpose

We all experience loss or grief in our lives; however, a tragedy can pull us toward an issue that needs us to bring it into the light. When suffering, we have two choices. One, choose our attitude; two, decide how to respond to the situation. A grieving person will often seek a coping mechanism that makes them feel productive, as if in some way this tragedy is a call to act. Many movements, laws, and charities have come to fruition because of a tragic circumstance, and someone's need to do something about it.

Canadians Hanne Howard and Ted Horton found themselves in a series of circumstances that continue to guide them to become deeply immersed in the Lenana community, a slum in Kenya. It started with an elderly resident asking for their help, followed by witnessing a listlessness in children singing. Hanne explains:

> We were confronted with these little kids. When they started singing for us, Ted asked, 'Why are they so listless?' The guy next to us said, 'Because I wasn't able to feed them for three days.' They were truly starving. They were going to die if no one fed them. Ted ran out to collect milk and bread

to feed them. That was the beginning, because once you start feeding them, you can't stop.

If you feed them, you have to educate them. If you don't, you become part of the problem. That experience changed our lives.

In Lenana, there are many orphaned children. Mothers have died of AIDS; fathers have abandoned their homes, or grandmothers are in poor health. Many kids have no place to go, and no place to call home. As a result, there is little parental influence. The Hanne Howard Fund helps fill this gap.

Hanne and Ted's trip to Kenya was intended to be a sabbatical, or as Hanne describes it, a holiday to "escape all our commitments in the first world." Ironically, they were seeking a carefree life, but circumstances took them on a detour and confronted them.

They were in a position to embrace their newly found circumstance, which led to helping raise 130 children on a quarter of an acre complex. They provided them with a refuge before school for breakfast, and a haven after school. The children now have access every day to an oasis in the Lenana slum where they receive care, hope, and life lessons. They are encouraged to live their dreams and not to be victims of their situations. Hanne and Ted take them in, feed them, educate them, care for them, and don't leave them until they are well on their way to university. Two Canadians moved from comfort to compassion, a demonstration that our lives will lead us to where we need to be if we are open enough to acknowledge the signs.

Evolution — *evolve to your purpose*

Joyce Muraya, country director of Amani ya Juu in Nairobi, Kenya provides thoughtful insight on the evolution of purpose: "To find your purpose, focus on just a next step. We don't see our purpose lit in neon. Just take the next step that is in front of you. Take opportunities."

Christine Asiko, a Kenyan English teacher now living in the UK, followed that advice. While in Kenya, she was tutoring a young girl named Maria, who was a gifted storyteller. When Christine read Maria's compositions, they were laced with spelling errors. Though they worked together for hours, both became frustrated because although Maria learned how to spell a word one week, she would forget how to spell the same word by the following week. Eventually, Christine received a book on a reading and writing disorder, dyslexia — Maria's diagnosis.

The more Christine taught Maria, the more curious she became about dyslexia. She found herself diving deep into understanding it, then began educating others about it.

Christine founded Strive International with the goal of building awareness of dyslexia in Africa and supporting discussions to help children with this learning disability succeed in school. She also addresses issues to transform the perception of dyslexia and provides tools to teach children, minimizing the marginalization of students.

Although Strive International has helped hundreds of African teachers understand the condition, Christine recognized the continuing challenge of teaching many African educators who use memorization as a learning tool: they are averse to different thinking patterns. She broadened her scope to incorporate various learning difficulties, including the challenges of learning in a different language or in a different culture. Christine evolved to be a neurodiversity specialist consultant, who acknowledges that all brains are unique, and all have different learning patterns — a purpose that grew from her compassion and curiosity.

Conscious quest — pursue your purpose

Rehmah Kasule, founder of C.E.D.A International in Uganda, saw her path in the corporate world as limited. "I knew my wings were too big to fit into someone else's office." Armed with a marketing background and a purpose to prepare youth and women for entrepreneurship, she pursued her path. As a Muslim woman, she would have to go against the cultural norm "of being seen, not heard," and find her voice to educate, inspire, and ultimately prepare women and youth to pursue their purpose. Rehmah takes youth and women on a journey of self-reflection, coaches them, and provides skill development to transform them into successful entrepreneurs.

Her purpose is to create a new generation of women leaders who are economically independent and socially responsible. She runs special income-generating programs for women, youth, people living with HIV/AIDS, and rural communities. She made a conscious decision to change course when she felt her job was not living up to her purpose.

Your purpose, however, can also be lived where you work. Find an organization with a mandate that aligns well with yours. Search social enterprises, benefit corporations, charities, not-for-profits or businesses and assess their purpose, vision, and mission.

Alternatively, explore an opportunity where you can realize your purpose at your present job. If you are in technology, perhaps you want to contribute to youth in distress; you could program an application that assists youth to connect to help.

If you are a marketer passionate about the environment, you can recommend solutions that could make your colleagues more environmentally aware. Employees can lead from any position; it requires the ability to take ownership of an idea and execute it in line with the overall mission of the organization.

Many of the women we interviewed found their purpose because of a calling, circumstance, or evolution. For those on a conscious quest it is less evident, primarily because exploring a purpose is a process.

Purpose personified

Once you understand your purpose, you will find yourself in an alpha state — awake relaxation. Here is where your awareness expands. Ideas emerge, and creativity flows because you are calm and peaceful. People often experience this state when they are highly relaxed, such as taking a shower, waking up from sleep, walking in the woods, or meditating. From this alpha state, it is as if everything happens to serve your purpose.

Once we re-engage into our beta state, we are fully awake and alert. Ironically, it is sometimes when we need to be most creative, we produce the least original ideas. In the beta state, we can lose the feeling of surrendering to our higher purpose. As we tactically move our aspirations forward, we can become consumed with the challenges and barriers rather than our resilience and the possibilities. Although you are still conscious of your purpose, in the beta state, you can become laser-focused, actually stifling progress. Allow it to guide you not consume you.

Merging the enlightenment of your alpha state with the strategic execution of your beta state will expedite your purpose realized.

Make your contribution count

To maximize your meaning, your conscious-contributions need to be aligned with your purpose. Is there a relationship that needs more attention; an area of growth that can benefit others; or has the universe conspired to direct you how to serve? Succumbing to your purpose, requires staying in the moment. As the universe sends you energy, be it through your God, spirit, or gut, accept its guidance. Acting on the signs is a steppingstone to our ultimate potential.

Reflect on how to make your conscious-contributions™

1. How would your life change if you were to serve a purpose?
2. Have you received signs that you are to do something specific with your life? What signs? What do you think they mean?
3. When do your best ideas emerge? What can you do more regularly to access them?

Chapter 10
Discover your purpose

Words of Wisdom

Lead your best life. Whatever your calling is, don't make any apologies for it. Do what you feel in your heart of hearts.

Joanne Mwangi, CEO, PMS Group, Nairobi, Kenya
Pioneer: founder of the Federation of Women Entrepreneur Associations

On my first trip to Kenya, the 18 women I traveled with had multiple suitcases filled with teddy bears, clothes, toiletries, sewing materials, and art and medical supplies. I arrived in Kenya with my clothes, hiking boots, and good intentions.

In preparation for our Kenya experience, the well-intended women discussed what they could contribute to Kenyan society. Not knowing what I had to offer that Kenyans would want, I surrendered to the experience. I would let Kenyans inform me if I have a skill that could serve its citizens.

One evening, one of my travel companions and I were invited to dinner at the home of Samuel, a student pursuing his master's degree in divinity at Africa International University.

I was curious. "What type of work do you hope to do?"

Samuel proudly responded, "I want to continue with the work I'm doing now. I started the Africa Frontier Initiative, a charitable organization that will transform the lives of pygmies in the Congo and other communities in the region. Pygmies lived in the deep forest between Rwanda and the Congo and at the end of the 1994 genocide, many of the militia backed by the Hutu ethnic group that provoked the genocide, ran to the forest to escape. The militants murdered and then cannibalized the pygmies for medicinal purposes."

I was horrified but completely enthralled. Not only had I not heard the word pygmy in years, I had thought it was a derogatory term. I also couldn't believe that these small, non-violent people were being brutally killed.

"For the pygmies to survive we need to get them out of the forest and assist them in establishing a new way of life." Samuel continued.

"How are you going to help?"

"We are teaching the pygmies how to farm."

"Do you know how to farm?"

"I don't know how to farm," he said.

In that instant, I couldn't help hearing the echoes of many Africans' belief that Westerners often arrive in their countries with bravado, teaching what they don't know, and trying to fix what they don't understand. Samuel, a Kenyan, was attempting to assist pygmies in the Congo by teaching a topic about which he had little knowledge.

He continued, "But some of the people I work with do. We will teach the pygmies to farm so they can survive outside the forest."

"And your role?"

"To raise money for the seedlings and the travel to get there. It takes days to travel by bus to get to this remote region in the Congo."

Watching my travel companion fidget, I leaned in. "So, Samuel, have you ever fundraised?"

"Would you be interested in training in how to fundraise?"

His answer was a resounding "Yes."

Now, a Kenyan had informed me of a skill I had that would be of service.

I had planned to stay for a full two months, originally to sightsee, but now I had a purpose — to provide people who discovered their purpose the skills to amplify their message.

Within the month, I was conducting training programs on fundraising and persuasive presentation skills, and yes, Samuel was a participant. He went on to expose the struggles of the pygmies in the Congo, Rwanda, and Kenya. He has written a book, *The Pygmy World*, and he is the founder and executive director of Pipes International. The NGO's focus is on serving indigenous pygmies, vulnerable children, and marginalized groups to help provide opportunities and hope through education, health awareness, resettlement, small businesses development, food security, missions, and outreach programs.[53]

Samuel knew his purpose was to assist the vulnerable; his mission was to help the pygmies thrive; he just needed further skills to realize his vision for both.

Living my purpose started years ago by training people to communicate their company's message influentially. Now my intention developed. I was to train Kenyans to persuasively communicate their mission to garner support — a shift in a purpose being lived.

In reflecting on each milestone that offered clarity to my purpose and evaluated socially conscious leaders, an interconnected framework emerged on how to maximize meaning: B.E.L.I.E.V.E.

B – Being authentic: Who is your authentic self?

When making decisions to shape a meaningful contribution to your profession, community, or beyond, it serves to act in line with one's authentic self. If you execute decisions from this perspective, you will minimize regrets and maximize the feeling of contentment, knowing it is consistent with your authentic being.

Jane Wathome, founder of Beacon of Hope, Kenya, suggests, "Visit with yourself." Self-reflect, create a list. Acknowledge your skills, talents, wisdom, strengths, fears, weaknesses, and perceived obstacles. Most importantly, identify who you are at your core —your unique, uplifting characteristics that yearn to be expressed.

Doo Aphane, a renowned women's activist from eSwatini, states that responsibility emanates from *me*:

> I believe that *I count*. No matter what came before me. When I ask God to help, I have to be there to ask the question. The individual counts.

I / me is the strength, motivation, inspiration, and the engine to make our purpose emerge.

Be present with yourself by finding the silence between your words and thoughts. Focusing on the now perpetuates a calm that will expose your authentic being; a benefit often realized through the practice of quiet meditation or meditative movement, such as walking amongst trees or yoga. Another approach to exude your natural essence is to uplift the life of another. From here, your purpose may emerge.

E – Empathy and compassion: To whom do you feel connected?

Empathy means you have an understanding or share feelings of another. It can manifest because of an intense life experience, such as a friend's family member being diagnosed with a disease that your family member suffered. Often people are connected to a cause because someone they know has been impacted by it.

Although empathy can be a valued trait, it can also appear as unempathetic. In our attempt to comfort another, we share similar experiences and feelings. Sometimes the focus shifts to us, leading to being consoled rather than us doing the consoling! To be effective, when being empathetic, we need to ensure the interaction is about them, not us.

However, you don't need to share similar circumstances or feelings towards another to be compassionate.

Consider who or what you are connected to, a particular group of people, animals, architecture, or the environment. For some reason, perhaps unknown to you, that specific group or issue pulls at your heartstrings. The feeling is unmotivated by a circumstance; it just is. I call this your *compassion-connection* — profound concern or care. Its interest is not passive, but active. You don't only feel for another or a situation; you're prepared to do something about it.

Knowing who you are compassionate towards, regardless of personal circumstances, will drive the realization of your purpose because it comes from your authentic being.

Your compassion-connection chooses you. Reflecting on who or what you are compassionate towards, will likely influence your career choice, volunteer efforts, and charitable giving while filling your mind and heart, en route to maximize your meaning.

L – Love and joy: What motivates you?

What you love motivates you to act. You love different things to different degrees. Some people love competition, camaraderie, the outdoors, being accepted, being challenged, being inspired, inspiring ourselves, money (usually it is what money can buy that motivates us rather than money itself) — the list is vast. The combinations of what drive us are diverse.

Motivations are rational, emotional, social, and cultural. Regardless of what or who motivates you, at the core, people want to love, to be loved, and to have joy in their lives.

Emotions have a high degree of influence on your decisions. When deciding on where to contribute, you tap into those emotional motivators. Knowing what motivates you will help identify what you love, and what you love will help motivate you.

As a lover of community participation, Yetnebersh Nigussie, an Ethiopian, focused on her abilities, not her disabilities. Blind at five years old, she was compelled to get involved in school, clubs, and councils as a way to prove herself. She wasn't going to be a victim, and her love for participation propelled her to create a school to empower others who had a similar fate.

> As a baby when you are born into a family, you need to be taken care of. You need to be provided with things. I needed to show my family and the community that I am a person that can also contribute, not only consume contributions from other people. I also need to contribute to the world.

> What I am proving for others is that I can do things by myself. I can do things, not as a blind person, not as a young person, but just as a person.

When exploring your purpose and evaluating what you love, also consider pursuing what brings you joy. Doing what you enjoy can help you discover your strengths, leading you to what motivates you.

Norah Odwesso transitioned into a role in public affairs and communications at Coca-Cola, Central East and West Africa, from a career in accounting. She was a good accountant, but she didn't enjoy it. She started seeking new opportunities within the organization to connect with her colleagues and communities. By pursuing a career in communications, Norah now loves her job because she has the opportunity to make a difference in the lives of others. By taking the leap, Norah believes "I am living right in the middle of my purpose — that is a success."

Similar to Norah, when deciding where I wanted to participate during my first trip to Kenya, I struggled between my strengths of business development and what I thought I would enjoy. My option was to work with women entrepreneurs or paint a school alongside teenage girls. Although both options would provide unique insight, I had an opportunity to gain access to a place that tourists often don't go. Speaking to Kenyan teenage girls would offer me a perspective I may never otherwise experience. The road taken proved to be transformational.

The insight gained from these teenagers was another motivator for me to establish the YouMeWe Foundation and to pioneer WisdomExchangeTv, to provide teenagers with a platform to learn from leaders within their culture. Conducting interviews connected me to pioneering women and allowed me to learn about their leadership and social impact, all of which I love.

Your joy will bring others joy. Pursuing what you enjoy can lead you to what you love.

I – Inner strengths: What is your strength thread?

You were born with natural strengths. Take the time to identify and build on them. When evaluating inner strengths, you will often see a thread that connects them. I refer to this as your *strength thread*.

Meaza Ashenafi found herself always wanting to protect those who could not defend themselves. At a young age, she was a guardian of her siblings and later an advocate for the rights of domestic workers. Her *strength thread* led her to become a women's rights lawyer and activist in Ethiopia, where she has a national platform. Meaza shares, "I think we need to reflect continuously on our internal strengths and never settle. We need to pick up on those strengths, push ourselves."

As one of the first female pilots, and commander of the first all-female Boeing crew in South Africa, Jane Trembath self-reflects on her journey to discover her inner strengths. In attempting to find her place in a male-dominated world as a commercial pilot, she continued to try to gain acceptance. It was through extensive journal writing and asking herself: "Why did I react and how could I be better next time?" that provided insight into her authentic self. The journal writing allowed her to vent her emotions so she could ignore them and better evaluate the behavior and reveal her strengths.

> I had felt inadequate because I believed that I had these personality traits that got me into trouble. When I realized those perceived weaknesses are actually strengths when I use them in the right way, I was able to be the best version of who I was. We have to appreciate our uniqueness because we are built the way we are to fulfill our unique niche on earth.

The director of African Programs at Computer Aid Africa, Gladys Muhunyo, describes how to use your inner strengths best:

It is all about what you have, not what you don't have. Begin with what you have, and you will be able to achieve your objective. Know your skills and talents, and your business [and you] will grow.

Be aware of your weaknesses but put effort into developing your strengths. Too much emphasis on improving deficiencies will leave you feeling exhausted and discouraged.

If, however, a weakness is a skill that you require to achieve your purpose, well dig in. Overcome it.

E – Environment: What environment brings out your best?

I attended a Big Brothers Big Sisters fundraising event. This international charity works with young people by providing voluntary mentors. During the dinner, one of the speakers explained the various roles someone can play to contribute to youth. She suggested you could be a donor, sit on the board, be a big brother or sister, or participate in fundraising. Each position is distinct, and you will want to consider where you are most motivated, what you enjoy, and where you can utilize your strengths.

If you like to brainstorm ideas, you may choose to be on a board of directors to have a voice in the strategy of the organization. You may prefer to work solo and find yourself drawn to fundraising where you can get things done on your terms. Perhaps you like to experience your impact firsthand and therefore want to be involved at the grassroots level. In this case, providing mentorship to youth could be the most fulfilling.

Your purpose may connect you with a cause or initiative, but you may not know how to serve it. There are many roles available, be it at your child's school, on her sports teams, with a charity, or at the boardroom table. Assess which environment brings out your best, a discovery that will propel your impact.

The environment best for you may be closing a social gap by establishing a not-for-profit. Lydia Muso, the oldest child of seven, was drawn to taking care of others. She followed her inner strengths and enjoyment of care to become a nurse in Sudan, where she saw many neglected children.

Returning home, Lydia researched the state of child neglect in Lesotho. She found there were no social programs available for vulnerable children and decided to be part of the solution. After being educated in counseling and social work, she started The Lesotho Child Counseling Unit. She now lobbies for policy change to protect children's rights. Although Lydia takes on many roles, the one that gives her the most fulfillment is one where she can connect with the children. She opened her home to abused children giving them a temporary place to feel safe while preparing them mentally and emotionally to go back into the world. Lydia excels in an environment where children are safe and happy under her full-time care.

V – Values: How do your values influence your purpose?

The most influential element of deciding how you will contribute to society, will be dictated by your values. Values are your moral compass, guiding you to make the smallest or the most life-altering decisions.

Values are composed of your ethical standards, religious beliefs, and personal values. Two people can hold the same ethical standards and religious beliefs and yet have very different personal values. You choose your ethical standards and religious beliefs; your personal values choose you.

Many of your values are so deeply submerged in your authentic self that they unconsciously impact the way you live. Your values are often not apparent, and it is not until you are in a moment experiencing inner tension that you realize authentic being is at risk. It causes you to make a choice that will be in line with your core values, which will calm your agitated state. Through this tension, your unconscious values become conscious. You will identify and experience your core values as they guide you throughout your life. Those values will influence your purpose, and therefore your conscious-contributions.

Once you are aware of core personal values, you can alter them to emulate your evolving purpose. Your authentic self is reflected in the intensity of each of your values lived. For example, you may value transparency and privacy. When presented with a situation where being forthcoming may be perceived as interfering in someone's personal life, you will need to decide which value to honor.

While in Kenya, I spent many hours with missionary friends Lois and Mark Shaw, discussing topics such as divinity, university life, and the Kenyan culture. Of all the conversations we had, the one that was most enlightening was about values.

Sitting over dinner, they advised me of the importance of a husband and wife creating family values and a collective life mission. Their commitment to their marital values and mission helped them stay connected over 25 years while they continuously relocated between Kenya and Virginia. When making a decision, they let their family values and mission guide them.

I live, teach and breath values in my work, but it was Lois and Mark's suggestion that prompted Mike and me to discuss what we value in our marriage. We then created a collective mission. Eventually, that conversation would change our course. When we were considering whether to sell our home and most of its contents to go to Africa to conduct interviews, the values and the mission we wrote together guided the decision.

Becoming fully aware of the values that you exercise consciously or subconsciously will guide your actions and help define your purpose. Visit YouMeWe.ca book community to consider your top 10 core values.

Consider adopting the YouMeWe's guiding values of: consistency, consciousness, contribution, care, collaboration, courage, empowerment, and inclusivity.

E – Empower: How can your passion empower you?

Empower your purpose with focused passion. Passion emanates from a combination of being, empathy and compassion, love and joy, inner strengths, environment, and values.

Passion comes from deep inside. It is an intense desire and enthusiasm, and it will empower your purpose. It will energize you to do what others think can't be done. It helps you stay the course when obstacles seem insurmountable. It will carve through any shame people attempt to bestow on you. It gives you the strength to endure when the mountain is high, and the criticism is constant. It will make you feel rich, even if you are poor. It will make you feel supported, even if you are alone. It is the passion for your purpose that will imbue you with courage.

When your purpose is to lobby for the voiceless, to protect against abuse, to raise the suppressed, your passion will inspire you to persevere.

A word of caution, passion can be the fuel to keep you going, but it can also empty your tank and leave you stranded. Exhaustion happens when you give too much of yourself at the expense of rational discourse and self-care.

Consider authentic being and your values to ensure your passion stays directed for good.

B.E.L.I.E.V.E a framework to discover your purpose

To maximize your meaning, your purpose needs to be in service of others. It is the synergy created by the interaction of your authentic being, who you are compassionate towards, what you love, your inner strengths, the environment in which you like to contribute, the values you hold, and the passion that empowers you.

Contributing in line with your purpose in a small way, or with complete devotion, is dependent on the time, resources, and your motivation. To have a social or environmental impact, you may find the need to streamline your life, to reduce distractions to accelerate meaning.

Perhaps you want to incorporate your social or environmental contribution into a model where you can also make a living fusing an equilibrium of profit and purpose.

THREE EVENTS INSPIRED MY journey to establish the YouMeWe Foundation Fund. The first was the late Dr. Carew's message that the biggest problem in Africa is leadership. Second was the realization fundraising could assist in preventing the pygmies' demise. And third, when I painted the school alongside teenage girls, they shared their need for mentors.

While providing fundraising and persuasive presentation training, I started to question if a Kenyan could provide this skill development. Free training is challenging to compete with, so, whose job was I taking? The question led to creating WisdomExchangeTv.com. My *strength thread* prevailed — to question, listen, isolate a gap, explore solutions, and to implement a course of action.

The interviews exposed the one characteristic that bonded all the women pioneers — their practice of conscious-contribution. This realization is infused into the YouMeWe ethos and reflected in the social enterprise and movement.

Make your contribution count

Explore your *why* and B.E.L.I.E.V.E. It will guide you to living your most meaningful life. Take one conscious step at a time and your purpose will unfold the way your higher power intended so you can *make your contribution count.*

Part 2: me — make your contribution count — maximize your meaning

Reflect on how to make your conscious-contributions™

1. How would you describe your authentic self?
2. Who or what do you feel the most compassion toward? Why is that?
3. What motivates you? How would you prioritize those motivators?
4. What is your strength-thread?
5. What environment brings out your best?

Chapter 11
Unblock blocks to live your purpose

Words of Wisdom

Nothing is ever simple on your path to reach your dream or your goal. Accept that and don't see it as a stumbling block. Have a plan A, B, C, and still be able think on your feet.

Tisha Greyling, founder Manyaka Greyling Meiring, partner at Golder Associates
Pioneer: founder of first public participation company in South Africa

Johannesburg, South Africa is a city with a reputation for carjacking, home invasions, and other violent crime. When Mike and I arrived in Johannesburg to conduct six interviews for WisdomExchangeTv, I felt more trepidation than in any of the other African cities we had visited.

We were invited to stay with a friend of a colleague in the suburbs of the city, a beautiful gated home in a wealthy community full of trendy restaurants. Our new friend went away on business for a couple of days and left the run of the house to us and the houseman. The houseman and his wife lived in a room on the back of the property. They were a kind couple who ensured our comfort.

At midnight, the lights suddenly went out. Rolling power outages are common, but after a few minutes of scrambling for the flashlight, Mike and I looked outside to assess the situation and noticed that all the neighbors' homes were still bright. Anxiety set in.

On the way to the guest room, we locked the metal door separating the living area from the bedrooms. I nodded off around 2:30 a.m. only to be woken up at 3:00 a.m. by clattering along the side of the house, followed by an engine leaving the driveway.

Where was the houseman going? Did someone think we are now alone? Was his leaving the signal to now break-in?

Thank goodness Mike was calm, at least on the outside. My imagination was inflamed with violent conspiracies, as every story I'd ever been told about Johannesburg entwined and swelled in my head.

When the morning finally arrived, we were safe in our bed. The lights were still out, and the houseman was still gone. In the daylight, Mike searched for the breaker, but with no success. Out of ideas and unsettled, we called our host, who guided us to the hidden breaker. Lights fixed. I inquired about the houseman leaving in the night.

"Oh, I didn't think to mention to you, but he had to pick up a friend at the train station last night."

A couple of hours later, the houseman returned home and asked us, "Did you notice the lights were out last night? I couldn't see while making my way to the car. I hope I didn't wake you."

It is human nature to make assumptions when we lack details. Information gaps are often filled with experiences or fears that can impede progress. The best course is to seek information to dismantle blocks brick by brick. Alternatively, if facts are unavailable, stay open to all possibilities and prepare accordingly.

Assumptions can be the most paralyzing block, as we don't take advantage of all the resources at our disposal. Conjecture manifests as biases and limiting perspectives, rather than innovative solutions that address social, economic, or environmental advancement.

Citizens of developed countries often assume that the inhabitants of emerging countries don't have the knowledge, ingenuity, or perseverance, to transform their circumstances. The thousands of Western organizations that have gone to developing countries to teach, not to learn, substantiate this claim. Similarly, states internationally don't take full advantage of women's leadership abilities and feminine energy on boards in executive roles or politics. Assuming a lack of talent, or not integrating all citizens' strengths and opinions, can block societies' progression. Limited participation stagnates the communities we live in, the companies we work for, the governments we elect, the countries we invest in, and organizations with which we collaborate.

Barriers start from an individual's perceptions and can restrict a group's advancement. To unblock a block, first, we must become aware of personal biases and limitations. Shine a light on them by trying to understand why they exist. Challenge our perceptions by approaching a block in the opposite direction. For example, if we have a bias toward a particular group of people, seek opportunities to work alongside them. Biases often exist because of a lack of understanding; creating a connection can often diminish any predispositions. A new appreciation can lead us to fulfill our conscious-contributions.

Pioneering African women have had a profound community impact because assumptions, propaganda, or their own perceived shortcomings did not stifle their performance. We assess some common barriers and how determined women converted what could paralyze them into an opportunity to propel them to live their purpose and *make their contribution count*.

Guilt — curse or choice?

Several conscious-contributors interviewed shared a common perception. They prioritized their contribution to society before their family's needs, and they believe their pursuit negatively impacted their family. In one case, a child overdosed. In another, a marriage collapsed. In another, a woman felt she should have been there more for her daughter, and yet another, more for her sons. Women often feel guilty for not feeling guilty!

A perpetual sense of guilt is a curse that plagues many women, as mothers, as partners, as daughters, and as sisters. It represents internal conflict at having done something that we believe we shouldn't have done, or conversely, having not done something we think we should have done.

Many women are compelled to take on all their children's ill-informed decisions and carry them as their burden. All choices impact our children and the people around us. However, there is a point in life when someone else's decisions are just that — their decisions. So many external influences impact our lives. — to bear the burden of every choice our loved ones make is a heavy load to carry.

Guilt often rears its obnoxious head when we are achieving what many would not dare and listening to naysayers. It sabotages our success by masquerading as social correctness. It's as if we are encouraged to defy our place in the world, rather than execute our purpose for the benefit of the world. Consequences seep into profound achievements as questions that force us to contemplate whether we made the right decision. If we broke through the proverbial ceiling, what did we sacrifice at home? If we were a stay at home mom, what could we have achieved if we focused on our profession? Laid off from work, what must we do to be productive now? It never stops. We always feel we are letting someone down, yet a feeling of guilt only lets us down. It consumes our minds and influences our actions.

So, let's be clear: Feeling guilt is wasted emotion. The reality is that we often feel guilty about circumstances in the rearview mirror; you can't change what you did — only what you are going to do. There is always something else we could be doing or something else someone thinks we should be doing. You have one journey. The past informs the path you will take; the next choice lays a steppingstone for the direction you will walk.

To live a life with limited or no feeling of guilt, make the best choice with the information you have. To move forward take responsibility for your choices. If your choice backfires, feel assured you will make a better decision moving forward. Joanne Mwangi, founder of PMS

Marketing Groups in Kenya, advises "follow your hearts of hearts," a wise antidote to feeling remorse.

When endeavoring to live your purpose, your choices will not always produce favorable results, although they will minimize your sense of obligation to others. With every path taken, however, another is not. Choose the way that provides you with the most meaning, and that is the decision you can emotionally defend.

Criticism — foe or friend?

Receiving feedback can block you or build you. It depends on a few factors:

- Who is giving the criticism?
- What is your mindset when receiving criticism?
- What are you prepared to do with the criticism?

Who is giving the criticism?

There will always be critics. Understanding their intention in providing you with this information is critical to assessing its value. Some will share malicious feedback to sabotage your spirit, in hopes of elevating their own. Accept this fact when leading an innovation or pursuing an unorthodox path. Being aware will render a foe's criticism powerless.

Where there are critics there are also supporters. Naturally, if someone you trust and respect provides feedback, it is insight to consider. Friends often experience our personalities from a different perspective and shed some light on how we are perceived. Our respected advisors have earned trust over time, or they too have put themselves in the line-of-fire and are compassionate toward our quest.

These friends encourage your success and can become ambassadors to amplify your initiative. Listen to these allies, assess their feedback, and consider how to implement information to make your efforts more compelling and sustainable.

Just before leaving on our extended African mission, a friend gave me a T-shirt with the slogan, *Well-behaved women seldom make history*. I always found comfort in the message. Behavior is often a judgment bestowed on us, rather than a self-assessment. It can lead to a block of perceived acceptance of our actions, again limiting our courage to do what needs to be done to live our purpose. Women seeking to make history, or to have a socially conscious impact, need to embrace a reality that if every idea we propose is accepted without resistance, our opinions and pursuits are likely redundant.

Self-criticism can be the most destructive. It is a good practice to reflect on our character and elements that we enjoy, as well as parts that we can improve. However, it is detrimental to our well-being to focus continuously on what we need to improve. Neuroscience suggests that what we focus on grows. When consumed with our unfavorable characteristics, we perpetuate the very traits we may be trying to avoid.

If we try to change an aspect of our personality, it can feel like we have put on a tight costume. Wear it too long and it eventually cuts off our circulation. We no longer recognize ourselves, and we can't breathe. This impostor gasps for air and ultimately has no choice but to take off the restrictive facade to survive. Who we are and how we express ourselves is *our authentic being*. Flexing our personality will exhaust you, and can be maintained only for short periods, so finding a *friend* in yourself can help you to thrive.

If we continually criticize ourselves, we will start to believe it. Expressing gratitude and celebrating what we have accomplished can reverse this endless spiral. Another approach to change the focus is to express appreciation or contribute to someone else. Help a neighbor, a friend, family member, or a colleague. By placing the emphasis elsewhere, your authentic self will shine through. When doing for others, you find that friend in yourself.

What is your mindset when receiving criticism?

Criticism is best received with an open-mind. The further removed from tension the more likely we are to hear the gems. Try to emotionally detach from the feedback by regarding it as information that we have the choice to act upon or ignore.

Being in the right frame of mind is essential. It is difficult to be receptive to criticism when being barraged with negative feedback and receiving little positive reinforcement. The delivery of the critique will also have a significant impact on whether we can digest it. Are the tone, intention, and environment appropriate for providing that feedback? If not, remove yourself from the dialogue, requesting another time for the comments. When the time, tone, environment, and intention are well-aligned, the critique can be transformed from a *foe to a friend* possibly altering your course and setting you on a desirable path.

Jane Wathome, of Beacon of Hope in Kenya, was blocked by constant criticism for leaving her professional marketing career to embark on creating a haven for women with HIV/AIDS. Although this judgment was her *foe*, she shielded herself from the bombardment by staying focused on her purpose. Pulling oneself up to a higher calling is the ultimate protection.

What are you prepared to do with the criticism?

Fikile Nkosi, the managing director of Nedbank Swaziland Ltd., says women are often held back not only because of their fear of the unknown, but more specifically, by their fear of criticism.

> We are so afraid to take an opportunity and run with it. We are so scared of being criticized. Once you believe that criticism is part of building your character, you can identify critics that are constructive and destructive. You will be criticized as a leader and as an individual. Take what is positive from that and move on.

Unshackle yourself from the boundaries that criticism can place on you, by consciously altering your mindset and actions. Through this practice, your *foe* will become your *friend*.

Sylvia Owori, an East Africa fashion icon, designer and publisher from Uganda, admits, "If someone really wants me to fail, then they should not criticize me — it just motivates me to be better."

Ability — weight or buoy?

Your ability can be a weight or a buoy; the difference depends on your consciousness. Ironically, a lack of education, experience, and physical restrictions can be more of a float the less consumed you are with its absence.

Education — obstacle or opportunity?

The countries with the highest Gross Domestic Product are in direct correlation with the most educated societies. However, few would argue that formal education alone makes us prosperous. One-third of the richest people in the world did not graduate college, according to extensive research by Steve Siebold, who spent three decades studying over 1,200 of the world's wealthiest people.[54] Education, however, is the admission ticket to the corporate world.

Zulfat Mukarubega has demonstrated that a lack of formal education doesn't need to be a obsticle. She founded the University of Tourism Technology and business studies. It started as a pioneering tourism school that provided tertiary degrees. She got inspiration for the school from her travels and observation of how hospitality could elevate a society. Zulfat hired professors, engaged leaders in the business community, and invested in bricks and mortar.

Armed with her secondary school education, she decided she had enough smarts to change the circumstances for the Rwandan tourism industry, and she did. Zulfat operated with what she did know, where anything is possible. As a divorced woman, she managed to do it her way. Now one of the richest women in Uganda, she proves that lack of education does not negate opportunities. She believes, "A wealthy woman shouldn't be perceived as a threat to a man, but rather an opportunity for the family."

There is underlining social bias that the more educated you are, the more you should be heard. That bias can skew perspectives and limit where solutions to social or environmental problems can be found.

Sheila Freemantle, the founder of Tintsaba Master Weavers holds a mirror to her education biases:

> When I first came here [eSwatini from South Africa], I associated success with education. I learned very quickly that the most successful of our women could be illiterate. It was such a big learning for me.
>
> The strength of the personality, honesty, and calmness are more important than having an educational background.

Tintsaba employs approximately 900 rural women. Watching these women go from being second-class citizens to becoming the primary family breadwinner gave Sheila a front-row seat to progress among the undereducated.

Having an education provides access to people, systems, and solutions that may be more challenging without a degree. Some studies, however, can force us to seek solutions within parameters, limiting our view.

Gita Goven, the founder and CEO of ARG Design, an architectural firm in Cape Town, South Africa, shares how her education was an obstacle to opportunities. She was seeking solutions to development in a low-income community. Her gut was conflicted for two decades by implementing the conventional rules of planning and architecture to meet the needs of buildings in rural settlements. It wasn't until she was challenged by the suggestion that there might be a different way to think about this, that Gita recognized the endless possibilities.

> It was a like a logjam got unblocked and possibilities started to surface opening up the opportunity to have different conversations. We have [designed] for 20 years, and we haven't solved the problem. We are now seeing the unfolding of a whole range of possibilities that are coming out. We are now thinking differently about how we can solve some of those problems: rapid urbanization and informal settlements, which are the only way cities are being formed in Africa mostly. Now we can begin to transform that game. Now and then, you have to think, you have to think again, look afresh.

Gita is no longer interested in sustaining the present, which she believes is unsustainable. She evolved from being an architect to being someone who creates "evolutionary futures." She discovered that drawing inside the lines could limit her influence and impact.

Lack of Experience — mountain or molehill?

If we don't have the experience, many of us will change course. However, what we want to achieve may require us to blaze through the lack of knowledge, not seek another path.

To hear an accomplished woman who has received a multitude of awards for her work in television production say "I don't like asking for money" is a common barrier. This mountain wasn't going to stop Maria Sarungi Tsehai from pursuing sponsorship. She is the founder and director of Compass Communications and needed funds to produce televisions shows that would earn the company international acclaim. Without overcoming this barrier, all she would have is a dream. Instead, with the support of a sponsor, her vision was realized when she received the UNICEF award at the Zanzibar International Film Festival with her hard-hitting journalism that exposed child abuse in support of the Say No to Abuse campaign.

Experience in asking for money, or expertise in providing it, can be an overwhelming mountain to climb. Meaza Ashenafi and Nigest Haile, two accomplished women in their fields of law and export, respectively, became two of the eight women founders of Enat Bank. Being the first Ethiopian bank to have the majority of equity infused by women, built to assist women-led small to medium enterprises, they had many barriers to overcome. The biggest was that none of the co-initiators had banking experience. As Meaza said, "The need outweighed the limitations." They had difficulty finding staff and selling shares. As a result, the bank was idle for a year. They never gave up, and on July 9, 2011, the bank launched.

Experience is a relative term; it doesn't need to be in the same job to count as worthwhile. Skills are transferable, and these pioneers demonstrated faith, confidence, and willingness to take a risk to have an impact. Many people would perceive such obstacles as mountains;

they approached them as molehills — inconvenient, but nothing you couldn't step over.

Physical restrictions — disability or ability?

No caring human being would wish disability on anyone. However, a person with a disability may be grateful for their fate depending on their attitude, culture, and unique experience. Yetnebersh Nigussie considers her blindness a gift. Doors were opened rather than closed. It was not easy to co-create her legacy at the Ethiopian Centre for Disability and Development, or to launch a school for the disabled and abled. Raised by her grandparents in Addis Ababa, the capital of Ethiopia, her lack of sight gave her opportunities to see.

> I would never say that I would not want to be blind, as my grandparents would never have allowed me to come to the urban areas. I would not have been educated, and I would not have been the person I am today. I would never say I would not want to be blind as it is the secret to my success. The challenge is my opportunity.

Marsha Gabriel would agree with Yetnebersh's sentiment. She is the founder and president of the CSI Business Congress, an organization that leads research, advocacy, and capacity building on sustainability matters contributing to the social reform in South Africa. Marsha's ability was realized through her disability in 1999, when a back injury paralyzed her from the hip down. She had to resign from her position in the South African Post Office, and she believed she was no longer employable in the open labor market. Marsha started by writing a list of her mandates — the catalyst for their fruition.

> Everything stemmed from that lowest point in my life. When you do reach a point where it is enough, you always remember the point where it started, and it gives you the energy to go further.

> Over the last 10 years, I have had major treatment on my spine. I do have a chronic situation that I need to manage, but when you do something that gives you energy, you jump beyond the boundaries of your disability. I was told I would never wear stilettos again, but I imagined my feet in green crush shoes. You cannot wear a suit without such shoes.

Marsha proudly wore her heels as she walked into the restaurant, which she also owns, to be interviewed. Her vision and perseverance transformed her own disability into abilities for entrepreneurs and NGOs to achieve long-term sustainability.

Fear — flight or fight?

Fear manifests in many ways: fear of the unknown, fear of consequences, fear of regret. Response to fear is frequently described as fight or flight, where we either fight for our survival or run for our life.

For Doo Aphane, fighting for women's human rights in eSwatini was the only option, "Nobody is going to come and do it for us Swazi women. It is something we have to do ourselves." And few women would stand by Doo when she was fighting for land ownership, achieving agreement for having 30 percent of women represented in the government, or protecting women's human rights. Many of these battles she fought alone. Regardless of her fellow citizens' belief in equality, they feared for their participation.

However, Doo understood that flight was never an option. She would have to ensure women's rights were part of the conversation in eSwatini parliament.

For Sibongile Sambo, flight was her business. She is the founder and managing director of SRS Aviation in Johannesburg, South Africa. SRS is the first 100 percent black female owned aviation company, offering clients professional and personalized flight options to destinations around the world. As Sibongile pursued this ambition, fear was a non-existent emotion. "I fear nothing. I'm a risk taker." Sibongile always was ready for the fight.

> When I apply my mind to do something, I go for it. The worst answer I can ever get is a no, but no will never kill me. I just wake up the following day and do something different.
>
> For me, it is the positive attitude I have in life; it has carried me to today. I have gone through so much with the business, but I persevered with a

positive attitude. I woke up one day and said, 'This is where I belong. This is my industry.'

When you live your purpose, fear becomes a minor inconvenience, not something to battle.

Many pioneering African women experienced fear but don't succumb to it. However, if you experience fear of regret, ask yourself if you would be satisfied in three, five, or 10 years from now if you didn't walk a certain path. Your answer can lead to discovering possibilities. Regret, like guilt, is a wasted emotion because even in hindsight, we can change our perception of the missed opportunity, or take it now.

Make your contribution count

Blocks are just that, obstacles that get in the way and are often just assumptions based on limited information. It is wise to gather all the knowledge to make an educated decision. Alternatively, take Doo Aphane's advice: "We should not wait to be counted in. We should just count ourselves in."

So, jump in, don't wait for permission. If we give carte blanche to our blocks to rule over us, we may not be pursuing our purpose, or we would persevere.

Reflect on how to make your conscious-contributions™

1. Describe a situation where assumptions have held you back. What would you do differently?
2. When you hear criticism, how do you put it into perspective?
3. What has limited you in the past, and how can you use it to propel you into the future?

Chapter 12
Enhance your essence

Words of Wisdom

At some point, you need to stop thinking of yourself as a 'woman'. This is how you arrived, but your sex ceases to be important—your brain becomes all that matters.

Florence Zano Chideya, ambassador of Zimbabwe to Canada;
Pioneer: deputy dean, Diplomatic Corps in Ottawa, first woman, and first Zimbabwean

While we were in South Africa, we were invited to join a couple in their mid-twenties on a grueling five-day coastal hike called the Otter Trail. We were not in our best shape, as we had had little opportunity to hit the gym while traveling from interview to interview. However, our out-of-shape bodies craved the adventure. With this test came the reality of carrying all our survival gear on our backs, and the camera equipment on Mike's front.

The night before the hike began, we stayed at a hostel, where I overheard a conversation between our younger hiking companions and a fellow traveler. The young man was sharing the details of the challenging hike and then decided to share the particulars of his hiking companions.

My ears felt infected when he said, "We are hiking with the older couple." Who could he possibly be referring to? Surely not us! I have never been referred to as *older*, or at least not in my earshot.

At 40 Mike and I hiked Kilimanjaro; at 45 we hiked Mount Kenya, and now in the same year, admittedly a little less in shape, we were the *older couple*. If one needed motivation, I think I received mine — this older gal was going to push her edge once again.

I had no idea that pushing the proverbial edge of my comfort zone would include walking on top of a cliff face centimeters from the brink — in the dark. Plummeting to our deaths was not beyond possibility.

For six hours, I struggled with my fear of heights as our headlamps guided us along a narrow path where one foot apprehensively stepped in front of the other. When the sun rose, we should have felt relief, but it just made it easier to see the large river crossing that awaited us. With our backpacks now in dry bags, we swam across the river the brochure suggested we could walk across. Greeted on the other side with the reality of another rock face, this time we were to shimmy along the bottom, holding on tightly to the protruding rocks while keeping our balance with our heavy packs.

Was I having fun? Unequivocally no. However, the hike in the darkness, swim across the river with backpacks, and shimmy along the edge of a rock face was not going to make me succumb to my fear. What happened next, however, did.

After a few minutes of celebration for the obstacles we had just overcome, we hiked around a large rock, where we stood at the bottom of another 10-story rock face — this one we needed to climb. Once again, it was a straight drop into the raging ocean. I did not sign up for rock climbing. The brochure said this was a hike, nothing more. I had to make a decision. Take me, my bad knees, heavy backpack and lousy attitude up the rock face, or go back the way I came to the escape route — on the other side of the raging river as high-tide was flooding in. I apprehensively continued forward.

Mike led the climb. Because I didn't have the strength in my arms, or the torque in my legs to push myself up, I needed his help. He grabbed the top of my backpack and hoisted me up while the front of my body scraped along the rock face. For every step Mike took, he hauled me up. We had a system. It wasn't pleasant, but it was practical.

Stained with tears, bruised, sore, and exhausted, I rolled over the lip of the cliff.

Our much younger hiking companions awaited our arrival and greeted us with smiles. The young woman proudly proclaimed, "My mother couldn't have done that." Vindicated? Perhaps not, but we, the older couple, did finish the hike beside the younger couple, with a few more scrapes and bruises, but nothing that wouldn't eventually heal.

This is exploring *edgeness* which offers us the opportunity to enhance our essence. In that state of exploration, you quickly realize what you can sustain, what you can't sustain, and what you don't want to sustain — hiking rock faces is not for me. However, I'm glad I did it, as who knows, I could have discovered something I enjoyed, and I excelled at. On the other side of comfort is optimized potential. If we don't explore this place, our possibilities become limited rather than limitless.

Optimized potential

Edgeness is found just beyond the edge of our comfort zone to the area of unknown. It is sustainable. Here your performance is optimized, and your potential begins to be realized. It is not the area of complete discomfort — where your performance is unrepeatable and unsustainable.

So why embrace your *edgeness*? Because life begins at the edge. How do we know? Do a self-assessment. When have you felt most invigorated?

We are either moving toward or away from opportunities based on our perception of the degree of fear and the degree of pleasure. What if fear and pleasure became the same thing? You will need to venture into the unknown, and let go of some control, which can cause stress.

Industrial psychologist Dr. Richard Davis describes what happens inside our comfort zone. We relax, but soon become bored and even apathetic. Our concentration evaporates, resulting in poorer decisions. Under these circumstances, we don't do our best work. Too much stress, however, can lead to burnout. Boredom may be enough to push the edge of our comfort zone; however, there are also consequences if we push too far. According to the work by Robert Yerkes and John Dillingham Dodson, there is a correlation between peak performance and mental or physiological arousal. It suggests that if you push your edge just far enough, you will create an optimal level of anxiety. Too much or too little produce weaker results.[55]

Through my years of coaching entrepreneurs, executives, and sales teams, I have observed that when I provide uncomfortable skill development exercises, participants find someone they have never met before — an enhanced version of themselves.

The edge of where we start to experience fear, stress or anxiety is different for each of us. The question becomes, what is on the other side of that barrier that we want to achieve.

In the WisdomExchangeTv interviews, I asked each pioneering African woman, "What was the one thing you have done that pushed the edge of your comfort zone? The one that if you hadn't done it, you wouldn't have achieved the impact you had in your community or beyond."

Through diverse responses, a practice to optimize performance, enhance your essence, and social impact emerged. E.D.G.E.N.E.S.S also came into view.

E - Eliminate your self-imposed limitations
D - Deploy your gifts
G - Grab your greatness
E - Emulate your authentic self
N - Notice your accomplishments
E - Express your values
S - Stay your purpose
S - Self-transcend

Eliminate your self-imposed limitations

We impose many restrictions on ourselves emanating from fear, stress, anxiety, lack of confidence, and possibly the most potent, our ego. Identify your self-imposed limitations and then embrace them.

The reality is that we need some fear to optimize our performance. We need some stress, or we become apathetic. We need some apprehension to keep us humble. We need to question our confidence to drive our determination. Lastly, we need our ego, or we won't dare to try.

As discussed in Chapter 11: *Unblock blocks to live your purpose*, one approach to dealing with a self-imposed limitation is first to examine it and then eliminate it by breaking the obstacle down into digestible pieces. Creative thinking, willpower, and the ability to compartmentalize our emotions are required. From this perspective, we can tackle each limitation rationally, and not through the lens of social judgment, self-perceived ability, personal discomfort, or consequences.

Gita Goven pushed boundaries in many elements of her architectural career, but she struggled with one of the most common self-imposed limitations for a mother — balance.

> I think there is a concern about what it will be like when you get married and have a family and how to manage. If I had worried about that at that point, I wouldn't have done what I have done now. Going through everything I had to deal with — motherhood, having a family and still being a leader in my profession — you work it out. You put together a plan and then put support in place so you can get done what you need to do. It is not easy, but if you are doing something that you're interested in, you will do what it takes to make it happen.

Work towards eliminating your self-imposed limitations. The path may be laced with judgment, but it is your own appraisal that you need to live with. Taking responsibility to live your purpose is the road to maximizing your meaning.

Deploy your gifts

Your gifts are like beacons that guide you to optimize your potential. The most efficient way to isolate those glimpses of light is in the moments when you operate at your most powerful. When you feel vigor, consider what you are doing. What talents or strengths are you exhibiting in that situation? When you find yourself challenged, what forces did you deploy to tackle the encounter? Your answers will offer the opportunity to harness those powers when you need them most and help you move from competency to possibilities.

For Yetnebersh Nigussie being blind as a child put her in the position of dealing with her discomfort daily. What made her most uncomfortable wasn't being blind but coping with labels people imposed on her. People tried to define an indefinable woman. Yetnebersh deployed her gift of patience and empathy to create an atmosphere where dialogue could commence, and progress could ensue.

> I don't like to be labeled. People think I am *special*, but I am not special. Other people can do [what I do]. For example, if I succeed at something and they think my achievements are special, they won't try it. I think I am part of the ordinary system. This is an excuse for people not to do what I do.

> I let people call me *special* or *disabled*, but I am not comfortable with either of those terms. I feel uncomfortable every day. As long as you have movement in life, there is the opportunity for discomfort. When people come to talk to me in my director position, they see that I am young, a woman, and disabled; all of a sudden, the conversation becomes shortened. So, I give them time to adapt. I welcome them, so they feel comfortable.

Every experience is an opportunity to deploy your gifts, or to learn what they are in the first place.

Grab your greatness

To grab your greatness, you need to let go of what hasn't served you, ignore what is not relevant, delay what is not essential, disregard others' judgment, and lean into the opportunity right in front of you. Soon your greatness will emerge.

You can seize your greatness by defying your perceived confines. Zulfat Mukarubega pushed her edge every time she spoke English.

During our interview, I was surprised to learn Zulfat's first language was French and of her discomfort in speaking English.

"Did you know this interview was in English?" I asked her.

"Yes, although it is a little uncomfortable, I'm doing it anyway. I need to improve my English. It is limiting me to market to other countries," she replied enthusiastically.

Zulfat admitted that she also feels unqualified to evaluate and communicate with the very people she employs — professors.

> It is difficult for me to evaluate [people with a] Ph.D., Master, or Bachelor degrees, as I don't have any of them. To be in leadership, you have to be able to evaluate your company and your people. I may not have the education to evaluate, but I do it in other ways.

With all her achievements, she was still self-conscious about not having a degree. I couldn't help wondering how many professors who worked for Zulfat wished they had her drive, vision, and gumption to continue to develop and expand a pioneering Rwandan university.

Grabbing your greatness means leaning into what needs to be done to achieve your vision.

Emulate your authentic self

Your authentic self is the springboard for sustaining your *edgeness*. Have you permitted yourself to be authentically you within the various environments in which you work, play, or contribute?

One of the most difficult people to be is our authentic self. Years of conditioning, experience, and expectations creates layers over our authentic self, making it difficult to recognize our essence. Throughout our lives we adopt a performance persona to do what needs to be done, mainly when it is outside our comfort zone. It is so much easier to push our edge when we know where the edge is. By camouflaging any part our authentic self, we can't possibly define what is comfortable or uncomfortable; the only accurate compass is authenticity. Recalibrating provides us the opportunity to harness our gifts, talents and wisdom.

Modesta Lilian Mahiga has no problem being authentic. She admits her voice drew wanted attention, but unwanted speculation.

> Although I am comfortable speaking out, even if I do know there are repercussions. [Regarding] Maanisha media entertainment, we have had the government going out asking why we are building youth capacity. Then they want to know who is behind the show — Modesta. They want to know who is behind Modesta? No one. They want to know what my vested interest is in making a difference.

> When I interviewed the president, the State House told me to 'behave myself.' I guess I am bringing on a revolution, but not in arms; it is economic in nature. I am not actually uncomfortable speaking up, but it puts others in a precarious position to be associated with me. I am doing this to touch on social transformation.

Emulating your authentic being in all situations will precipitate diverse reactions. No doubt, the world needs more authentic people who unapologetically radiate confidence, and who have the best interest of society in their heart.

Notice your accomplishments

Pushing your edge over time can lead to burnout and sometimes requires hitting the pause button. Each time you extend yourself you move your comfort zone a little further out, and a new normal becomes established. Observe and celebrate your new abilities. Acknowledging progress is an essential element when finding and adjusting to your *edgeness* — a step often ignored.

Stop, reflect, celebrate, and share your accomplishments. It will not only motivate you and others, but it will also allow you the opportunity to assess what you can do better, and what you can do without.

One of the toughest decisions a leader has to make is to sever themselves from an individual who is holding the team back. As uncomfortable as it may be to part with an employee, it is sometimes necessary for the overall health of an organization. Antonia Mutoro, the first female executive director at the Institute of Policy Analysis and Research in Kigali, Rwanda, explains how this reality affected her, the team, and the organization.

> I am a people person, but one of my staff was not delivering, and I had to [fire] him. He was a senior member of our team. I was very uncomfortable. After that, there was a change in the organization. The younger researchers who were being mentored saw it as motivation. I found firmness in myself and realized that making a decision also affects the people remaining.

Asking someone to leave your team or taking responsibility for the actions of an organization are signs of a leader. Neither is comfortable, but both are necessary for the benefit of the whole. Antonia celebrates making the right decision for all, as it is an essential element of making a difference for all.

> Another [time when I pushed my edge] was when I started at IPAR, and I had to speak on the radio. I had to learn about the company, and I started to imagine what [the interviewer] would ask. I knew our reputation was bad, and I was going to have to address that. It taught me to take responsibility and not to blame others in the past. I knew I had to take responsibility for the IPAR actions. Once you have the opportunity, you need to make a difference.

Notice your accomplishments and celebrate your acts of courage to get done what needs to be done. It will serve you to do what is required when it feels as if your options are limited. Embrace what Nigest Haile, believes is one of the keys to her success.

> You don't get acknowledgment. I always congratulate myself, I say, 'Nigest, I have done a good job today.' There are so many things I have done that I acknowledge myself. I celebrate my successes and learn from my failures. That is what drives me.

This is an act of self-preservation. Noticing your accomplishment is such an essential part of elevating your purpose and your mission. If you don't stop and celebrate, it becomes challenging to persevere.

Express your values

Values are the fulcrum to conscious-contributions to the community and are instrumental in making all decisions on the YouMeWe journey. As highlighted in Chapter 10: *Discover your purpose,* values also assist us in deciding where we will contribute our time, skill, and knowledge to impact our lives and the community. When you want to expand your impact and push your comfort zone, you will have to challenge yourself in line with those values; otherwise, internal conflict will sabotage your authentic self.

While Meaza Ashenafi was advancing the women empowerment movement in Ethiopia, the government confronted her to retract a statement regarding violence against women. Meaza led the Women's Law Society, and in 2001, they were very vocal about a case where a woman was the victim of abuse.

> A government official asked us to retract a statement. We felt it was not right to retract it. The association was suspended. We continued to fight, and we had to go to court. This was a challenging situation in my career. Staying true to my beliefs can put me in uncomfortable situations.

Our values will always be our guide. Our authentic self must operate within them, even when it is easier to abandon them. Any deviation will make you vulnerable, and unlikely to enhance your essence.

Stay your purpose

Living your purpose, is a constant and contributes to your overall well-being. When you are discovering a more enhanced version of yourself, your purpose doesn't falter. It stays true. Your commitment grows stronger.

There is no doubt that once you push your edge in one area in your life, focus follows, causing other priorities to unravel a little or a lot. Different elements of living your purpose may need elevated levels of attention. It may be temporary, but it is necessary.

Living your purpose will expand its impact and your fulfillment. Focus coupled with patience, persistence, and knowhow makes achievement imminent.

Dr. Thandeka Mazibuko was the first black female student accepted to specialize in radiation oncology in KwaZulu-Natal, South Africa. She believes you must suffer and push limits or you will never realize your potential. Much of Thandeka's learning has created psychological scars, and each mark has its purpose in designing a life filled with focus and meaning.

> It seems like if you are going through hardships, you must not give up. You get pushed to your limits. You are told to stop fighting, but if you stop fighting, how are you going to get knowledge? I have to push the door to get in. Leaders don't like you because you are touching the areas that should not be touched. You lose friends. If you talk about issues, you are wrong. If you become silent, you're wrong. At every turn, you are wrong.

> There is a time when things get very dark, and you don't know which way to turn, but you persist because there is a goal you need to obtain. There is no room for giving up. Now that I realize I am the first African [woman] here [oncology doctor], I am staying. Now that I realize that the knowledge is available, I am staying. I have been suspended for things that I don't know I have done. I have almost lost my career many times, but I have stayed.

When staying your purpose, you may have to make sacrifices. The real reward of this journey is enhancing yourself, your performance, your purpose, and your impact.

Self-transcend

Abraham Maslow's hierarchy of needs, focusing on human motivation, was written in 1943. Today it continues to draw much commentary. Maslow popularized the concept of self-actualization as the last motivation of human beings. Each level of needs is sought prior to pursuing the next level.

The critical highest level of the hierarchy of needs is self-transcendence, where you are other-focused instead of self-focused.

Your concerns shift to higher goals rather than self-service. The greater-than-self can include a range of interests such as concern for other people or species, the environment, how you fit into the universal plan, or what your divine power wants for the greater good. Realizing your purpose can lead you to self-transcend, where your focus shifts to provide conscious-contributions to society — where you are most fulfilled.

When exploring one's *edgeness*, the ultimate of the enhanced version of yourself is when your actions elevate the people or environment around you. You heighten your performance and maximize your meaning. You are in service, and it can transform into your mission.

YouMeWe defines the difference between purpose, mission, and meaning as follows: Purpose is lived; a mission is pursued; meaning is realized. You maximize your meaning when you live your purpose, pursue a mission, and progress society.

Angela Dick gave up all she had for what she believed, which was the right to employment for everyone. She chose a path that meant every day she was working with impoverished employees, a route that almost cost her everything. Angela's compassion for the realities of her country's people is what motivated her to embrace her *edgeness*, an experience that provided her with the ultimate wealth — serving humanity.

> I think about, 'What do people of South African want?' They want the same thing I want. They want a home for their children, food for their children, they want transport to get to work, they want employment, and they want some kind of future for their children. That is what keeps me going.

For Angela to employ more than ten 10,000 temporary and contract staff, she had to choose to risk everything by leaving the security of a well-paying job as a sales executive. All her savings and the sale of most of her possessions financed the start of Transman. It took 18 months to receive a paycheck and five years to be established in the recruitment business. Angela's conviction eventually led to transforming the temporary job market in South Africa.

Self-transcendence is not easy. It does mean you find yourself in situations where the only option is to push your edge, become uncomfortable, and challenge your abilities. The reward is discovering an enhanced version of yourself — a journey worth exploring.

I continue to observe the women we interviewed with admiration. Many have expanded their impact exponentially. Some have taken on new challenges to amplify their voices and new roles to broaden their impact. Undoubtedly, these leaders continue to push their edge to benefit all.

Make your contribution count

Following the E.D.G.E.N.E.S.S formula to living your most meaningful life will cause you to reflect, identify, and act on opportunities that may previously have passed you by. Every possibility has a time, a place, and a circumstance when it is optimal to execute. Perhaps once you take time to process your *edgeness*, all the elements will align, making your time now.

Reflect on how to make your conscious-contributions™

1. When do you reveal your most authentic-self (work, play, contributing)? Physically draw a picture of your authentic self. Is that the best version of you? If not, draw a picture of your enhanced version of authentic you. Embed that visual, so that is whom people experience.
2. When have you been afraid and persevered? What did you notice about your performance? Your experience?
3. What strengths do you exhibit in your most challenging situations?
4. How do you reflect on your accomplishments?
5. Which value do you hold in the highest regard? How can you lean into it to push your edge?
6. How does what you do every day positively impact the whole? How far outside your comfort zone do you have to go? Can you sustain it?

Chapter 13
Capitalize on your cornerstone to propel meaning

Words of Wisdom

Have a vision for your family. [My mother] wanted education for all of us. She wanted her girls to have the same treatment as her boys, even if it meant we were outcast of our community.

Leah Ngini, founder and director of St. Christopher's schools, Kenya
Pioneer: first woman to serve on the board of governors of Africa International University (AIU)

Mike and I attended Evangelic Christian Chapel in Nairobi, along with approximately 1,200 worshippers. The preacher had just returned from the U.S. and shared an observation of a shift in Western values where it was acceptable for a husband to stay home and do the household duties, including taking care of the children, while his wife went to work. The preacher wanted to gauge how receptive the congregation would be to changing roles, specifically the husband shifting from being the breadwinner to be the homemaker.

He invited another preacher onstage so they could role-play a dialogue with two different perspectives. One supported the stance that it was acceptable for a husband to be the homemaker, and the other took the opposing view, that the husband should be the breadwinner.

The pro-homemaker preacher argued that it was important for the father to be involved in his children's lives, and it didn't make him any less of a man to take on a less traditional role. Women in the West, he continued, often made more money than their husbands, and parents often couldn't afford for both to work because of the cost of childcare in the West (the local cost of childcare is quite minimal in comparison).

The pro-breadwinner preacher stated that it was a man's job to work and provide for the family, and a woman's job to rear the children, take care of the home, and cook.

After each of the preachers stated his case, they encouraged questions and comments from the congregation. At first, many men started to stand up and share their perspective. Each one seemed to appreciate both views. Although they seemed to lean toward the husband being the breadwinner, they appeared to consider the homemaker role.

I felt encouraged. Evidence through my interviews showed that pioneering African women transformed communities. Therefore, if more women were in the workforce their influence would be amplified.

And then a woman stood up. I was feeling hopeful that finally we would hear unconditional support for a husband as the homemaker, and for a wife as the breadwinner. In a loud, emphatic voice, she proclaimed: "There is no way my husband is going to stay home. His place is at work!"

A ripple went through the audience. Woman after woman got up and shared this perspective.

There appeared to be some anxiety in many of these women's voices. They seemed to believe to capitalize on a husband as a cornerstone, meaning someone you depend on, he would have to monetize his day. This would offer the most family support.

Neither of the preachers addressed the issue of emotional support, and yet it could have changed the entire dialogue. Half of the pioneering women we interviewed saw their husbands neither as a breadwinner nor homemaker — but a motivator.

It doesn't matter who acts as your cornerstone, it is advantageous to have someone who will support, inspire, encourage, and celebrate your success especially if you are embarking on the arduous task of elevating society with your mission. Noticing your accomplishments is vital to continuing to motivate yourself to push your edge and reach your potential; however, if you have an advocate beside you, your conscious-contributions to the community can be even more gratifying.

Spouse as the cornerstone

Supporters can catapult us to new heights and encourage us when we are disillusioned. When that person is your life partner, you have the opportunity to hear the cheerleader in your corner every day.

Regardless whether a marriage is perceived as modern or traditional, pioneering African women believe the helping hand of a spouse can make all the difference. Leah Ngini attends Nairobi Chapel. She speaks of her husband with such fond memories and a sparkle in her eye when she shares that the school was her dream but building it and expanding on it was realized only with her husband's backing. Leah proclaims it was her husband's continuous support "as the head of the household" that made her dream of building a school a reality.

Leah shares that her husband believed in the power of women to do things and improve situations, so he had no problem supporting her. When Leah started her school, many banks in Nairobi were still reluctant to provide loans, so it wasn't just nice to have her husband's support, but necessary.

> My husband was with me all along. He would be with me to sign the loans. He would leave me to run the business. I am the educationist. He had his business, and I had mine. We never failed.

I was curious to know if Leah felt she would have achieved her success without the support of her husband.

> No, I don't think so. He encouraged me a lot. He would say: 'You can do it.' For example, when I went to get my driver's license, I called him to pick me up, he said: 'Didn't you just pass your driving test? You can drive yourself home.'

Doo Aphane's husband was less of a spring to her potential, but rather a refuge from it. Doo, being a women's rights activist confronts a barrage of naysayers. She receives refueling in her sanctuary with a husband who accepts her for who she is.

> When I am in public, I have to exude this fighting energy all the time. But when I am at home, I am accepted as I am. I have these two worlds. I get really energized because there is no fighting when I come home. When I come home, I get encouragement. Not to say that if he [husband] wasn't supportive I would have stopped, but I need to acknowledge that he fuels me in a big way.

A Parent as the cornerstone

Your cornerstone, the person who supports you, is often an individual who was there at the beginning. We observed how they treated others, demonstrated integrity, loyalty, dedication, and probably the most important, their belief in us. A father needs to set an example for his children, which was likely the root of the mock debate between the preachers at Nairobi Chapel. Culturally, a father's contribution as a dad who is homemaker doesn't constitute a familiar role model. Through my eyes, if a husband is making way for his wife to reach her potential by staying at home, he is someone to be emulated.

Regardless of whether a father is a homemaker or is the breadwinner, there is no doubt that his support can influence a child's aspirations. For Nouzha Chekrouni her father's words rang in her ears for years. His support propelled her potential and harnessed her obligation.

> I remember when I was six years old. I was about to go to my first day of school. Just before I left home, my father told me two things: One, you will be responsible, and you will be free to choose what you want to do in your personal and professional life. Two, freedom equals responsibility, and you have to act, you have to deserve it. This provided a path to how I was to behave in my life.

I asked Nouzha if it was common in the Muslim culture for a father to provide a young girl with such advice.

No, I don't think so, especially not at that time. It would be more common today as parents are more modern and open-minded. In my day, this was an exception. I feel very lucky that my parents provided this kind of education. That is why I want to pay tribute to them, as they are a big part of who I am today.

Lydia Muso's father also inspired her contribution as an activist for children and her sense of duty to society.

My father took in children from other families. He would tell us to give children food and clothes. Sometimes he would take my dress and give it to other children. He would just take it and wouldn't ask if I wanted to present my belongings to others. Now, of course, I understand that my father was teaching us to give and share. I am not saying I grew up in a rich family because we were also poor, but we were taught to share the little that we have.

Even though the interviewees lived in a patriarchal society, many fathers saw their daughters' power and ability to take the lead. Their fathers' encouragement and example were the guides to achieving their career accomplishments and contribution to the community. Perhaps they tapped into their feminine energy to encourage their daughters' potential.

Regardless of who is the head of the household, a mother can also have a transformation role. Leah Ngini's mother made bold choices for her daughters, which made them outcasts of the community. During the 1950s and 60s, her mother didn't honor the traditional customs.

My mother would tell us society doesn't think much of you. 'You have not been brought up like other girls in the village.' We were not going to be circumcised; my mother refused. We were not going to be part of village life, so we felt a bit isolated. From school, we had to go home. We were not allowed to go to friends' homes just in case if they were conducting such practices, they may take us also.

Our relatives were also circumcising the girls, but [my] mother could not see the advantage of what she went through. Those women could not stretch anymore because of the scars. She saw how women bleed to death, and children died. My mother was a midwife in the hospital.

Leah's love of education was the legacy of women in her family who instilled the importance of schooling. Leah's grandmother ran away from her village so that she could go to school at a time when girls were not considered worth educating. Leah's mother didn't go to school but ensured Leah did.

> My mother was the only daughter of a home full of boys. My mother saw boys playing like boys and decided that when she had her family, that she would treat the girls the same as boys. My mother had five girls and five boys. We all learned to wash our clothes, clean the house, cook, work in the garden, and all went to school. We were all encouraged. I remember my mother telling us girls that we all have to work very hard to excel in life. We have to work extra hard. The girls have done very well.

Leah seems to be a woman surrounded by support. She embraced her lessons learned, and her upbringing, and rolled them into the values of St. Christopher's School — where both boys and girls are valued.

One of Leah's daughters is a lawyer, and the other is an accountant. Both are significant assets in running the family business. In meeting them, I could see their spirit, insight, and determination. The most visible trait is their pride in their mother and grandmother for not succumbing to the status quo and providing the girls with the tools to create their opportunities.

Parents who treated the boy and girl child equally raise leaders such as Bience Gawanas, who had high ranking position in the African Union, and now in the United Nations. Bience attributes some of her passion and commitment to standing up for women's rights from being born into a family of 11. "My parents never discriminated against me, so I was fortunate. Even though we were very poor, our parents never distinguished between girls and boys."

Katherine Ichoya believes, "If you don't have a family that supports you, you will go forward two steps and back one."

Mentor as a cornerstone

The cornerstone in Meaza Ashenafi's life was a mentor: "I had a very good mentor. I worked for a senior minister. He helped construct my values in life, my focus, and prioritize on how to live a complete life."

Mentors can play a significant role. They can provide valuable guidance through obstacles. Jane Wathome suggests that you have both a personal and a professional mentor. Both can offer a unique perspective and allow for continued growth.

Many of the women we interviewed found support in women's business groups, or by having productive conversations with other women trailblazers.

If seeking a mentor, allow the relationship to grow organically. If a relationship has mutual respect and appreciation, a mentor may emerge. However, use a mentor wisely. Activate them by providing specific problems and solicit real solutions. If you need personal validation, talk to a friend, they will remind you that you are fabulous!

Faith as a cornerstone

Each woman we interviewed had one cornerstone in common — a strong religious faith. Regardless of her religion, it was integral to her character, and one each turned to often for guidance.

When we asked Dr. Thandeka Mazibuko, if there was someone along the way who helped her see the more significant opportunity, she replied:

> It has been all by coincidence. Being a Christian, I believed in God's plan. When He says: 'I knew before you were in your mother's womb, your future was planned.' I believe I am walking on a path like I'm blindfolded, but I am going somewhere. I only see the achievements when they happen. I never anticipate.

Jennifer Riria shares her belief that her faith helps her overcome all obstacles: "God has a purpose for me, and I need to live it. I changed careers because I knew my purpose should have even more impact than it was having. That gave me inner strength."

Faith is mighty and can keep you hopeful when you see no hope. You may be more spiritual than religious and find belief in that the universe has a plan for you. You may deviate from that plan and wonder where universal guidance is when you need it. That is where faith kicks in; knowing even though you are not experiencing the fruits of your beliefs, trusting that you are on the right path will bring you well-being.

The community as your cornerstone

As Doo Aphane continues to struggle with advocacy for women's equality in eSwatini, she experiences that the men who perceived her as an obstacle to their vision for society can become a cornerstone, making her mission a reality.

> There are men that are standing beside me. Most of the time, their sisters, or daughters have been affected. These men give more support because they have no fear. Some of them admitted that, before their sister had this problem and I helped out, if their family saw a picture of me on TV, they must switch it off. A wife knew that if she was in the same room as me, it was the end of the relationship. These are the men who call and follow up because their sisters and daughters have been assisted. And they are now looking at women's issues differently.

As each voice echoes your own, momentum occurs, and change is imminent. When it comes to women's human rights, equality will be achieved when men's voices are as loud as women's voices.

Janet Nkubana appreciates the generosity of her community. Being a young girl with little means, strangers and friends gave her a gift that was a cornerstone to launch her into a life of employing hundreds of women producing high-quality baskets in Rwanda and eventually distributed throughout the world.

> When I was in the refugee camp [in Uganda], I was fortunate enough to be picked by the church to go to school. I realized how much people paid for church dues that helped me go to school. I was humbled. One of my

callings was to give back. My sister and I embrace that responsibility, and that stems from our humble beginnings.

Just having one person who believes in you, challenges you, or helps pave the way, can make all the difference in a young person's perspective and confidence.

Your business partner as your cornerstone

Janet Nkubana had support from the community and her business partner. Janet relies on her sister, and best friend, Joy Ndungutse, to assist with raising her five children when she travels to promote Gahaya Links to international markets. It's a good thing that she is a sibling because most business partners wouldn't take care of your five children! No doubt, when families are in business together, they may be able to rely on each other for extra personal support; however, that same familiarity can impede progress and test patience.

Through all the travel chaos and complicated logistics of every single WisdomExchangeTv interview, there was one constant cornerstone — my business partner and best friend, who is my husband. Many of the women we interviewed looked on with curiosity at my husband following my passion, some with questions, others with admiration, but most with appreciation. In the West, the reception to our partnership isn't much different.

Capitalizing on your cornerstone is not always easy, especially when your spouse is your business partner. It can become confusing when work and life collide. As the visionary, you see the path to its fruition clearly, and yet for your partner, it can be like walking in a fog. A remarkable amount of trust is required on behalf of the partner, combined with an equal amount of strategy and belief by the visionary.

As the leader, you must have the right balance of patience and driving results. That trail is often strewn with land mines, which can set the project and your romance back several paces.

Regardless of how much passion you have for each other and your mission, sustaining it will only be achieved if you let go of the small stuff. As allies you need to continuously remind each other of your collective values, your mission, mutual respect, and that your differences are what will make the vision a reality.

Since 2011, my husband has placed himself in unfamiliar territory. He had to learn new skills to help grow and sustain our business. He had to embrace uncertainty. He had to have faith that I was leading us in the right direction (even when I wasn't sure where we were going). As we have evolved as life partners, in every sense of the word, he has taken the lead in so much of our home life.

Thank you, Mike, for being my cornerstone.

Make your contribution count

Capitalize on your cornerstone. We all have someone that can elevate us; we just need to find them. If you are fortunate to have someone in your corner who supports you, energizes you, or has helped you build a stronger base, you can harness that guidance and build off the foundation. It is nice to have support when the going gets tough.

Reflect on how to make your conscious-contributions™

1. What potential does someone see in you that you don't see in yourself?
2. Who can you count on for encouragement and perspective? When do you reach out to them?
3. What role does faith play in your decisions? Can faith further serve you so that you can serve others?
4. How can your community or a mentor assist in reaching your conscious-contribution objectives?

Chapter 14
Volunteering the good, the bad, and the opportunity

Words of Wisdom
When something is crucial, never be flexible, so you never lose your essence.

Nouzha Chekrouni, ambassador of the Kingdom of Morocco to Canada, Morocco
Pioneer: first woman Moroccan Minister

The first time I walked through Kibera, the largest urban slum in Africa, located in Nairobi, we had a local guide. We engaged a resident to walk with us so no one would challenge our presence. Our guide led one professional and three amateur photographers, including me, on a photo exploration.

Each of us had different reasons for wanting to experience the muddy pathways, feces-filled streams, and mountain-high garbage piles. For us, this was an excursion. For approximately 250,000 residents, this was their home. We walked by hundreds of 12 by 12 mud homes with corrugated tin roofs and dirt floors. Women washed clothes, children played, and men made changaa, a cheap brew of more than 50 percent alcohol. Female dwellers that agreed to a photo to promote women leadership, welcomed our presence. Some were only welcoming if I paid for the privilege. The illegal brewers chased us out of Kibera and wanted to confiscate our cameras. Thankfully, our guide finessed our extraction, cameras intact.

Perched on a hill on the perimeter of the slum was a new apartment complex. Our guide informed us that it was built by a charity. According to his understanding of the community, having its shadow cast over the corrugated tin homes was a mockery to those who lived below. The apartment's presence would further emphasize the difference between the haves and the have-nots and would likely induce resentment followed by looting.

I couldn't help wondering who built the apartments. With over 50 percent unemployment in the Kibera, did the charitable builder capitalize on community engagement, or did they rely on well-intentioned volunteers who had come from other countries to give to the less fortunate?

Although in recent years there has been a shift to local community participation in building, I'm a little suspicious when someone says, "I / my son / my daughter was in a developing country, building a school." Often this proclamation is made with pride in the individual's contribution to helping make the world a better place. Perhaps we could have a more significant impact if we paid the locals to construct the schools or homes. If needed, a qualified builder could teach locals to build and maintain it.

Building a school, when not in construction, teaching entrepreneurs skills when you are not an entrepreneur, or hand-rearing orphaned wildlife in rehabilitation centers when you are not a conservation expert, is voluntourism. Often Westerners are drawn to traveling to new destinations under the banner of voluntourism, meaning: I'll give my time, energy, and money to temporarily contribute in exchange for the helpers high. Internationally volunteering is to be celebrated if the beneficiary needs it, wants it, and it consciously advancing society.

Volunteering as a practice has other considerations.

Volunteering the good and the bad

Nigest Haile encourages her teenage daughters to volunteer. They often contribute as a family, and she advises young people:

> Do volunteer work for your country. Everyone expects remuneration at a very young age. Everything is about payment. If we continue to have such

a culture, I don't think we will have a generation of successors. My children are involved in many volunteer activities, such as the Rotary Club.

There is no shortage of volunteer opportunities. You might join a local service club, become involved in your organization's volunteer program, give your energy to your professional association, time at a charity, or provide your expertise on a board of directors. All are ways to *make your contribution count.*

A volunteer contributes time and energy to a task that is not necessarily related to your profession or area of expertise. Without volunteers, not-for-profit's mandates would not be met.

There is another case for volunteering and ensuring you put the best foot forward. Modesta Lilian Mahiga founded the Maanisha! Foundation, whose goal is to help youth positively change the way they think, perform, and present themselves for business success. Modesta offers that volunteerism can demonstrate to a prospective employer your abilities and eventually your expertise.

Although volunteering may provide an opportunity to enhance a resumé, or round out skills, it is most rewarding when the motivation is to enhance a community. There is deeper fulfillment for you and the organization you contribute to.

How you volunteer can vary between being an able body available in a pinch, to contributing your expertise to assist in skill transference to locally-led organizations and their teams. Expectations of volunteers, however, are limited, and performance does not always equate to professional ability. Often volunteers give their time when it is convenient to do so. There can be lack of accountability in volunteer work effecting others who are counting on the commitment and impacting delivery of a project.

Because of the vast difference in execution and expectation, I have coined the term professional-contributor to replace the often less accountable implications of being a volunteer. Both these concepts suggest unpaid participation in a cause or initiative to advance the organization's mandate, whether that organization is an NGO, professional association, community group, charity, or foundation. The primary differences are embedded in your talent and attitude. When you are a professional-contributor:

1. You are engaged in providing a specific skill/service in which you have talent or demonstrated **expertise**.
2. You hold the same **attitude** toward your unpaid role as you would a professional position.
3. You are **accountable** and therefore deliver to the best of your ability on any promised task.

The opportunity

At our core, humans have a desire to live a life of significance. For some, that means starting a social enterprise or working for an organization with drivers beyond the mighty dollar. Others seek an opportunity to live a life of meaning outside their workplace by contributing to their family or the community.

Within organizations, there has been a significant shift from conducting social responsibility programs, where the employee is a bystander, to providing volunteer programs that encourage sharing of expertise with charities, financially supporting employee causes, and tracking volunteer hours. The catalyst for the shift is primarily the desire of the millennial generation to be part of something bigger than themselves. Without organizations providing these opportunities, millennials will search outside their work environments, or look for organizations that offer the opportunities they seek. Navigating additional volunteer time for this generation who are in career growth mode will be a challenge, so having a place to work that meets employees' holistic needs would optimize engagement.

Although many organizations are recognizing employees' vital shift from seeking a job to obtaining a meaningful career, those of us over 45 seeking more meaning at work often lack the experience to be employed by the mission organizations. We grew up in a profit-before-purpose era limiting our accesses to the not-for-profit or socially conscious enterprise sectors. There are alternatives.

The Purpose Economy, by Aaron Hurst, founder of Taproot Foundation, drives social change through pro bono services. He suggests that of the 25,000 requests his organization receives each year to volunteer their expertise pro bono, do so because their 9-to-5 jobs are not fulfilling their need to make the world a better place.[56] These people are seeking inspiration and desire to be part of something bigger than themselves.

Regardless of your motivation, all you need to professionally contribute is passion, time, talent, and a professional attitude.

How to make your professional-contributions count

1. What is your purpose?

When considering a professional-contribution opportunity, it is essential to *B.E.L.I.E.V.E to discover your purpose*. The seven essentials to evaluate your purpose will lead you to where to contribute professionally. A variety of opportunities await your capabilities and commitment, including professional associations. Selecting a cause most in line with your mission will keep you engaged through the ebbs and flows of your contribution.

If you're not clear on your purpose, providing your energy and time can assist you in evaluating it. If you are not attached to a particular mission, volunteering will help expose the difference you want to make in the world.

2. What are your objectives?

Susan Muhwezi could be called a serial professional-contributor. Her contributions are vast and include being the senior presidential advisor for African Growth and Opportunity Act; vice chairperson of Uganda Hotel Owners Association; chairperson of Uganda Women's Effort to Save Orphans; and chairperson of the Women's League, Western Region. She contributes to her nation, to her professional association, to the community and her peers. Susan is clear that each of these roles has a distinct objective.

> The most important question is, why are you [contributing]? Are you doing it as a service, or to benefit you? It is fine to do it for both reasons, but when you go in, make sure you are going to make a difference.

Knowing one's contribution has made a difference is the best recognition a volunteer can receive. The impact you have can often correlate with the objectives you set out that motivated your participation. Consider some personal and professional goals you may have in contributing to a community group, not-for-profit, or professional association such as: develop a new skill, expand your network, or connect to the community. Visit the YouMeWe.ca book community for a downloadable list of objectives to mull over.

Pick two or three objectives and keep them at the forefront as you engage in any non-paying initiative. If any of the goals align with your professional persona, recognizing the opportunity as a professional-contributor may alter your execution.

3. What knowledge and skills do you offer?

A professional-contributor seeks opportunities that align with their knowledge, skills, and talents so they advance a particular initiative, and therefore, experience a higher level of satisfaction. If an impact is felt, particularly in an area we are passionate about, such as contributing to our compassion-connection, our engagement increases.

When evaluating your purpose, I encourage you to assess your inner strengths. Through that process, you will identify your knowledge, skills, and talents. Do you have expertise in marketing, communications, leadership, social media, project management, engineering, driving, design, teaching, caring, housekeeping, fundraising, or perhaps making friends? A young woman in Canada created a business based on providing friendship, and although I'm not sure if it will be lucrative, as a free service, it does fill a void for people, particularly some elderly who could benefit from more compassion through companionship.

Contributing your talents is not to suggest, that you can't also use an opportunity to experiment. Many professional-contributors still have the desire to learn something new, have a unique experience, or to challenge their skill in an area where the risk isn't as high as it may be in a paid environment.

Boards and community groups rely on the present acting members to execute previous strategies or hone the new way forward. Unlike paid positions, where an employee is hired to implement their knowledge and skill for a specific task, when you are professionally contributing, you are frequently in the role of creating the direction and accompanying responsibilities. This allows for more ownership, and personal accomplishment. Consider the knowledge or skills you have and would like to expand upon will help asses if the opportunity is the right fit. Download questions to assist the process at YouMeWe.ca book community.

Regina Ingabire, a Rwandan national, was raised in Tanzania then moved to her native country after the 1994 genocide. After co-founding a youth network, Never Again, she went to the United States for further education. Although Regina was comfortable in the United States, she returned to Rwanda when the opportunity arose. "It is my debt to come back to do something. Other Rwandans have built Rwanda, and it is my duty to come back and build on what they have done."

Regina uses her network and the skills she developed internationally to professionally contribute once again to a community that will never forget its history.

4. How much time do you want to commit?

Any professional-contribution opportunity can take as much or as little time as you want. However, what you intend and what is anticipated of you can be very different.

How much time you commit will be dictated by your contribution objectives, and how in line an opportunity is with your mission. If you have two commitments, however, that meet your goals, which will take priority, and under which circumstance? Although this may be a difficult decision, the answer is in the attitude — be it a volunteer attitude of "I'll fit it in," or a professional-contributor attitude of, "I will follow through on my commitment." If at an impasse, identify all contribution commitments and place each in priority based on what you value most. The analysis will assist you in making several decisions on your time allotment. Life brings us all sorts of surprises and knowing our values and priorities will allow us to more easily make decisions about where we allocate our time and with a lot less guilt.

Cautionary note: Trying to respond to all the demands on your professional-contribution time could eventually breed resentment. If you are overwhelmed, pull back and re-evaluate what your motivation was in the first place. Then assess what alterations are needed to get your objectives back on track. Also, proactively communicate with the local president or directors about your time and perhaps how to best reallocate it. Solutions could stem from innovative thinking, both about your approach and the time required.

Allocate your contribution time, but allow opportunities to seep in, or you may close the door on what could be a life-changing or a phenomenal experience. The trick is to balance how wide you leave the door open for new opportunities. A professional-contributor leaves it ajar enough without the door swinging in the wind.

5. What is the right opportunity?

Of the myriad professional-contribution opportunities that exist, research the one that is in line with your mission, that will reach your objectives, require your skills, and will have the appropriate time commitment. There are many ways to research what is available. Start with your government volunteer agency, such as *Volunteer Canada*, or search *Volunteer Match* in the United States, which makes finding an opportunity locally and abroad easy. Join your local service club; connect with not-for-profits in a country of choice; or just Google "volunteer opportunities in [name a country or demographic]."

Before making any commitments, do your due diligence. Inquire about their mission, vision, impact, and sustainability practices. Garnering references and first-hand experience will provide you with the confidence to commit.

6. What are your expectations?

Regardless of your role, it is in everyone's best interest to communicate expectations at the beginning of the contribution experience — both yours and the organization's. Ensure you have agreement and confirm timelines.

It is also valuable to communicate expectations continuously. Once you become exposed to the depth of the issue and the expanse of opportunities, expectations can change. Continued communication will allow for constant engagement. Without it, a contributor can become non-contributing.

Also, consider communicating your objectives to your fellow professional-contributors so they will have clear expectations of you and context for your participation. Disclosure will also encourage them to be aware of other opportunities within or outside the initiative that could help you reach your objectives and goal.

7. Brand yourself

The reasons you choose to contribute will influence the impression people have of you, so make your professional-contributions count. People make decisions about whether they respect you, trust you, or will refer you. Judgments are made, consciously or subconsciously. Everything you do helps to form someone's perception of you.

Contemplate how you conduct yourself as a professional-contributor. Many people volunteer to enhance their professional careers, while their interactions with other volunteers may jeopardize the professional impression they wish to impart.

As a professional-contributor, consider a brand vetting technique: "Do I always need my voice to be heard or my way to be had, or can I move past some issues to move forward on others?" For more branding considerations as a professional-contributor visit YouMeWe.ca book community for a download.

To be perceived as a professional-contributor, treat the opportunity as if you were dealing with a client, and each fellow contributor as an influencer. This approach will promote respecting the process, putting your best forward, and not becoming overly familiar with anyone. As you build trust and rapport with your fellow contributors, moving toward a respectful colleague relationship will allow for camaraderie and connection that will promote continued engagement.

Also, it's easier to be a professional-contributor when there are limited demands on your time and energy, but when it gets tough, would you choose to quit? That decision will create an impression of you, whether you like it or not.

8. Evaluate

Evaluating impact will directly relate to what your objectives were in contributing. Assess if you achieve what you intended, why or why not? Did you overestimate the organization's values alignment or underestimate their objectives? Was it the right time for your goals?

As the president and a director on a national board within the Canadian speaking industry, I experienced the sobering reality that although I had clear goals, it doesn't mean the board is ready to implement them. Some stages need addressing before a vision can be the logical next phase of evolution. It is often not until we are in an organization and contributing our time, skills, and energy, that we realize what needs to be done before our goal can be achieved. Reflecting on your mission and passion could help prioritize. However, if your mission is aligned and your passion is enough, it will be amazing what you can endure, not to mention learn on the way.

Immy Kamarade, managing director and founder of Dallas Investments Ltd, and formerly president on three boards, is also the mother of five children. Immy explains why she has taken such an active contribution role in her community:

> When you look at our lives here, especially African women, not all of us had the opportunity to go to school, the opportunity to gain exposure, nor the opportunity to exploit our talent and wisdom. The moment I realized God had made me be among the few, I knew I needed to share it with others. I often say yes and rarely say no.

Many women can relate to often saying *yes* and rarely saying *no*. However, Immy shares the rewards of surrendering to *yes*:

> Through Benishyaka Association, we have educated over 10,000 orphaned children. I have had the pleasure of seeing these children grow up and many go to university and have good jobs, supporting themselves, their mothers, brothers — personally, it is powerful. It motivates me. It shows possibilities. We are building our nation. I'm building a future for myself, my children, my nation, for the continent. All of these things make me want to continue.
>
> [Sitting on the board] in my business associations has no financial benefit, but it is all about community development. We are also building people and their purchase power. It won't work today, but it will work in 20 years.
>
> [Another benefit] is learning. I learn from my colleagues. Many of them have a lot of experience. I learn leadership. I develop my mind source.

Of course, evaluating the impact also influences who or what you want to help, uplift, or advance by your participation. Many not-for-profits conduct surveys that can provide you with perspectives. Keep the lines of communication open with the organization and the beneficiary of your efforts will assist in the assessment. One of the most compelling measures of your impact can be by having a discussion with the recipient and assessing if they felt the contribution was helpful, how, and what else is needed and why.

Gaining their perceptions can motivate you to continue as planned, or to recalculate how you consciously contribute. Either way, insight is instrumental in ensuring your professional-contributions count.

Make your contribution count

Volunteer burnout occurs at a faster pace when we are doing something that doesn't align with our purpose, objectives, expertise, skills, or mission. When everything aligns, not only do you feel fulfilled, but you also will amplify your impact. No matter where you contribute, make it conscious by committing to provide your talents that will assist progress, hold the professional attitude when executing, and deliver on promises. Visit YouMeWe.ca book community for questions to guide the journey.

Reflect on how to make your conscious-contributions™

1. When volunteering, what objectives do you have?
2. When volunteering, are you demonstrating the level of professionalism you want to be associated with you?
3. What opportunity will align your purpose, mission, skills, time constraints, and values?

Chapter 15
Move from messenger to the mission

Words of Wisdom

[Women] are the backbone of this continent. Not the rib, like they talk about in the Bible. We need to move towards reshaping and redirecting the continent. The way it is going now it's not going to work for the women of the continent, nor for the children of this continent. Let's rise up like the backbone we are.

Gcina Mhlophe, writer, director, storyteller, founder of Gcinamasiko Arts and Heritage Trust, South Africa
Pioneer: African Storyteller

I wasn't a journalist. I wasn't a writer. I wasn't a host. I had none of these qualifications when I started WisdomExchangeTv. Regardless of my eligibility or title, I was able to gain access to interviews. High profile African women responded and expressed their honor and appreciation. Some women influence the direction of the continent. Many have the ear of the President or King. All have an impact on either the social, economic, or environmental well-being in their community or beyond. Regardless of their position, influence, or schedule, they gave me time.

My network in Africa was almost non-existent. I had two supporters, who offered a few introductions, but for the rest of the interviews I relied on my own devices. My name means nothing to most people. With no qualifications, no connections, and no name cachet, most of the women I reached out to interview graciously accepted. Sometimes they traveled to me, but mostly Mike and I went to them. We were welcomed into their offices, homes, or favorite retreats. They graciously opened a door into their minds and hearts.

I'm astounded that we were granted these interviews. I question whether, if I were to ask in the West or in other countries, if I would receive the same reception. By the time this book is published, I will have that answer as WisdomExchangeTv.com is relaunching with interviews of conscious-contributors globally. Based on the feedback of the African women interviewed, there were many reasons they accepted the invitation, but the two that were repeated most often, were the ones mentioned in the email invitation. "We are celebrating African women leaders with the hope of educating future African women leaders" and "It is a *how to* interview, not a *what you achieved interview*. It will provide practical insights to assist other women to succeed."

Both comments focus on the mission, not the messenger.

We focused earlier on self-transcendence, by looking at how you can serve others by moving from your purpose to your mission, through conscious-contributions — from *me* to *we* — from messenger to the mission. In this personal evolution, marrying what the world needs with your talents and what you love takes center stage.

To contribute in the best interests of the whole requires a very healthy dose of humility, because the focus shifts from *me*, what we want, need, or get, and moves to what is in the best interests of all (or *we*). When focusing on the messenger's needs, it is often our ego driving the goal, subconsciously or consciously wanting acceptance, acknowledgment, or appreciation. However, when the mission is the motivator, we step aside, making room for the mandate to take hold and grow. We demonstrate humility when we see ourselves as a conduit of a mission, rather than the sender of it.

We celebrate missions with the increased presence of TED Talks and TEDx in communities. Speakers deliver a provocative idea to change attitudes, lives and, ultimately, the world, all in 18 minutes or less. The mission of Ted Talks is *ideas worth spreading*. The presenter is just the messenger delivering a thought much more magnificent than themselves. Social, cultural, or environmental movements are also good examples of a mission, strategically bringing an idea forth in hopes of gaining momentum. A good definition of a movement is described by Wikipedia, a resource that is another example of placing a mission before the messenger: "They are large, sometimes informal, groupings of individuals or organizations which focus on specific political or social issues. In other words, they carry out, resist, or undo a social change."[57]

Ignitors of movements communicate a message to prospective followers accompanied by an action in the hope that it will gain traction. The campaign may have begun because of the messenger, but it doesn't create energy until it has a follower. It is the first follower that validates the mission and starts its momentum. Erica Chenoweth, an American political scientist, conducted extensive research on violent revolutions versus peaceful civil participation. She found that it takes a minimum of 3.5 percent of the population to provide active and sustained involvement to make a change.[58]

A messenger is a catalyst, and if she requires continued self-gratification, her ego may monopolize the energy necessary to create a substantive movement. Tapping into one's feminine energy helps keep the ego in check.

Contribution continuum — individual participation

Starting a movement can be overwhelming; however, to have a sustainable social influence, the chasm between our ego and impact requires reflection and a shift in mindset. A contribution can be progressive and doesn't have to be all-consuming. Individually, we can become more mission-focused through various pathways of conscious-contributions. Some of these opportunities are more passive, meaning they require less of our time, energy, and focus. Bear in mind however, these passive opportunities often need the commitment of money. On the other end of the spectrum are active contributions, which require more time, energy, and focus. Here you don't lead with financing; the commitment is more holistic. Active contributions are woven into our lifestyle. Within each marker, there are degrees of commitment. The easier penetration point is passive and often financial.

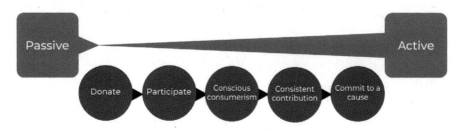

Donate: An accessible access point to any contribution is providing a donation. It can be as passive as supporting a crowdfund, or a giving pledge, or as significant as a philanthropic gift. Regardless of what you give, it is likely more passive as it requires less time, energy and commitment to a specific cause. Often passive donations are based on the relationship you have with the fundraiser rather than the connection to the cause itself. Examples include Salvation Army, Boy or Girl Scouts, clothing donations, or children selling chocolate at the supermarket for a school trip.

Participate: Participation is moving toward a more active involvement, but still leaning heavily toward passive, as this marker refers to attending fundraising events, causal volunteering, or voluntourism. Participating in these events is often motivated by your relationship with the invitee, or the experience promised. Examples include Ride for Heart, Run for Cancer, attending a gala supporting anti-violence and building stoves or bikes in a developing country.

Conscious consumerism: This starts leaning toward a more active contribution, as it is a lifestyle choice, and is woven in many, if not all, your consumer and waste decisions. When making purchase decisions, there is consideration of the provenance of a product. A conscious consumer is asking questions about a company's values and ethical practices and how they adhere to them, e.g., to ensure clothes are manufactured by a company that doesn't use child labor. Perhaps you value buying local; only purchasing products from your nation or community. Maybe you value not purchasing products from a state that violates human rights or endorses unfair animal treatment. Conscious questions support some or all your considerations.

Consistent contribution: This refers to actively and consistently contributing socially or environmentally. This progressive marker or entry into the continuum accepts our responsibility as citizens to participate and recognizes it as a significant part of our authentic self. One may choose to give to a wide variety of initiatives and join a service club to appeal to the diversity. However, one may also want to exclusively commit to their compassion-connection — a group of people or issue for which a person has a profound concern or care. The interest is not passive, but active. A person may want to focus their time and energy, and align all initiatives benefiting that group or issue. There are many activities to participate in around fundraising, from hosting an event, to starting a foundation, or a donor-advised fund. Alternatively, engage at grassroots by assisting the beneficiary; this could include anything from helping neighbors to teaching in Peru.

Commit to a cause: Here you are most active, and put all your energy, time, and focus into a singular contribution. More personal time and energy is required. There is likely ongoing interaction with the beneficiary in some capacity. This level of commitment may morph into a not-for-profit or establishing a social enterprise.

Many not-for-profits can turn a passion for a cause to an opportunity for beneficiaries to make an income empowering her to make her own decision on health and life choices — a key marker for empowerment and equality.[59] The Hanne Howard Fund is likely to stay a not-for-profit because they don't have a product or service that can be paid for by the community. However, Jane Wathome's Beacon of Hope was founded to assist women, and this not-for-profit can transition into a profit center by providing capable women with income from the production of goods to sell to the general population. In the spirit of sustainability, many not-for-profits attempt to transition to a more social enterprise structure, an evolution that would rely less on the good nature of donors and promote beneficiary dignity.

Contribution continuum – organization participation

Traditionally the founding of a business pursues a goal of generating profits for shareholders. There is a shift these days where companies are moving from the messenger and money, to the mission and meaning. Small businesses are leading the charge. Regardless of what stage or phase your business is along a continuum, there are various entry points to have a social impact and progress your business from money-driven to mission-motivated.

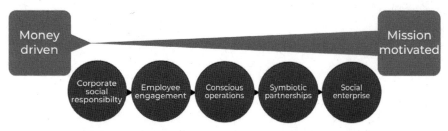

Corporate Social Responsibility (CSR): Organizations often start with committing part of their resources to a cause. Although there has been an increased commitment from companies toward supporting social or environmental initiatives and increased impact, there is still a reluctance to believe the motivation is genuinely for the benefit of the issue, instead of bolstering a company's reputation. Some CSR initiatives are directed from the c-suite or are an owner's or leader's pet project. It is launched with fanfare and enthusiasm, only to eventually be greeted by fizzle and flop, because the only person committed to the cause is the one who cared about it in the first place. If embracing corporate social responsibility is to have a long-term social impact, it needs stakeholders to be engaged. Those who are successful at appealing to a broad stakeholder group receive the benefits of employee retention, customer loyalty, and enhanced reputation.

Employee engagement: This is a movement towards shared value where social responsibility initiatives consider employee needs to contribute to society. Within this evolution, there are various opportunities including donations, such as automatic payroll deduction, matching gifts, fundraising matches, dollars for doers, annual not-for-profit stipend and more.

Small businesses tend to want profit before committing to financial contributions. Another alternative to donating dollars is employee participation, which also can incorporate many levels of involvement. Organizations may sponsor their employees' expertise to a not-for-profit, or encourage company-sponsored team community projects, internal employee fundraisers, or paid time off for employees to volunteer. Some companies are even tying skills-based volunteering to their development plan.[60]

As a small business, consider joining a service club so each employee can get involved as much or as little as they want, while respecting their interests and aspirations. Another option is to promote employee engagement to advance the Sustainable Development Goals through Impact2030.[61]

Conscious Operation: At this marker, you will identify the business's vision, mission, purpose, and values, and then select suppliers that align. Regardless of what a supplier provides, product or service, evaluate whether they incorporate an ethical distribution channel. From sourcing, producing, to managing and distribution, each element is considered to maximize conscious business practices that promote inclusivity, human dignity, sustainable resources, and limit the negative impact on the environment.

Becoming a conscious organization requires dissecting each element of the company to assess how to transform it to a more ethical execution. Although this procedure can be time-consuming, the rewards are tremendous. As a leader, you are departing from the sole focus of being money-driven, and moving toward being mission-motivated, where all stakeholders feel part of an ecosystem in which their contributions count.

To take steps to becoming a conscious operation, embrace the mission-motivated philosophy and adopt from any position — from being a volunteer, manager, leader, entrepreneur, or employee.

Symbiotic partnership: At this stage an organization is moving toward being more mission-motivated. Here there is an increased emphasis on shared value with beneficiaries of a contribution, partners to deliver on the mandate, and customer participation. Conscious-contributions are baked into the organization's DNA.

A symbiotic partnership is a sustainable long-term partnership where collaborators benefit from an ongoing relationship and refer to each other for strategic insight and synergies. To spawn such a connection, mutual respect, trust, and aligning values are all required. Parties have each other's best interests in mind.

First, there are beneficiaries of the contribution. They may provide a product or service offering. The business is structured to elevate that group. For example, Gone Rural is a handcraft business formed to help provide rural women with jobs to produce an income for their families. The beneficiaries make products to sell to consumers. Without the beneficiary partnership, there would be no product for sale. This relationship is significant, and the beneficiaries are consulted regularly to ensure an initiative that was developed to empower a group is reaching that objective.

Second, there are the partners in the supply chain. For this relationship to flourish, the mission and values of the organization have to be well-aligned. This symbiotic partnership engages all allies in the overall mandate, working together to reach a common good. An example is the food distribution initiatives, where grocery stores donate food (whose sell-by date is close to or recently expired) to a food bank or other charities.

Another significant partner, and the one that can have a profound impact on your business, is the consumer. Of course, product or service purchases mean profit, but just as revealing is that when consumers buy from a mission-motivated organization, they are supporting your conscious-contribution. Consumers' purse strings support this claim as indicated by Nielson Research, that 40 to 55 percent of consumers will pay more for a product or service if it has a social or environmental impact. Beyond paying more to do social good, there is an increase in customer loyalty.[62]

A business can engage customers by creating an experience. Implement an initiative where they can spread the mission's mandate through social media, such as in the Bell Let's Talk campaign. The communication company donates five cents to Canadian mental health programs with every Bell specified social share, text message or phone call.[63] Up to 2019 they have committed over CDN$100,000,000 to mental health initiatives.[64]

At YouMeWe we create a customer experience by encouraging people to celebrate others' contributions in the community on our #YourContributionCounts Campaign page. For every listing, we invest US$1 in a woman's education or business, helping her move from poverty to prosperity. Although we invest in line with our mission to create and promote social and environmentally conscious companies, we also celebrate the many people who contribute to that mandate.[65]

Social enterprise: More organizations are becoming conscious, and more social enterprises are being established. A social enterprise intends to improve social, economic, and environmental well-being. Social enterprises often include not-for-profits that use commerce to help create an income but reinvest all profits into the organization. However, YouMeWe encourages a profitable social enterprise. With net income generated, there will be increased motivation, sustainability, and, therefore, social impact. In other words, a social enterprise validates its success by providing a social return with an equal balance of profitability.

With any business where the mission is the central focus, it needs to articulate the difference it wants to make in the world. Why is your business important now? How will it fulfill its mission? How will it be determined that the enterprise is successful? If the enterprise didn't proceed, what issue would persist?

Social enterprises were created by many of the pioneering African women we interviewed 20 or 30 years ago, businesses which now impact thousands. Although they didn't consciously create a social enterprise, they followed their instincts to respond to what society needed. These women are visionaries and social transformers. Without their ingenuity, thousands of people would have been left with little to no income, and communities would have stagnated.

WE HAVE BEEN IN the information economy since the early 1970s. We have seen the evolution of business with technology disruptions in virtually all industries. Now, more of the private sector is taking the reins of social reform. There is a rise of conscious-companies that are ethical, inclusive, and fill social, cultural, or environmental gaps. Because of this transition, power can lie in a democracy where profit is not the only guide. Consumers, collaborators, employees are speaking with their money and their loyalty. Economic evolution is underway where the information economy is primed to make a shift into the mission economy— where everyone will profit.

Personal evolution

The evolution of businesses from messenger to mission relies on the person at the helm to optimize their meaning by collaborating with well-aligned individuals. The catalyst for the shift is the business leader's progressing values.

Looking at the money-driven to mission-motivated continuum, one can also enter from the mission side, by starting a social enterprise. This is where an entrepreneur is motivated to implement an idea that fills what the world needs (such as an issue on *The World's To do List*) and is well versed in creating and delivering a product or service to address a gap. The mission is the motivation. From here, an entrepreneur starts researching the beneficiaries and seeking symbiotic partners to bring the offer to the market. She may then decide to immerse herself in complete conscious execution. From here, engage congruent employees who seek to do work that provide meaning. Finally, one needs to promote to the masses to enhance the business reputation. Many of these phases can overlap regardless of which direction you enter the continuum. Where you enter depends where you are now and how you engage with an opportunity that can provide you more meaning.

Make your contribution count

If you become committed to a cause or a mission, you can marry what the world needs with what you love, what you are good at, and what you can get paid for. Your mission converges with your passion, vocation, and profession. In the Japanese culture, they call this *Ikigai*, where a lifestyle balances between the spiritual and the practical on route to maximizing your meaning.

Regardless of where you are on your journey to contribute, there is a pathway to a profound impact. In Part 3, we will look at how to lead a conscious-contribution sustainably to create a ripple effect.

In Gcina Mhlophe's words of wisdom at the beginning of the chapter, she was referring to African women being the backbone. I don't think she will mind if I suggest feminine energy is the heartbeat of continents. The more we connect and collaborate, the more we will pump love, care, and inclusivity through societies' veins.

Reflect on how to make your conscious-contributions™

1. What is your motivation to contribute?
2. Where are you on the contribution continuum? Where do you want to be? What actions do you need to take to progress to your goal?
3. What contribution idea could you implement into your organization?
4. What mission could you support and become an advocate for?

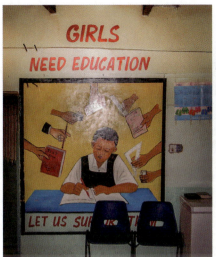

Girls school in Kibera slum, Nairobi, Kenya

Girls school in Kibera slum; Nairobi, Kenya

Typical rural roadside store; Uganda

"Take interest in your partner's passion and spend more time together to avoid the sexual network." Uganda billboard

Smiles for miles; South Africa

Mike meets a young man with a Canadian hockey jersey; Kampala, Uganda

Mike spending time at an orphanage; Uganda

Suzanne connecting with young girls in an urban slum; Kenya

Suzanne spending time with differently abled children; Kenya

Attending Christmas pageant in Lenana slum, Nairobi, Kenya. The beneficiary of the Hanne Howard Fund

Leah Ngini, founder and director of St. Christopher's Kindergarten and Preparatory Secondary School with a welcoming class of teachers and students in Karen, Nairobi, Kenya

Celebrating life in Kibera slum, Nairobi, Kenya

Suzanne hanging with local children in Swakopmund, Namibia

Mike being charmed by a local Mama in Swakopmund, Namibia

Rendille Tribe attending school under a tree in North Eastern Kenya

Small group tavel with our dedicated overland crew. Cape Town, South Africa to Nairobi, Kenya. Namibia, Botswana, Zimbabwe, Mozambique, Malawi, Tanzania

Rural water collection; Kenya

Washing day; rural Kenya

YouMeWe baskets are hand crafted from sisal by local artisans of Tintsaba, eSwatini

Sisal being prepared by the fabulous artisans at the Tintsaba workshop in Piggs Peak, eSwatini

The welcoming party at Rusia Orikiriza Bariho rural compound. Women wearing the traditional Ugandan dress, the gomesis. Outside Kampala, Uganda

Suzanne with Janet Nkubana of Gahaya Links after interview in Kigali, Rwanda

Suzanne with Meaza Ashenafi after interview in Addis Ababa, Ethiopia

Gone Rural market day in eSwatini. Artisans come from miles to trade newly woven merchandise for a Fair Trade living wage, and obtain raw materials for next months production needs. A micro-economy has emerged and health services are also provided on trade days.

Suzanne and Mike at our home away from home in Kenya with Lois and Mark Shaw

Suzanne interviews Rehmah Kasule, Kampala, Uganda

Suzanne & Mike attend a Valentine's Day party with Mary & George Ogalo and their church congregation. Nairobi, Kenya

Suzanne with Ela Gandhi, Durban, South Africa

Suzanne interviews Christine Asiko, Kenya

Suzanne with Mulu Iori, Addis Ababa, Ethiopia

Suzanne with Katherine Ichoya, Nairobi, Kenya

Hiking Mount Kenya for Suzanne's 45th birthday. The awesome crew (above left) got us to the top, cake and all (below left). Top right: Hiking Heights for Higher Education awareness campaign makes a stop at the forth highest peak in Africa.

Hiking the Otter Trail in South Africa

Hiking Heights on the Otter Trail with fellow Canadians

All smiles before swimming across the river, Otter Trail

Rest camp hiking Mount Kilimanjaro, Tanzania

Participating in the ceremonial bonfire as part of the Meskel celebration in Addis Ababa, Ethiopia

Part 3: we — make your contribution count — sustainably

Chapter 16
Generate a ripple effect

Words of Wisdom
Women must understand that inherent in each one of them are powerful jewels. They need to value themselves and they need to value what they bring to their families and corporate tables.

Norah Odwesso, public affairs and communications director for Coca-Cola Central East & West Africa, Nairobi, Kenya
Pioneer: co-founder Footprints of Faith

Perched on the side of a mountain, 50 artisans gather in the rural highland in eSwatini for the Gone Rural market day. Every month the handcrafters give Gone Rural the finished woven products in exchange for income and dyed lutindzi grasses used to produce the newly ordered products. Mike and I were invited to visit one of 13 production groups spread over 53 communities. The women have come from near and far, skillfully carrying dried grass, mats, baskets, placemats, and coasters. These products will be sold through two local stores and exported to 32 countries.

Handcrafters anticipate this monthly ritual because they are paid 47 to 52 percent of the wholesale price (a Fair Trade income). They also have an opportunity to connect with their broader community. Artisans share tribe stories and catch up on the latest community goings-on. Many are still trimming rogue grasses to complete their weaving before presenting the product to the quality examiner.

Although Gone Rural was the catalyst to bring these women together, grassroots businesses capitalize on the micro-economy that has emerged through these regular gatherings. Vendors set up to provide weavers with easy access to home-made food for lunch, used clothes, and fruits and vegetables. NGOs are present to offer social programs where handcraft producers can talk with a local specialist about health issues, their children, and school fees.

The micro-economy and social services are among the many ripple effects that transpire from being one of the leaders in establishing the eSwatini handcraft industry. Another is being able to feel the energy culminating from the collection of motivated rural women who can provide for their families.

Mike, feeling a bit like an intruder, stood back and watched the market unfold. I, feeling more like a guest, engaged with the women and chatted about their families, their craft, and how Gone Rural has changed their lives.

Philippa Reiss Thorne, managing director for Gone Rural, recognizes the significance of building an organization and how it can influence the industry and create a hive of activity in a small country.

> I feel very proud to see our handcraft industry becoming world-renowned. We have big buyers coming here, and all the handcraft companies work together because the buyers would not just come for one of us. They come to see 10 or 20 high-quality handcraft companies.

Like Gone Rural, many of the social enterprises interviewed rely on sustainable local resources such as grasses, plants, or recyclables to create a ripple effect throughout their community, while working to elevate it out of poverty.

Businesses that have a social impact provide more than an income; they provide the methodology to uplift society. Mother Teresa summed up a philosophy that describes these social transformers: "I alone cannot change the world, but I can cast a stone across the waters to create many ripples."

One of the most personally enlightening fiction books is *The Power of One*, written by Bryce Courtenay, a South African. I loved it so much, I also saw the movie.

In the movie, there was a dialog between the main character, PK, a teenage boy in South Africa, and St. John, his headmaster at university. Hearing this message in my mid-twenties influenced me to transform from a dreamer to realizing that any movement can create the momentum that can be the difference.

PK: How will they ever be included if they can't ever read or write English?

St. John: I quite agree with you PK, but at the end of the day, it's only about a dozen people you're talking about teaching. How much difference will that really make?

PK: A waterfall begins from only one drop of water, sir. Look what comes from that.[66]

A ripple effect starts with one drop. It begins when a morally courageous person goes against the current and doesn't succumb to the status quo. She tosses her wisdom, energy, and values into a sea of unknown and trusts that with perseverance the ripple they create will eventually have a remarkable impact on the whole.

Throughout the book, we have highlighted courageous women, who refused to accept mediocrity and embraced their role in the evolution of human potential. Their goal was to transform societal circumstances, raising the well-being of all; they know it starts with *me*. Through the eyes of these pioneers' unique perspectives, they embarked on establishing a sustainable social enterprise or spearheaded a social or environmental initiative. Each threw *me* into the vast waters of the unknown and perpetuated a ripple that impacted hundreds, and in some cases, thousands of people. They chose to be the drop.

Be the drop

Our presence has created a ripple effect through this vast interconnected human ecosystem. Everything we do has a cause and effect. Perhaps unconsciously, our efforts have impacted the environment or society. We often don't know what our actions will initiate, until one day we see a flower grow on a lifeless shoreline, or we run into a child or a colleague who tells us our words set them on a new trajectory. Learning we are the *drop* can also cause a positive effect in us, making us more conscious in our interactions, our selection of issues, and generating a power that can turn into living our most meaningful life.

Gcina Mhlophe, freedom fighter and internationally renowned storyteller from South Africa, feels her most significant impact is reflected through the experience of others.

> The number of people that I meet, young people, or people in different professions, [that say] 'I believe in what you said, and I'm so grateful I got to hear you,' and it carries them forward. I may not be their biological mother, I may not be their older sister, their cousin or their aunt, but I'm related to them, because I believe in making a difference in this life. I know the continent needs people like me. I can't be down; I must rise up and make a difference.

Gcina admits, "I'm just living my life most of the time." To create waves of transformation on how future generations think, work, act, and ultimately affect the ecosystem is often subconscious. We focus on our desires, ambitions, and eventually recognize that our struggle paves the way for others to make their journey less arduous. It is when this subconscious becomes conscious that we realize our responsibility and the opportunity to create a path for others to follow, powering them to empower others. Jane Trembath, a pilot, realizes that what was once a lonely cockpit opened the way to a historical moment. Jane is the drop that started the waterfall.

> When we did the first all-women flight on a Boeing, it was something that just happened. It meant women can operate this aircraft and we didn't need men to operate it. So many people have acknowledged that women have taken their place in aviation. For me, that was very significant. It helped others realize the sense of their power as well.

As we initiate the first drop, we are often unaware of the possibilities; however, following our purpose will guide us. Antonia Mutoro, executive director of the Institute of Policy Analysis and Research in

Rwanda, believes that economic growth and development is impossible without sound policy and responsive governance. She sought to strengthen the evidence base available to the government, civil society, and development partners regarding pressing social, economic, and political issues facing Rwanda. The institution's purpose was to provide real-time solutions to everyday challenges. With a research-based approach, Antonia's organization identified gaps that shone a spotlight on Rwanda's poorest of the poor.

> The study identified that if the government, NGOs, and investors supported household-level enterprises, Rwanda would get out of poverty much quicker than doing anything else. No one seemed to realize that something smaller than small enterprise was there and these people need to be uplifted, especially the youth and the women.

Antonia's research points out that poverty alleviation starts with understanding, then creating policies and practices that focus on household enterprises that do odd tasks for income. The Rwandan government embraced this research. Although the ripple effect hasn't reached its potential yet, there is a lot more attention internationally being placed on household-level enterprises, making the smallest of the small enterprises relevant.

Innovators are often the drop to uplift a person, country, or continent. Gladys Muhunyo, director of Africa Programs at Computer Aid Africa, was instrumental in meeting the demand for people to access computers all over the continent. As the first woman to be appointed head of an Information Communication Technology (ICT) network in all of Africa, many people wondered who she knew, rather than what she knew. Leading her team to provide computer access to over one million people and setting up regional offices was the evidence needed to demonstrate she was the right person for the job. Computer Aid Africa is replicated all over the continent with the mission to empower the developing world by providing access, education, implementing technology, and supporting environmentally responsible solutions. The mandate is achieved through many initiatives, including recycled computers to educate future generations. It also assists refugees in camps to connect, leading from isolation to hopeful liberation.

Computer Aid started in 1997 in the United Kingdom. It now operates in 100 countries helping over 14.5 million people through its distribution of 260,000 computers.[67]

With mission leaders at the helm, a force of energy can create a wave so powerful its wake can address some of the most challenging issues of our time.

Mission leadership, the drop that generates the ripple effect

Each interaction with an African conscious-contributor left me mesmerized with their similar characteristics. Although each woman was unique, each leader appeared to be grounded in service, and displayed humility despite her accomplishments.

These women embrace mission-centric characteristics. They recognize that it is critical to be invested personally while being mindful of their impact. Embedded in the YouMeWe ethos are the qualities exhibited by the women interviewed, where inclusivity and consciousness are the cornerstones of a mission leader:

She is ethical: No matter what the consequences, a mission leader stays true to her moral fiber. She looks fear in the face and persists while honoring her faith, culture, and family. She is fair, ethical, and adheres to a higher social standard. She reveals her integrity in how she conveys herself, makes decisions, and interacts daily.

She is genuine: She focuses on what is in front of her, and graciously gives her energy to another. She demonstrates intention in every interaction and initiative. She leads, speaks, and acts from the heart, with grace, purpose, and consciousness. She is authentic and doesn't apologize for who she is. She celebrates all facets of her character, even when society suggests some don't serve her.

Gladys Muhunyo suggests, "Be an authentic leader. If you are authentic, people will stand by you." A mission leader does not put on a facade. She exposes her genuine self consistently to her team, her partners, and her stakeholders. She knows it is an honor to be followed and doesn't take it for granted. She recognizes it is not her *title* that gains respect, but how she performs every day.

She is willful: To make any vision a reality, a mission leader needs the confidence in herself to persist regardless of the naysayers. She needs the will to persevere when obstacles seem insurmountable. Fighting a crusade alone doesn't defuse her determination; it inspires her to find new approaches to gain momentum for the mission. She doesn't seek others to fix her community's circumstance but empowers the citizens around her.

To influence social transformation Nouzha Chekrouni, Ambassador of Morocco advises:

> You need to be confident. You need to have a mission in your life and define it, then find ways to achieve it. Secondly, [realize] you are not facing an enemy. Society is not our enemy. We should build with it. Many people aim to build in different ways. We need to understand others and find ways to become a part of the group that we are well-aligned with. As a group, we can be stronger and go so much further. Thirdly, we should be humble.

She is humble: She focuses on *we*, rather than *me*. A mission leader recognizes that while she can progress independently, momentum only occurs when people align with, act on, and amplify a message. The combination of alignment, action, and amplification make a messenger's mission multiply and eventually creates a movement worth following.

She is loyal: A mission leader caters to her employees, extended family, and community, and takes that responsibility very seriously. She approaches her role with love and care. She acknowledges that she is accountable to the ecosystem and to the mission. She serves with integrity in the best interest of the whole.

A mission leader invests in developing her team and herself. She believes in realizing a vision by inspiring growth and bringing out the best in people around her by allowing them space to pursue their purpose, whether that means a colleague stays alongside her or travels a new path. She is inclusive, and doesn't leave anyone behind, but will part with a rogue team member if they are not in service of the whole.

She is inspirational: A mission leader is curious, and therefore wants to learn about others. She listens, and as a consequence, is heard. She has the power to mobilize people who are engaged or to bring those who hide in dark corners into the light. She communicates to each team member their value and appreciates them in unique ways. She understands that each person is motivated differently, has different priorities and a different personality. She harnesses their uniqueness and inspires them to be the best version of themselves. She recognizes that some colleagues may have ambitions outside the scope of the organization's mission; she elevates them to have the courage to pursue their path and purpose.

She is collaborative: It has been said that *women collaborate; men negotiate*. Feminine energy leads horizontally and empowers a team to make decisions.

Mission leaders promote mutual respect and trust in forming symbiotic partnerships — sustainable long-term partnerships. She recognizes and appreciates that she can't do everything. She is transparent, accountable, and inclusive, resulting in loyal collaborators. She acknowledges the importance of establishing a culture in which she cultivates trust and care.

One distinct difference that sets a mission leader apart is their core motivation to consciously advance society, while collaboratively working alongside stakeholders.

Generating a socially conscious enterprise's ripple effect

The largest socially conscious enterprises we interviewed have five strategies in common:

1. They implemented social, economic, and environmental solutions to increase, harmony, health, and sustainability;
2. The beneficiaries of the social initiative are also the producers of the product brought to market;
3. The quantity produced dictates their income;
4. The enterprise employs the marketing and administration team and sub-contracts the producers;
5. The enterprise continuously tweaks the process to produce the highest quality product and enhance the beneficiaries' lives.

In the African context, harmony at home has many factors; two are to honor the family's culture and traditions. Making products at home part-time appeals to the way of life where women can also adhere to traditional roles. Between plowing fields, cooking meals, washing clothes, fetching water and wood, and taking care of her children — a mother weaves a masterpiece. There are times when farming will take precedence, resulting in a handcraft production lull. Socially conscious enterprises like Gone Rural and Tintsaba Master Weavers, both eSwatini companies, bring the raw materials for output to the producer to facilitate the ease of production.

For most of these women this part-time job is her family's only source of income. Many men are unemployed in the rural areas or work in the mines, away from home for months at a time. Women rely on innovative social enterprises for the income to sustain the homestead.

There are challenges for businesses when relying on individual artisans from remote production hubs, otherwise referred to as their hut, homestead, or communal tree. The well-founded concern is the struggle between an artisan's ability to provide food for the family and to educate her children. As a socially conscious enterprise, the responsibility is all consuming. Strategies need to be in place to ensure there is enough demand to keep everyone employed, including those around cash flow, timely delivery, and consistent product quality. These are, of course, similar to the challenges of many businesses.

Tintsaba Master Weavers created a competition to elevate quality. Founded in 1985, the first eSwatini handcraft company, impacts over 900 rural women and their families. Sheila Freemantle implemented a key strategy for sustainability, which was to acknowledge performance through a leadership and quality hierarchy. In both cases, rural women have to demonstrate their ability to master their craft. In leadership, they can move from weaver, to community leader, to full-time employee. As a quality master, Tintsaba has pioneered an approach in their part of the world, where women climb up the various skill levels en route to becoming a coveted Master Weaver. This is an initiative that Sheila talks about with pride:

> Out of 300 baskets weaved, 20 to 30 are considered using the finest technique. What is interesting about the entire competition is master weavers get a money prize, and they share in the profit that we make from that basket if we sell it in the Santa Fe consumer show. It is becoming a career, as opposed to a craft. These master weavers now have a status in their community. They start to be mentors for budding weavers or newcomers.

Leading a socially conscious enterprise in a country with one of the highest rates of HIV/AIDS per capita in the world has other unique challenges.[68] Although it is tragic to lose a life, it also has an impact on productivity. Sheila pulls herself out of her natural optimism, and her face morphs into a weary businesswoman, "When we lose someone, there is a person involved and a relationship, but also there are years of training invested in that person." As a business that prides itself on transforming women into highly qualified master weavers who can provide for their family, there is a high rate of loss to disease.

Hellen Acham acknowledges the challenges of local circumstances in building a business. When she established the North East Uganda Chilli Producers Association, the region was volatile. With the assistance of the cooperative, 65 percent of the women who have children are now able to pay their university fees, and peace and unity between tribes have ensued.

Hellen uses her experience in agriculture, leadership, and education to empower chili producers. As a mission leader whose goal is to create a sustainable business that has a profound ripple effect on the production and quality of life for all, her most important role is to lead her team to empower others, to galvanize co-operatives.

> As an organization, I have 22 field staff, based in various districts and sub-counties, who coordinate activities. These farm groups all have their leaders. We have more farmer leads than staff.
>
> We have mainstream training to assist them to handle the challenges that they face such as conflict development and sensitivity programs in place, i.e., gender sensitivity. We encourage the communities to take the lead. We achieve this by giving them the skills to deal with diverse situations.

Through this process, North East Chilli Producers and Hellen have managed to advance peace in Northern Uganda by promoting collaboration between tribes, and husbands and wives.

The key to the success of many social enterprises and cooperatives in the production business is through establishing a system to make a quality product and forming partnerships for export to markets. In the African context, this means the more recently realized opportunity of South-South trade, which is exporting on the same continent and region. With less restrictive export parameters and reduced transport cost, it is natural to look closer to home for expansion.

Generating a human rights ripple effect

Creating a ripple effect is displayed in other professions, such as the Women's Law Society in Ethiopia, that transformed women's rights. The society is determined not to rest until Ethiopian women have equality, respect, and dignity. As the founder, Meaza Ashenafi is proud of the ripple effect the society created through its perseverance:

> We have managed to do research and mobilize public opinion and present the case to the government in terms of discriminatory laws stating what needs to be done. We were part of the initiative that has led to the reform of Ethiopian family law, reform of criminal law, and reform nationality law that affected women rights.
>
> Also, the legal aid program is an important contribution to women. It has been in place for 12 years, and it provides access to legal aid for women all over the country. [We put] women's rights on the national agenda. When we started, there was no such name for *violence against women*.

Influential groups of women from Ethiopia to Morocco, and much further South, did *not go gentle into the good night*. Nouzha Chekrouni, was the delegate minister in charge of the issues for women, family, childhood protection, and integration of the disabled in Morocco. Nouzha explains how society transformed because a group of women persisted, and that determination was the first step in showing Moroccan society that it can't grow and develop without women's participation. With the support of the King, a political strategy was launched.

> We set up a national strategy to fight violence against women. We signed The Convention on the Elimination of All Forms of Discrimination Against Women. We had to implement all the laws.
>
> Secondly, we focused on how to get women involved in politics. We had to work on how to get women who were involved in political parties elected. We were able to bring approximately 11.2 percent of women to parliament. This was the first time there were such a large number of women elected. This completely changed the political landscape. Society discovered that women provide different input and as a result were making our society richer.

Creating a ripple effect often starts at home — mentoring your children. Hellen Acham shared the pride she felt in paying for six adopted children's university education. Tereza Mbire, serial entrepreneur, shared her most significant impact in addition to helping women at grassroots succeed in business, "After my husband died, I managed to educate my children because of the success of my businesses."

Make your contribution count

Know that you are significant, and any action that you initiate can have a constructive ripple effect. Those forks in the road lead to opportunities; it is about selecting the one that will give you the most meaning, impact the most people, and will be sustainable once you are gone. If you utilize mission leadership techniques in a for-profit business, or a not-for-profit organization, no doubt you will be the *drop* that creates a following where everyone will be able to *make their contribution count.*

Reflect on how to make your conscious-contributions™

1. Describe a time when you discovered you had a profound impact on someone. What did you do or say that induced their response?
2. Which, if any, of your leadership characteristics need to be elevated to optimize your life and your conscious-contributions?
3. Where would generating a ripple effect provide you with the most satisfaction?

Chapter 17
Make your conscious-contributions™ sustainable

Words of Wisdom
You win when others win with you. You grow as your network grows with you. As growth brings social impact, it will definitely improve your bottom line.

Gladys Muhunyo, director of Africa Programs Computer Aid Africa, Kenya
Pioneer: first woman appointed head of Information Communication Technology (ICT) network in Africa

Artisans gather from all over eSwatini for the annual SWIFT Fair Trade product competition. Each artisan sets up their table with their creative designs, carvings, weavings, jewelry, clothing, or pottery, with the hope of being acknowledged as the producer with the best business potential. All the competing artisans have completed the SWIFT training program, providing them with the skills to establish a sustainable business locally, with the goal of eventually being able to export to international markets. First, they had to get past the judges.

As one of three panelists we set out to assess the newest products and the artisans' business potential. We graded quality, value for money, branding, and presentation. We asked questions to prepare the producers for the realities of customer curiosity and business longevity. Creating a unique and appealing product wasn't good enough. The artisans needed to know how to market, price, and distribute to transform their craft from what is often called in Africa an *informal business*, into a formal enterprise.

And the winner is…eSwatini.

Philippa Reiss Thorne, of Gone Rural, indicates that buyers are coming to eSwatini to visit several of the handcraft companies, as they wouldn't come for just one. Therefore, there needs to be synergy amongst the local businesses to lure international buyers. In 2005 established handcraft companies, with the financial support of Comic Relief (from the UK) founded Swaziland Fair Trade (SWIFT), which has been instrumental in synthesizing eSwatini businesses for sustainability.

SWIFT is a member-based organization whose mission is to provide training, trade, and advocacy for businesses by promoting the ten Fair Trade principles for the sustainable socio-economic empowerment of producers and communities.[69] The principles consist of fair employee payment, capacity building, no child or forced labor, no marginalized small producers and gender equality.[70] SWIFT and its 48 members believe that lifting people out of poverty requires trade, not aid.

They instituted a multi-level program to promote entrepreneur handcraft evolution. They have been able to attract members, accounting for 5,000 producers, of whom 97 percent are female. On average, these women earn two times the minimum wage. Since 2011, 25 new businesses have been established and 330 new jobs created. One of SWIFT's key objectives is to provide training in business development. They have contributed over 900 hours of training, coaching, and mentorship. Each member of the organization has the goal of providing a living wage for producers.[71]

Establishing opportunities for entrepreneurship and trade, not aid, will empower citizens to make decisions for their futures, their families, and their communities.

Stay the course to sustainability

When considering this principle, I can't help but reflect on a rafting trip down a rapidless river. Before our departure, the guide instructed us, "If you fall out of the boat and get stuck under it, don't panic. Walk your hands along the bottom of the raft and continue in one direction.

Don't lose patience and start turning around in a different direction — you will start going in circles leaving you exasperated and under the boat." This turns out to be excellent advice for many situations.

When making a conscious-contribution, it is most efficient to continue in one direction — in other words, to make it consistent and focused; this will offer the most significant impact on the beneficiary and on our personal gratification. However, there are times we can get distracted with the latest opportunity, and in doing so, dilute our contribution impact.

YouMeWe Foundation learned the wisdom of the rafting guide firsthand. Although we were focused on raising funds to provide university scholarships, there was a new opportunity in town that friends were supporting — building the Leah Ngini Community and Women's Center at AIU. I wanted in. Under the raft I went, not having the wisdom of my guide, I was stuck going around and around unfocused.

After two years, the ground for the center still wasn't broken. The charity I funneled my fundraising funds to stepped in. They redirected the monies to scholarships for deserving women.

Today, I would ensure that we had a memorandum of understanding (MOU) stating that if monies slated for a specific project were not used by a particular time, with the agreed upon specified parameters, the funds could be redirected within the charity's mandate.

Continuing in one direction means not deviating from your mission, as discovered by TSiBA, a higher education institution that focuses on *igniting opportunities through education*. When the school strayed into microfinance, they achieved less than stellar results. Gia Whitehead, founder and sustainability director, explains:

> We have an Ignition Centre, where we support entrepreneurs in our community that are not students. One of the first things we started to do is give loans because we thought you needed the money to start growing these businesses. We realized that wasn't working, so we stopped the loans, recognizing the real value was around the mentorship and skills that they

needed. Now we put a lot of focus into mentorship, just like we do in our curriculum to grow entrepreneurs.

Having the courage to expand is admirable, but first, a contribution needs to be entrenched before you deviate. Without a strong foothold into contributing to what and whom you care about (your compassion-connection) you will sabotage your efforts, minimizing your gratification and beneficiary benefits.

Donor dependency, the good, the bad, and the sustainable

The good

The definite advantage of a large donation is the infusion of capital, especially in the early stages of launching an initiative. Some donors will also be able to provide strategic insight and give access to networks to advance your cause. A directed donor may become an indispensable advocate and ambassador for the cause and have a significant influence on garnering other supporters.

The bad

Unfortunately, there are consequences for entirely relying on donors. Many benefactors require an immense amount of time and energy to appease. In addition to the financial due diligence needed from not-for-profits, donors' high demands can increase those administration costs. There may also be obligations tied to the donors backing. The dollars can be connected to a different direction, taking the mission off course or requiring you to collaborate with their contacts. The more dependent you are on a donor, the more you may have to succumb to their demands.

If desperate for donor dollars, you may subconsciously (or consciously) abandon your diligence to ensure your donors' values and sources of income align with your cause's mission. Doo Aphane shares her perspective on the limitations of acquiring funding:

I wish I could be self-funded. Funding comes with strings. We do things on the terms of other people. Sometimes I don't even consider where I am getting the funding from. We don't make the time to find out where they are getting the funding from. All we want are these enabling monies to meet our objectives.

In the end, a large donation can get a conscious-contribution launched, but what will happen if the donor's flow of finances stops?

There is another caveat, mainly if your cause is proactive rather than reactive. Human nature suggests we tend to respond to a problem rather than prevent it from occurring. The lack of universal engagement on prevention of further climate change is a case in point. Relying on donations alone is a shortsighted model. It relies on the goodwill of people with disposable income. Preventive causes will require more innovation, strategy, awareness, cost, and persistence to prompt social action.

The sustainable

The idea is simple — provide an experience in exchange for financial support — however, the execution could prove more complex.

Running, cycling, rowing, cocktail receptions, banquets, social media challenges have one thing in common — they create a donor experience. A benefactor can be prompted to support a cause by appealing to their interest through fundraising efforts. From large events such as CIBC Run for the Cure, to small events such as YouMeWe Spin from Cape Town to Cairo (a spinning/stationary cycling fundraiser with photos projected on the wall) can produce meaningful experiences in which the public wants to participate. Although the YouMeWe Foundation has a donate link on its website, our most significant fundraising initiatives have always been hosting an event. To host a successful event, one needs to be innovative, strategic, persistence, and have a good contact list.

There are several advantages to incorporating an event or social media experience in your fundraising strategy. Firstly, an experience brings more joy than material acquisitions. Millennials particularly have subscribed to the belief that *things don't define me; experiences do*. It has the extra benefit of lasting longer than the actual event. Momentum can be built pre, during, and post the experience allowing for long-term emotional connection. Secondly, funds come from a larger group of people, leaving you less reliant on a single funder and offering you more control to stay directed to your mission. The experience can garner participant loyalty year over year. Events also attract media, drawing the attention and participation from many, versus donations from a few.

Donors can kickstart your contribution reality, but understand they come with a cautionary note. If you are only relying on donors, you may minimize your overall impact. Implementing a commercial strategy to address social, economic, and environmental problems will foster sustainability because a business needs to utilize ingenuity to solve an issue while offering something of value to consumers.

Self-sustaining contributions

One of the biggest challenges in executing a business motivated by a social mission is maintaining demand for a product or service that is often more expensive to bring to market. Sheila Freemantle of Tintsaba, perceived this to be her most onerous obligation in managing her social enterprise:

> The cash flow and maintaining the bulk of work that women depend on was my biggest challenge. Many of those women don't have any other income and many of their husbands don't have any other income, so they rely on us. That is the biggest responsibility at Tintsaba.

Considerations for self-sustainability

Whether you build a social enterprise in a developing or developed country, maximizing local resources will engage and employ people long-term, mainly when utilizing untapped resources.

Sibongile Sambo offers some sage advice. Although she is the founder of a for-profit aviation company, her philosophies can make the difference between a social impact that can fly or flop.

Make your conscious-contributions™ sustainable

Go into business with an open mind. Know you can have a very good business idea but be prepared that sometimes the environment will not allow you to achieve it. Be flexible. Think out of the box. Think about ways to diversify. Think of ways to be profitable at all times. It doesn't help to be so passionate about something that is not bringing in money for you. You should be able to realize profits. If you can't make money from the initial idea, then alter it to help keep you afloat.

We can get caught up in living a life of doing good. Doing good without doing well, is not doing good for long.

No matter what type of business or conscious-contribution that you start or support, certain principles will assist with sustainability. Two of those are expanding the offering and diversifying the targeted market. Jennifer Riria, CEO of Echo Network Africa in Kenya, advises on the first:

> Grassroots companies need to learn the art of saving, moving from survival to investing. Women need products that make sense to them. If they get it, and it makes sense they will promote it. Then you think what complements that product. This is where growth will occur.
>
> Growth companies: when businesses are borrowing US$5,000 to US$10,000, they are still at the service level, but in order to grow, they need to get into production and manufacturing.

Hellen Acham's business success embraced expansion of their offering through production and manufacturing. She knew that taking the cooperative to the next level would require manufacturing at home, rather than exporting the unprocessed chili. Hellen believes the gap in optimizing production and profitability lies in the technologies for post-harvest handling.

> We are also looking at making chili sauce. We only have one company that is producing chili sauce in Uganda. We think if we can make chili sauce concentrate, then export it to other factories that can dilute chili sauce to use it.
>
> If we can acquire these technologies, it would really assist us in expanding our market. The chili oil is essential because pharmaceuticals need it. It is the most expensive element in the chili industry. All the drugs for humans

or animals, injectable or tablets, are preserved using the chili oil. All the garment industry uses chili for color separation.

Through increased processing of fruits like chili, the cooperative expanded to central and western Uganda, also growing the collective, as well as the members' bank accounts. Since our interview with Hellen, the North East Chilli Producers Association now manufactures red bird's eye chili in many districts. The association was the first to initiate commercial chili production in Uganda. By 2013, members had increased to 32,750, of which 60 percent are women and 40 percent men, supporting Hellen's mandate to provide income for women. As the cooperatives grew, they introduced production of other high-value non-traditional crops such as sugar beans, sunflowers, soya beans, and sesame in the same districts.

The Association is currently the biggest producer and supplier of chili to the two leading exporters of chili in Uganda. With a vision for the association to create "self-sustaining and financially prosperous communities," they are meeting their mandate.[72] Perhaps Hellen was right, "Our chili is the best in the global market so far."

TSiBA business school in South Africa not only expanded their offering but also diversified its target market in order to reduce donor dependency. Gia Whitehead shares some strategies they implemented to become less reliant on funding.

> We have had to be innovative, so we don't see our main income coming from donors, although we are reliant on them. We are looking at how we can generate non-donor-based income through generating activities. We have a number underway. We are also thinking creatively about how we can offer corporations our intellectual property using the knowledge that we have, skills we can offer to their employees, and other ways we generate income rather than it being perceived as a handout.

Approaching a contribution to society with business acumen can boost sustainability. Upon donor insistence, after a decade of TSiBA offering students full scholarships, they had to change the model. Students are now required to financially contribute to their education, with the goal of establishing a sense of ownership. Students pay what they can afford, leaving no financial barriers to a student's education or future. Payment can be as little as 30 dollars a month and has reduced the financial pressure on the school and made more scholarships available.

Marsha Gabriel, founder of the CSI Business Congress in South Africa, consults with many not-for-profits and educates them on how to look at their business profitably. She encourages them not to rely on donations, but to be self-sufficient. Some of the considerations to be self-sustaining include:

1. Be selfless, but not self-destructive. Create a sustainable project by making it income generating. You can be passionate about what you do, but passion doesn't pay the bills.

2. Target the right market — Marsha has developed three projects that are income generating, sustainable, and at the same time very attractive to corporations and government. She believes governments cannot make all the changes needed in South Africa; they need people on the ground who understand the hearts of the people.

3. Implement a project that affects the intended beneficiaries.

4. Develop staying power. You cannot tire of what you are doing.

If your primary objective is to have a social impact, the implementation of these strategies is critical. There are, however, many alternatives for capitalism to spread the wealth.

Finance a social impact with profits

Another alternative for sustainability is to donate some of your profits to a cause you care about as part of your social responsibility, marketing, and business strategy.

Marsha Gabriel has multi-streams of revenue including the CSI Business Congress, Mainstreaming Gender into Trade, and the Business Action Against AIDS, along with her restaurant. A portion of her profits help support and sustain all her other conscious-contribution initiatives including food distribution, and orphanage renovations.

Marsha continues to seek opportunities to capitalize on business relationships while assisting NGOs to operate profitably. As a marketing specialist, Marsha was offered a good income to design a public relations program for *Unite Against Hunger* campaign for a South African packaged goods company and an events company. She recommended they give her company food products in exchange for her public relations work. Her negotiation started a sustainable food distribution program and she is able to distribute food to orphanages, retirement homes, prisons, and babies at hospitals.

> We distributed food to the value of 500,000R per month and distributing to 102 organizations. There are still cost factors to get this food to these organizations: in terms of trucks, diesel, fuel, salaries, and cost for warehouse and distributors of our projects. I had to create a marketing initiative outside of that to move into promotions and personally to sustain that project. I created an initiative to where I would give away three cars a year so that I can put the message throughout South Africa: 'If you give $10R, not only can you win a vehicle, but you also will save lives.'

To make this program work, Marsha had to have strong public relations, advertising, negotiating, and speaking skills, combined with the vision to draft a plan that was sustainable long-term. Any social enterprise, charity, volunteer, or professional-contribution opportunity could benefit from such skills. Although Marsha is receptive to government funding, her profit models do not qualify. She relies on her ingenuity, experience, and business acumen to fill social gaps.

If inspired to transform a social, economic, or environmental situation, you may choose to build a business around the issue or establish another organization (such as foundation, fund, charity, nonprofit, or social enterprise), to finance what you care about. Pioneering African women use both strategies. Both can be sustainable solutions, and the latter can be an effective strategy, particularly if a business is well-established.

Regardless of the approach to making a social impact, a thorough strategy is essential.

Launch a social enterprise

Like any new business, a social enterprise needs to assess its potential for sustainability. It will start with industry, competitive, and customer analysis and cash flow forecast. The research will help form the business plan, which will include the purpose, vision, mission, values, strategies, tactics, timeline, goals, business model, financial plan, distribution channels and marketing elements that will inspire confidence in the business growth.

A social enterprise uses commercial practices to have a social, economic, or environmental impact and measures its success in equal parts of providing a *social return on investment* and profitability. To become sustainable, one needs to find the sweet spot between making enough money and creating the desired impact.

Achieving the sustainability starts with your commitment to the mission. In Part 2 of this book, we provided strategies and anecdotes on how to *maximize your meaning*. Assessing authentic being is essential to whom you can sustainably impact. This means holistically merging what the world needs with what you love, your talents, what you can be paid for. By fulfilling this gap in society consciously, as highlighted in *Part 1: me — make your contribution count — consciously*, you have done your due diligence. You recognize that how you address the world's needs means bringing your product or service to market to promote beneficiary participation, ethical practices, collaborative execution and creating opportunity, not dependency. A strong foundation will prepare you to launch a sustainable business.

Unlike most businesses, a social enterprise's inception is inspired by the impact it will have on society, the environment, or both. Therefore, at the outset, articulating an impact statement will guide all your strategic efforts. An impact statement focuses on the effect you are going to generate. It incorporates what you will achieve (outcomes), for whom (beneficiary), by when (timeframe); the more specific the statement, the more directed your efforts.

A well-crafted statement will assist with accountability and therefore should include targets that are measurable and realistic over three to five years. Once you commit to an impact statement, you will be able to write a strategic plan with much more clarity. You will also prioritize strategies accurately, make decisions faster, incorporate measures that matter, communicate more persuasively, and align with colleagues, clients and collaborators. They in turn will then be able to more precisely identify where they can contribute to your initiative.

Incorporating a statement of impact in your business plan will make it more robust and directed. Indicate clear, actionable milestones en route to reducing a social, economic, or environmental gap.

Once an impact statement is clarified, establish a theory of transformation, which focuses on *why* and *how*. Isolate the approaches needed to achieve the goals. A theory of transformation is a gauge to measure the progress between strategies implemented, the performance expected, and results realized. Develop a logical model that will identify progression on your journey of social impact.

By nature, a social impact isn't achieved alone. Many organizations, businesses, not-for-profits, community groups, and associations can assist you in expanding your reach. This chapter started with a focus on SWIFT. Like other organizations, they promote the use of Fair Trade principles, and guide how to adhere to them while having financial success. The next section concentrates on various networks in which you may want to consider participating to bolster your social initiative.

Connecting to networks

Without a doubt, having a network of people can provide perspectives and connections, essential for sustainability. Gladys Muhunyo summarizes it best:

You win when others win with you. You grow as your network grows with you. As growth brings social impact, it will definitely improve your bottom line.

Internet access is improving in many corners of the world. As a result, online communities are growing and belonging to more networks is easier than at any point in history.

There is a plethora of avenues to connect where you can expand your knowledge, gain alliances, find suppliers, and discover a mentor. There is a network for everything, including having a social, economic, or environmental impact. Consider making connections with people in your field, where your customers congregate, and within a group of shared interest. Of course, one group can meet two objectives.

Associations: Regularly connecting can provide an excellent networking experience. Are you seeking knowledge, suppliers, clients, or collaborators? A clear objective will assist you in selecting the right association for your development. Attend a couple of meetings and ask members about their experience. If you choose to become a member, get involved. Become a board member or volunteer for a committee. Participation will strengthen your networks and expedite your learning. (Chapter 14: *Volunteerism, the good, the bad, and the opportunity* can be your guide to finding the optimal position for you.)

Business networks: If you want to connect locally, an effective avenue is through the local Chamber of Commerce. The Chambers are located all over the world where businesses congregate to network, learn, and affect policy. Another resource offered in Canadian communities are the Small Business Centers which provide support to establish and grow a business. Many of their services are free because they receive tax dollars.

LinkedIn: Check to see if your business has a LinkedIn profile. (This may have been generated automatically.) Take control of your brand by populating your business and personal profile with relevant and engaging information. Then join related groups. Participate in a group conversation. Groups can help you find suppliers, get answers to a business challenge, demonstrate your expertise, and eventually receive referrals and LinkedIn written recommendations. The more people see you, the more they will feel connected and answer your questions.

Facebook: With this social media platform there are a few ways you can connect with your customers: a company page, an exclusive group, a community, and a personal profile. If you desire to engage customers beyond your official company page, a group offers the most control and encourages two-way dialogue. Members are allowed to post questions, opinions, and photos and anyone in the group can respond. Administrators have the ultimate power and can choose what is posted and by whom.

Join a club: There are professional clubs, sporting clubs, social clubs, service clubs, and hobby clubs — the options are endless. These are excellent ways to get to know people in a more casual setting. Often removing yourself from the business environment can provide the most productive alternative to connecting and ultimately leverage each other's sphere of influence.

Participate in a forum: This can be either face-to-face or online. Spend time conducting research on which forum will meet your objective. Many courses create forums for discussion allowing long-term connections. There is an increase of women-focused forums. Most focus on leadership, entrepreneurship, equality, and living your best life.

At YouMeWe, we too have a community, and focus on all these areas, with one key differentiator. Our value proposition includes supporting and growing women-led small-businesses and not-for-profits to lead a social, economic, or environmental transformation required for a conscious, inclusive, and caring society. The community offers women the opportunity to cultivate their social impact by learning from experts in business, consciousness, and sustainability. They can collaborate with other leaders who want to make an impact to discuss marketing, leadership, and develop strategies to attract, retain, and engage clients, customers and collaborators while contributing to the community.

Professional forums are available for people with specific accreditations. These are worthwhile networks because experts pull back the curtain on issues and share a depth of perspective.

Associations, business networks, social media, clubs, and forums provide access to knowledge and networks, both essential for sustainability. Select a combination of communities based on your objectives, the participants, and your available time. This will help gain a foothold in delivering conscious-contributions.

Networks are only as good as the support

In order to maximize a network experience, there needs to be the attitude of support. As Dr. Jennifer Riria's suggests, "Women need to unite. They need to support each other, and we need to put women into leadership positions."

When Beti Olive Kamya ran to be the President of Uganda, she shared that no fellow female trailblazers called with congratulations. As Beti said:

> It is now okay for women to run for parliament, in any position, but presidency? The society doesn't believe that a woman can succeed in that seat. I didn't receive any support from any of the women activists or women leaders. None of them gave me a phone call to encourage me.

> Even the top women leaders internationally demonstrate that there is only so far a woman can go in politics. In a seminar, one of the resolutions was 'We will demand President Museveni appoint a woman as vice president.' I told them they don't need to demand an appointment when they can elect a woman president. This group of internationally high-profile women didn't see the presidency as the option for a woman in Uganda.

> I would have appreciated some acknowledgment from my countrywomen, regardless of their political beliefs.

Citizens can elevate society by providing support, offering collaboration, or at the minimum — appreciation. Collectively we are more powerful.

Make your contribution count

Seeking a sustainable solution starts by looking at who your advocates will be and by assessing what they will support. Creating an experience promotes an emotional connection. An emotive bond, whether experienced through an event, a product or service offering, will breed loyalty. Innovative solutions will allow you to take the brand recognition and expand on your offerings or provide a well-established product to a new market.

Whether creating a new initiative or growing a business, leaders have a tremendous opportunity to address the social, economic, and environmental issues of our time. The key to success: stay the course.

Reflect on how to make your conscious-contributions™

1. What are the objectives of your contribution?
2. What innovative, well-aligned experience could you create to promote support?
3. What sustainable structure is well aligned with your contribution objectives?
4. What is your impact statement? What strategies can you utilize to make it a reality?
5. Which combination of networks will provide the knowledge you need, the contacts you require, and the support necessary to elevate your mission?

Chapter 18
Shift from competition to collaboration

Words of Wisdom

Women alone cannot achieve equality. Men also have to be involved. It is not a woman issue; it is a society issue.

Nouzha Chekrouni, ambassador of the Kingdom of Morocco to Canada, Morocco
Pioneer: first woman Moroccan Minister

We are interviewing among the flowers and trees in the backyard of the former home of Kenya Women Finance Trust (KWFT) with CEO Dr. Jennifer Riria. Jennifer now leads Echo Network Africa, a new venture where the development institution works with other like-minded stakeholders to empower, position, and advocate for women.

Although Jennifer has received numerous accolades throughout her career for her leadership and innovation, she humbly admits that not all her initiatives were successful. When she was the leader of KWFT, she designed a mentorship program matching aspiring entrepreneurs with established business owners, with the goal of skill transference. Unfortunately, the mentorship was short-lived because in Jennifer's opinion, "The established businesses felt they were creating their competition."

This issue of women competing against each other, however, goes deeper than gaining an economic foothold over one another. It is embedded in human nature to suppress something that feels like a threat to our success according to the survival of the fittest theory.

Survival often conjures up images of a violent struggle rather than a helping hand; and *fittest* often is perceived as winning a competition, rather than being resilient. Success is not achieved alone. Some of the most influential leaders of the twentieth century, such as Mahatma Gandhi, Martin Luther King, Jr., and President Nelson Mandela knew that in order to gain consensus one must advocate for collaboration.

Societies need more collaboration and less competition, particularly when it comes to solving social, economic, and environmental problems. Feminine energy can be used collaboratively to address local and world issues. If more leaders tapped into this power, we would see the transformation of companies, communities, countries, and continents.

Although competing is prevalent in most cultures, collaboration can produce the most innovate solutions. We gain new perspectives when we synergize, regardless if we are the perceived competitor or collaborator.

When there is a critical mass of a cohort, in positions of authority or influence, there will be less perception of scarcity. That same cohort will reduce competing and start more collaborating. Instead of pushing feminine energy down, society needs to pull feminine energy up, so more citizens will act in the best interest of the whole.

It is critical for women in developing or developed economies to look to each other and not away from each other. Only when women help women will their voices echo, and we can shift from singular success to a movement of the masses.

Jennifer Riria proclaims, "Women need to work together and see each other as resources to escalate their vision." She measures her success with that objective in mind. The more for-profits, not-for-profits, governments, and institutions embrace collaboration as a viable alternative, the more we will start behaving with the respect, integrity, and grace required to sustain them.

Make the shift

Competing strives to gain or win by defeating or establishing superiority over others who are trying to do the same. A competition pits one against another. Collaboration is the action of working with someone to produce or create something. Collaboration is focused on co-creation. After discussions with small-to-medium enterprises (SMEs), it was apparent that few were capitalizing on collaboration. Perhaps, as Dr. Riria said, there is a reluctance to invest in one's competition. However, an entrepreneurial mentorship program can be a vital strategy to pull people out of poverty, to elevate an aspiring business owner to make their vision a reality, or to help a successful entrepreneur to expand exponentially. As well as, collaboration can build a stronger marketplace. Through mentorship, budding entrepreneurs can become employees, advocates, and partners.

Investment in micro-enterprises (usually less than five employees) is growing in many African countries and internationally, as evidenced by the increase in microfinance solutions. While an investment can boost a woman out of poverty, far fewer financial initiatives and organizations focus on supporting small business growth. A company that wants to expand may hire employees and could benefit from hiring a micro-entrepreneur. The new entrepreneur could benefit from income and business training while offering their expertise.

Many small businesses fall into the *go it alone* trap. Entrepreneurs continue to be hands-on while trying to grow and expand. For these enterprises to get to the next level, they need to remove themselves from the day-to-day operations and seek new avenues for growth.

Become a competition mentor

One solution is to become a competition mentor. One of the signs of a proficient leader is a person who elevates employees enough that they have confidence and ability to pursue their purpose. Perhaps in the case where an employee requires the basic needs for survival, a leader creates an opportunity where he or she can build the confidence and ability to pursue other avenues of income to feed their family and educate their children. That is an objective of Philippa Reiss Thorne at Gone Rural. "The way I see it, if more women go out on their own [and build a business], the more women we can help."

Investing in competitors' success is why I applaud Mulumebet Iori, founder of Byogenic Beauty Spot. After establishing a successful business, she established a beauty school to foster her competition. Mulumebet pioneered the industry in Ethiopia. Like so many women we interviewed, she saw another woman's success as her own.

If a small business cultivates a mentee or two, they are preparing their enterprise for growth. When hiring a mentee, it is prudent to outline objectives and expectations. In addition to a salary, you offer her an opportunity to learn various elements of starting and growing a business: the skills, the business acumen, and the management of people.

As a business owner, what benefits do you receive from mentoring others?

In the short-term, you receive motivated employees. In the long-term, you may create your successor or lead her to become an entrepreneur. She can start a similar or complementary product or service. As the mentor, you can provide the seed money in exchange for a percentage of her profits.

If establishing another income stream is your goal, share this objective. If the mentee is the right candidate, she will be very motivated. No longer is the mentee competition, but someone to whom you can refer customers or be an emergency back up when you receive orders too big for your organization to fulfill.

Mentoring your competition can be the evolution of microfinance initiatives. Seed money is not enough to grow a business, but lots of guidance can unite the mentor, mentee, and multiply the profits.

I was fortunate to prove this theory. When I was leaving for Africa, I needed to reorganize my company, so I sold a license to train clients using my intellectual property to one of my colleagues. The financial structure of the deal was partial payment upfront, and residuals every time he used the material. He built a lucrative business, and I received residuals for several years. Without this arrangement, pursuing my passion would have never come to be. When I returned to Canada, he became my collaborative competitor.

Become a collaborative competitor

Philippa Reiss Thorne attributes some of Gone Rural's business success to becoming partners with other companies to create unique and superior quality handcrafts. She has expanded this philosophy to a new business she started in 2013 called Khokho, the siSwati word for great-grandmother. Khokho is an accessories brand that combines leather artistry with traditional weaving techniques. The mission is to preserve and elevate the craft with a modern aesthetic while creating income-generating opportunities for its artisans. She partners with talented international fellow designers and local leather crafters who are internationally trained. They transform woven panels into fully lined handbags in an eSwatini workshop.[73]

Philippa's believes collaborating with perceived competitors can create strength.

> Often in business, we are afraid of competition, we are afraid to work together; we try to keep our own ideas. I think it can be a really powerful way for Africa and craft to grow, by seeing partnerships as a really powerful way to market products.

Making the mind shift from competitors to collaborators continues to increase the unique product design and the demand for exports.

Become a client collaborator

Depending on the objectives of a business and its growth opportunities, a company's established client can assist it to achieve the next level of maturity. The client could provide guidance on how to run a thriving organization and contacts to expand distribution. In exchange the client receives a percentage of the growing business's sales.

When I founded my training company, a client had the foresight to see how his public relations company's clients could benefit from face-to-face communications development, which my company provided. He provided strategies and financial security, and I provide him with another income stream. Collaborating with clients in a similar way can also amplify a socially conscious enterprise's confidence to bring an idea to market.

Become a collaborative investor

We have seen that women work together in Africa, and there is a rise in the West. Women are coming together to invest in other women through SheEO founded by Vicki Saunders. The model brings together 500 women each year, who contribute $1100 each. The money is pooled and loaned out at zero percent interest to five women-led ventures selected by what SheEO appropriately refers to as the *activators*. All ventures are revenue generating with export potential and are creating a better world through their business model or their product and service. The fund is perpetual, which is why they refer the initiative as *radical generosity* because women are investing in women, and the return on that investment is expanding women leadership, entrepreneurship, and impact.[74]

Collaborating to generate a ripple effect

An old African proverb says, "If you want to go fast, go alone. If you want to go far, go with others." When it comes to filling a social gap, going fast can be the only option to get started. However, if you want to create momentum and long-term social impact, collaboration is essential.

Olive Luena founded the Tanzania Gatsby Trust in 1995; it wasn't until 2007 that she shifted to collaboration as a core business strategy, which created a ripple effect in helping the vulnerable.

No one succeeds alone, not even athletes. They too need support. If you want to succeed, bring in as many partnerships as possible with different expertise and motivations. Align goals and missions to forge the way forward.

There is no need to reinvent the wheel. Someone somewhere has the expertise. You need to tap into that expertise to move forward. I always look around to see whom we can form alliances with, so I have people around me who can cheer me on or put in resources. Organizations with experience can help create the path since they have been there before.

We are a foundation, and we want to make sustainable change; even when we are not there, it continues. These alliances are helping to achieve sustainability.

Many conscious-contribution initiatives start with passion, but for sustainability they need partners.

Evaluate prospective collaborators

When assessing partnerships, start with what you need. Evaluate your organization's abilities to isolate its inabilities. Olive described some of the strategies used to secure partners:

> Firstly, you need to know what you need in a partnership. Once you've established the type of partnership you need, then look to the market and identify who is there. Which partnership will make a difference in your work? What we look for in a partnership: skills, experience, resources, the personal touch — look at whom you connect with. Look at the road you have traveled and see who can assist with your goals.

In development of any business, there are so many players. Assess who they are and who you can create an alliance with. Olive advises to identify the competitors. What are the competitors offering that you are not offering? What can you provide to make yourself better? Sometimes, through competitors, you bring alliances. Through people who do similar activities, you bring partnerships.

Gaining insight into prospective partners by learning about their collaboration history including approach, expectations, and tenure, will provide a glimpse into their collaboration character.

Assess mission alignment

Eva Muraya provides some vital considerations when assessing the right people or organizations to collaborate with:

> Sometimes we are too hasty in selecting people that we collaborate with. It is critical that you find a like-minded person or organization that shares your vision. You share a value system.
>
> Ensure that your style and process is very close to your partner's. You need to discuss very early your values, style, and process. If this is not done, it will compromise the collaboration. Your competencies should be complementary. No one is lagging behind. You both are putting the same amount of energy into delivering a solution.

Morocco has integrated the value of women as *equal citizens* throughout the country. Nouzha Chekrouni explains the importance of society in collaborating to embrace social change.

> Firstly, no one can succeed alone. We have many similarities to other Islamic communities, so Morocco is very open to sharing our experience with other countries.
>
> Secondly, you cannot do it alone within your society either. Women alone cannot achieve equality. Men also have to be involved. It is not a woman issue; it is a society issue. Everyone should be concerned about this issue, and work in order to achieve equality. Equality will impact society, it will impact the children, and it will impact our entire lives. We need the will to govern. Everything becomes possible, but we must work together.

Collaboration can move masses; it starts with aligning missions and values to maximize social impact.

Hire well-aligned employees

At Beacon of Hope, founder Jane Wathome uses her emotional intelligence to hire the right people to promote a haven for vulnerable women. To ensure new employees align with the mission, values, and culture while being able to collaborate with colleagues, she implemented a systematic hiring process inspired by her pastor, Oscar Muriu. She hires employees based on the five Cs.

1. Competence — look at professionalism. Although Beacon of Hope is philanthropic, Jane wants to be a center of excellence. She only hires people with the credentials required.
2. Committed — can Beacon of Hope rely on the employees to do their job and support others?
3. Character — do they have integrity and compassion to connect with the team and the benefactor?
4. Chemistry — do they fit in, understand the vision, and work well with the team?
5. Cost — can we afford them?

Because of their work, compassion is mandatory. Jane and her team thoroughly evaluate a prospective employee's character allowing her to feel confident in meeting the not-for-profits mandate if she is at work or not.

When looking to hire an employee with well-aligned values and to determine if collaboration is part of her DNA, asking *why* questions will expose the underlying character of your candidate. Asking *Why is that?* Is a direct method to reveal an individual's values — like a magnifying glass into their soul. To access questions, visit YouMeWe.ca book community for a free download.

The same questions you use to assess a candidate's values, character, and skills can also apply when considering organizations with whom to collaborate during your conscious-contribution.

Hiring candidates and partnering with organizations who are aligned is critical to sustainability. Without assessing their character at the beginning of a relationship, you may find yourself down a path of investing a large amount of money and energy into a person or organization that has a conflicting mandate.

When Eva Muraya struggled to start a new business to help African brands excel during the market downturn, she appreciated the power of partnership:

Bring in as many partners as possible. The strength of collaboration is often underestimated. I think collaboration in today's world is the way many of our initiatives will be realized. When you collaborate, you can stay focused on your area of expertise.

Make your contribution count

Who can you collaborate with to expand your mandate and expedite the mission? There is an often-overlooked truth about collaboration: organizations tend to choose partners who have already demonstrated success and are less likely to seek people they need to pull up. Although there are methods suggested in this chapter on how to engage a budding entrepreneur, there is the expectation that they have a skill that would be advantageous to the growth of another's organization, business or initiative. So, when seeking collaboration, consider what you can bring that will benefit the other. Who and what can you expose them to — what clients, sponsors, donors, ideas, and expertise?

Reflect on how to make your conscious-contributions™

1. What does successful collaboration look like to you?
2. Is there a competitor, or a complimentary organization that you could collaborate with to have a more significant social, economic, or environmental impact?
3. What values do you want to ensure your collaborators have?
4. How could you engage your team in the hiring, retention and collaboration process?

Chapter 19
Develop symbiotic partnerships

Words of Wisdom

The most important thing is to trust your inner instincts. Look at what you respect, who you respect, and who you believe in. Who do you believe is genuine? Don't be swayed by material or superficial things. What is the genuine essence of what it is you are trying to achieve?

Angela Dick, founder & CEO, Transman, South Africa
Pioneer: the recruitment businesses in South Africa

Angela Dick's *words of wisdom* get right to the heart of whether a collaboration is worth pursuing. When YouMeWe created the foundation fund, engaging collaborators on the onset would have improved momentum. By soliciting a board of directors, or partnering with like-minded contributors, we could have shared knowledge, challenge perspectives, and collaborated on the work required to achieve increase scholarship distribution. We could have formed a *conscious-contribution circle*, which is a gathering of like-minded individuals who collaborate on a meaningful project or a cause that contributes to society. Collectively we could have sought out collaborators to expand the contribution's impact.

With due diligence, you will find the right partner. Tapping into your experience, strategy, and feminine energy will prove useful in finding the ultimate collaborative relationship. Seek out symbiotic partnerships. Earlier in Chapter 15: *Move from messenger to mission*, the importance of establishing symbiotic partnerships with well-aligned stakeholders was introduced. These are sustainable long-term alliances where collaborators benefit from an ongoing relationship and refer to each other for strategic insight and synergies. Mutual respect, trust, and aligned values are essential. Parties have each other's best interests in mind.

When looking to establish a partnership, start by researching who is serving your targeted beneficiary. Can you collaborate with a well-established social enterprise, NGO, not-for-profit, company, government, institution, community service, colleague, or supplier? Consider whether it would be advantageous to partner with their initiative in a support role.

Tisha Greyling consults on public participation and shares strategies on how organizations can collaborate with the communities in which they wish to operate.

> You make very sure before you approach people [to understand] what is the local protocol. Sometimes you have to go through the local university, or you ask someone in the know. What we do when we work in countries outside South Africa, when we are not familiar with the culture, we always team with a local counterpart organization. In the process, we help build up their capacity. They can pave the way for us culturally and by using local languages. They help us make sure that we don't make a mistake. These people know the local situation. We may have better expertise in communication, in message management, development of materials, but they know what the local circumstances are.

There are multiple stakeholders that you may want to collaborate with to make your conscious-contribution a reality and then sustainable.

Collaborate with mission-driven individuals

Depending on where you are at on the contribution continuum, consider starting with the people you know, like, and hold shared values. Alignment provides a good opportunity to form a *conscious-contribution circle*.

Nigest Haile along with seven other women entrepreneurs and activists chose to collaborate to establish Enat Bank in Ethiopia with the mandate to provide women with financing, particularly to help SME women-led businesses to aspire beyond microfinance initiatives. These women were business associates, and therefore collaboration worked, however, partnering with supporters you know may get you out of the gate, but may not necessarily help you stay in the race.

Joanne Mwangi recognized that those you know through your personal network are often not going to be your biggest advocates and supporters long-term. "Don't rely on the people you know for finances. It is the people you don't know that will make a difference in success or failure."

Networking is key. Consider who you don't know as you look for collaborators in your conscious-contributions. It may not be as comfortable as asking who you know, but it may be more sustainable to engage with who you don't know. Connect with those who can bolster your impact, expedite its reality, and help sustain a new existence.

Collaborate with NGOs

As NGOs are not-for-profit organizations usually driven by fulfilling a social purpose and engaged in long-term pursuits, local NGOs enjoy a high degree of public trust. They can be ideal organizations to collaborate with or be a conduit between a project and the community.

Throughout Trisha Greyling's career as a pioneer in public participation in South Africa, she has relied on NGOs to be the agent between her mining clients and the communities close to projects. After a mining company experienced strife in a community in the Congo, Trisha explains how they reestablished trust.

> The mining company got a trusted NGO to help people in the community to establish their businesses. Every brick that was made for the mine, every piece of road, and every doorframe was made by the local people in their own businesses. When that phase of the construction stopped, that money was circulating in the local villages with people [now able to afford to have] something done to their house. There was sustainability.

As we all know, we all have to work on relationships. It takes a second to break the trust, and it will take a long time to build it up again. With a lot of work, this company did, with the help of the NGO.

International NGOs can also assist in making a socially conscious enterprise a reality or improve on its impact. The need they are meeting and the approach they are taking could help you create your mission or redefine your vision. Hellen Acham of North East Chilli Producers co-operative transformed because of her partnership with an international NGO, which insisted that she sell the seedlings instead of providing them free. Production increased, because the members no longer felt they were growing *Hellen's chili*, but their own — instilling pride of production.

Collaborate with companies

The state of being *stronger together*, is achieved by merging of the minds where all the minds have a stake in an organization's success. Modesta Lilian Mahiga capitalized on mind sharing to build a transformational and socially conscious company. She relied on five strategic partnerships that are part of the overarching brand to assist with her mandate to provide organizational transformation. She says, "We are looking at Tanzania as the launch pad. We are always looking at joint ventures, constantly looking at what is not being served, or how it is being served and coming in and taking great risks." Modesta shares why she started to pursue collaboration:

> I got to a point I didn't need to prove myself. I knew I needed to find strategic partnerships. It would take too long to transform Tanzania myself. With strategic partnerships, someone has the funds, someone has the expertise, and someone has access to the markets. You bring your expertise to the table.

> Many people say they can't start a business because they don't have the money. You don't really want money; you want what money can buy. If you can find that without having to spend the money, partner with that person. What is the point of having 100 percent of a $10,000 business when you can have 50 percent of a $10,000,000 business? Make sure your position is not compromised. Make sure it is in line with the vision.

My team understands that we want to wow the world because this is the last place [Tanzania] you would expect greatness.

Partnering with companies under the same brand to expand into a market, harness social leverage, or working with talents different than yours, are productive collaborative approaches. Another is being the conduit to connect companies so that they can collaborate.

Nigest Haile puts women at the heart of everything she initiates, from co-founding Enat Bank to advocating for women exporters. She often represents women business owners in foreign markets to sell Ethiopian brands and provide them with not only a sustainable business but also one that will help sustain other Ethiopians. She engaged with WEConnect International; whose mission is to help women-owned businesses succeed in global value chains.[75] Nigest acts as a conduit to assist this collaboration.

> Exhibitions and trade forums, such as the one I participated in China last week, is where the international trade center is working closely with WEConnect International. They bring the multinational companies together so they can source products from women. Four of the multinationals signed a contract to buy 14.7 million dollars of product from women. Soon as I got back, I connected women with those buyers.

Looking at your mission, objectives, values, and strategy will assist in defining which companies can help leverage where you are today to where you want to be tomorrow.

Collaborate with government

You know your conscious-contribution is having the intended impact when the government is paying attention. Many pioneering African women have been able to escalate their mission to grab the attention of their governments and get them to carry their message. The King of the eSwatini would ask, "Is this Doo-approved?" to ensure women's rights are being considered. Janet Nkubana and Joy Ndungutse included the Rwandan president in a marketing campaign to distribute their peace baskets to large Western retailers. Mary Ogalo gained buy-in from a Kenyan politician to assist with funding County Girls Caucus. These pioneers collaborate with whomever they have to, to get the job done. However, integrity cannot be compromised.

Because Nigest Haile's business helps connect to the international market, she utilizes government-supported opportunities. One initiative that has raised exports is the African Growth and Opportunity Act.

> We usually organize visits of buyers to various Ethiopian producers, and the buyer may make a sample order. We organize this mainly through the US embassy, as there is a special provision where women can enter their products tariff-free.

Although tariff-free opportunities change with governments, we can still support socially conscious businesses.

Sibongile Sambo makes her contribution to society by assisting the government to achieve their development mandates. As the owner of an aviation company, forging a relationship with the government is critical.

> We spent the entire weekend with [young women] at a camp, showing them how to write a business plan, and then they compete on presenting that business plan. It is one of the areas supported by the department of trade and industry in South Africa. Because the government is a key stakeholder [in my business], I assist them in getting their objectives achieved wherever I can.

Social projects often look for collaboration with governments, who have money earmarked for specific initiatives. But filling out grant forms and aligning with their objectives can be mind-numbing and take months, or years. Many initiatives hire grant writers to help make their vision a reality.

Margareth Chacha of Tanzania Women's Bank Ltd, cautions collaboration with the government. She shares an alternative approach.

> I would have mobilized shares differently and not have relied on the government. I would have sold shares to able people and companies. Instead of running short of capital, I could go back and ask investors for more. It is much more difficult to ask the government, and it is retarding our growth. I can't go back, as my hands are now tied.

If possible, start a project by circumventing government funding, as your priorities will only be theirs as long as they stay in power. However, if government support would help you gain momentum, confine their involvement to the launch of your conscious-contribution. To sustain it, start to seek other partners. Meeting your mission is better navigated with you at the helm.

Collaborate with the community

A friend worked for a refining company and we were discussing how one gold mine engaged the community by employing them to build crates to transport the gold. It hired locals, so it must have been a worthwhile initiative, right? Not necessarily. Once the containers were shipped, they had to be broken open and sent off to be recycled. It did keep the community employed; however, once the mine was depleted, so was the community. Making boxes was a short-term solution without any production spin-offs for long-term sustainability; and to boot, they produced increased waste.

Locals need to be engaged in a collaborative solution that will enhance the lives of the community long-term. Trisha Greyling advises how companies can promote community engagement:

> If the project you are embarking upon in any way will affect people, by law in most countries you have to *consult* the people. Often companies are afraid to do that because they are afraid to lose power. They may feel that it is theirs or the government's decision to be made.
>
> One of our mining clients in West Africa in 2006 had work stoppages, roadblocks, and really bad press. We assisted them by helping build good relations with the locals. Talk to people, have a relationship. The research shows that the mining client spent 1.6 million dollars per annum less on security because they have good relations with their communities.
>
> If you view public participation in the right way, it is like getting free consultants to design your project. Whether you are developing a big project or small, you don't want to have 20 or 30 years of grief with your neighbors. Good social management can cost money, but bad social management costs a lot more.

When contributing to a marginalized community, consider how to reduce poverty, accelerate growth, and promote equality. Incorporate local opportunities that will develop skills across the district. It will establish an affordable long-term operation, which makes business sense. Contributing knowledge can be the best sustainable solution.

It is imperative to implement projects that engage the community long after the initiator is gone. Otherwise, the initiative only brings temporary hope and optimism to a town only to leave it in despair. The conscious-contribution rule of thumb is that who, what, or where we engage should be better off once we depart. Unfortunately, that wasn't the case where Lydia Musa creates programs to protect children. When Lesotho opened its doors to foreign assistance, it deviated from its core values, causing an escalation of child abuse problems.

> There are now helping-type professions that are coming in, and sometimes they are suppressing good practices that we have had in the community. Now we are trying to bring back some of those good practices. We are currently forming *child focus groups*. This means groups that are to protect children. We provide them with topics to talk about and give them insight into the child participatory mechanisms to protect themselves.
>
> We also have community child welfare forums. This is for ordinary people to attend to promote some of the old practices that we are all responsible for protecting the children. We have training for teachers also to pay attention to the children. It is the responsibility of the community to protect children. Communities should provide the first aid.

It is essential to collaborate with citizens on the ground who understand the culture to create an ethically sound and sustainable impact. It is the locals who will be left behind to either clean up or manage any community initiatives.

Collaborate with colleagues

A contribution started with colleagues is like pushing a boulder up hill; however, once it is over the crest it gains momentum on its own. According to American Charities, in a document entitled *The New Corporate DNA: Where Employee Engagement and Social Impact Converge*,

82 percent of the survey respondents wanted the opportunity to volunteer with peers in a corporate-supported event. Also, 70 percent said they wanted the ability to organize volunteer events, and 60 percent wanted to recruit peers to support their contribution efforts. The era of corporate social responsibility without employee engagement is going the way of the dodo bird.[76] It is clear that employees want to lead an initiative they are interested in and collaborate while they contribute. The bonus, it increases productivity and job satisfaction at an organization, promoting a more engaged and inspired workforce.

Leaders have an opportunity to initiate a project where they participate alongside colleagues by cleaning up the community, conducting a food drive, or collecting soccer uniforms for children in need. Consciously contributing together allows for an opportunity to get to know colleagues personally. The enduring benefit is elevated trust, deeper rapport, and flowing communication. From collaboration to co-creation, you are connecting and weaving your purpose together, creating a holistic bond that bridges personal desires with professional motivations and connects employees to the organization that provides the opportunity.

Different departments that are often in conflict can also weave themselves together through conscious-contributions. The fervor is taken out of disagreements when one connects to someone doing something bigger than oneself. Employees have a new frame of reference as they value each other's contributions, which will break down barriers and build bridges to effective communications.

According to the same study, more organizations are allowing employees to volunteer for their charity of choice during company time. Although this increases employee satisfaction, it doesn't offer the same opportunity to collaborate with colleagues in a unified community contribution. An organization may want to consider *conscious-contribution circles*, where a group of value-aligned employees who have the same compassion-connection contribute together. Either approach will enhance the culture of a company — benefiting all stakeholders.

Collaborate with suppliers

We have established the importance of the beneficiary, colleagues, and partners in delivering a conscious-contribution, but another stakeholder who can have a profound impact is a supplier.

Establishing symbiotic partnerships with suppliers is essential to being B Corporation or Fair Trade certified. Transparency and shared values are necessary when pursuing social procurement. According to Buy Social Canada, "Social procurement is leveraging a social value from existing procurement." [77] Based on the findings of Buy Social, in 2016 Canada as a whole produced $2 trillion worth of goods and services. If one percent was socially procured, that would equal 20 billion dollars slated for social or environmental good.[78] Buying from a social enterprise is the most direct way to accomplish social purchase objectives.

In developing countries, supporting women by purchasing ethically sourced and produced products can have a lasting, profound impact. Similarly, support any social enterprise by buying their socially procured products. Purchasing an item that is not mindful perpetuates poor production, and will likely end up in a landfill, ultimately harming the environment.

Therefore, when sourcing suppliers, consider their social, cultural, and environmental impact.

MIKE AND I BOUGHT handcrafts from many of the social enterprises we interviewed. One morning, the beautiful green and purple woven basket by my bedside captured my attention. I bought it from Tintsaba, the eSwatini master weaver handcraft company. The detail is impeccable. The colors are contemporary. The craftswomanship was unmatched. Not only do I love their work, but their company values are well aligned with YouMeWe.

I reached out to the new managing director, Richard Freemantle, the husband of the late founder, Sheila Freemantle. After a formal introduction through eSwatini Fair Trade, we started to engage in my vision of creating a YouMeWe logoed basket. Weaving a four-color logo with words was not going to be an easy task.

Richard was reassured when one of the master weavers said they could reproduce the logo. We decided to proceed with sample baskets. Weaving the baskets turned out to be much more complicated than anticipated. With all the challenges, I started to wonder if the supplier partnership was going to help them or hurt them. Was producing a specific logo just too much to ask?

Respecting a supplier's circumstances is a lot easier when you know you are both in pursuit of the same objectives. Looking at suppliers as people who are as invested in the success of an initiative as you are provides comfort and promotes patience. Eventually we received four boxes of vibrant colored, well-crafted baskets.

In the book *Conscious Capitalism*, John Mackey the CEO of Whole Foods sees suppliers as critical stakeholders:

> Today, as much as 70 to 80 percent of the value the average company provides to its customers is created by suppliers. [...] The bottom line is this: having weak suppliers leads to a relatively weak business. Strong suppliers are an integral part of the foundation of a strong and competitive business. We must never take our suppliers for granted.[79]

Make your contribution count

Consider the power of collaboration, regardless of whether you are starting a social or environmental initiative locally, advising internationally, or being the conduit to an opportunity.

Suffice to say all stakeholders should be seen as collaborators, as this will increase a social initiative's sustainability and the ripple effect on the beneficiaries and community. Just as valuable, establishing symbiotic partnerships increases personal and professional satisfaction. When we feel more connected to our organizations, colleagues, suppliers, and community, our well-being is enhanced. We appreciate that we are part of something bigger than ourselves. We are a *we*.

While implementing a project you need to continuously check how stakeholders are responding and alter course when necessary. A project can't drop in, create community chaos and expect to be a sustainable solution. As the African proverb says, *If you want to go far, go with others.* Collaboration can take longer, but it also will increase the likelihood of achieving sustainability.

A dear friend of mine, David Gouthro a professional speaker and facilitator espouses, "How different our world would be if collaboration triumphed over competition every time."[80]

This revolutionary thought could transform the persisting social, cultural, and environmental challenges of our time.

Reflect on how to make your conscious-contributions™

1. Do you know someone that you would like to contribute alongside?
2. Is there an organization that you can contribute to or collaborate with to advance your mission? Is there a gap that you can fill to complement their mission?
3. Do you have a group of colleagues you can conduct a fundraiser with? Is there a well-aligned corporate social responsibility initiative that you can supplement by taking a more grassroots approach?
4. Which of your clients or suppliers could you work with to address a social gap? How will they benefit?
5. Is there any government funding available for your initiative?

Chapter 20
Cultivate your capacity to influence support

Words of Wisdom

Women need to invest in their learning and knowledge. It is important to educate yourself and take risks. But first, know who you are before you start to lead others.

Gia Whitehead, sustainability director of TSiBA Education South Africa
Pioneer: co-founder of a revolutionary business school providing extensive scholarships and embedding paying-forward philosophy.

On my first trip to Kenya with the WOW group, I had the pleasure of traveling with three Canadians who used their expertise where there was limited local attention. When Karen Anning, Gail Pennington, and Susan Kawa first walked into Joytown in Kijabe, in 2007, there seemed to be little joy. Approximately 300 young children, born with physical disabilities were residents of the government-run institution. Fathers abandoned their children because they thought the mother was cursed. Mothers had been shunned by society for bearing an atypical child, left destitute, alone, and hopeless. They couldn't afford to give their children the therapeutic support to crawl or walk, never mind run. However, they gave them what they had — love.

Karen, Gail, and Susan arrived on Joytown's doorstep with a rented car full of diaper rash cream, wheelchairs, walkers, orthotic braces, toys, stuffed animals, socks, and clothing. They brought the joy of possibility to these young children. The three divided their week between

Kijabe Hospital and Joytown, working with the doctors, nurses, and occupational therapists. A temporary therapy room was set up. Karen and Susan, as licensed physiotherapists in Canada, worked with the African educated therapists and children in the clinic, showing them how to use the equipment, and then taught caregivers how to work with their children. Susan and Karen also engaged the mothers by teaching them how to hold and feed their children therapeutically and how to incorporate therapy into play. As a result, mothers felt hope.

At Joytown, children received primary care. There was a non-functional swimming pool, a play area with barbed wire around it, and rusted playground equipment. One occupational therapist aided all the kids. Gail describes their first visit:

> The sight of their tattered soiled clothes, old ill-fitting wheelchairs and braces, the physical isolation of the extreme cases, and the children lying on the bathroom floors, eating out of bowls with their mouths, stays with us to this day. However, we also saw that they work very hard to survive. The smiles on their faces and the hope in their eyes gave us hope and the desire to help. The joy needs to return to Joytown.

When the trio returned home in Toronto, they spent the next year gathering donated equipment. They paid for a shipping container and sent it. Karen and Gail returned to Nairobi to meet the container. They distributed its contents to Kijabe Hospital, Joytown, and a new rehabilitation center, Bethany Kids Children's Center. The institutions had never seen so much quality therapy equipment. The therapists were shown how to use, adjust, and care for the equipment, which started mobilizing lives.

The trio has continued to be a resource for Bethany Kids Children's Center. Their projects included financial support to the physiotherapist and ongoing therapy input. They provided educational materials, day-to-day essential therapy supplies, program suggestions, and organized healthcare work groups to assist with the implementation of specialized treatment programs.

Susan, Karen, and Gail's project started because they took into consideration their collective expertise, personal experience, and their passion for assisting children with special needs. Knowing whom they wanted to impact, they needed to find out where and how. Before arriving, Karen started communication with what would be the eventual Bethany Kids Children's Center. Her message was simple: "We are physiotherapists. We want to come and visit. How can we help?"

The impact these three women had is due to their diligence prior to, during, and after their arrival at the Children's Center. It all starts with the question, "Do they need what we have to offer?"

Karen's daughter has carried on the trio's legacy by encouraging her students to raise funds for Bethany Kids Children's Center. Kids helping kids — that is how to create a sustainable ripple effect.

Compassion isn't capacity

Marsha Gabriel is a socially conscious entrepreneur in every sense. When Mike and I interviewed Marsha in her restaurant in Durban, we discussed her other businesses. We considered how the compassion of a Good Samaritan doesn't always equate to sustainable social solutions. Marsha is very passionate, but also very pragmatic — characteristics much needed in the world of contribution where the heartstrings of the haves are preyed on to serve the have-nots.

> Most [social programs] are dependent on funding simply because they lack knowledge. This is Africa; most of the organizations have started not because they wanted to generate income, but their true motivation of not-for-profit organizations started because of diseases, unemployment, or lack of finance, where parents die early and leave children on the streets. A Good Samaritan comes along and takes these children under her care. Then she starts asking people for funding, then corporations, and moves further up to ask for support. She started from the heart of a mother; now we have to go and teach her business skills so [the project] becomes sustainable for life.

Just because you have the time and desire doesn't mean you will be able to add value. Expertise, skill, and ability are required to develop your capacity to contribute consciously.

Cultivate your capacity through one of three viewpoints:

1. **Create** a contribution — start a socially conscious initiative
2. **Lead** a contribution from within — obtain organization support
3. **Influence** a contribution — gain donor support

In all three cases, understanding the perspective of beneficiaries and enlist their support is critical.

In the case of *leading a contribution from within* an organization, you also will need to gain buy-in amongst your leadership team. Learning their values and experiences will be essential for contextualizing your conscious-contribution.

When *influencing a contribution*, understanding a donor's giving motivations and patterns will provide the nuanced context needed to align your mandate.

Beneficiary analysis

Every conscious-contribution starts with soliciting the beneficiaries' perspectives. Even when tragedy strikes, and we put on our capes, we still need to ask the question, "How can I help?" Then we must ensure it will benefit the whole.

Asking beneficiaries about their objectives, experiences, and values will help you understand what they want. Their cultural norms will dictate how to deliver it. Rehmah Kasule is a Muslim and Ugandan pioneer who contributes by training a new generation of women leaders. In her work she experiences the cultural barriers that often inhibit women, from being able to learn what people want.

> Ugandan and Muslim women are often taught not to speak up. We are quiet. We are at a disadvantage due to our culture. Because of our culture, we don't speak up when we have an idea, while a guy will. Next thing you know, he receives a promotion.

A cultural norm can be the barrier to communicating effectively and building the capacity required to implement a contribution.

Through Rehmah's training, women find their voice. She starts the transformation by understanding their perception of why they didn't have one in the first place.

Dr. Thandeka Mazibuko understands the importance of having an ear to the ground. To assess the treatment required for rural settlement dwellers outside Durban, Thandeka urges patients away from their dependency on the advice of the witch doctors.

> This woman had a lump and had it for a long time. She was offered surgery. She declined. 'If they cut my left breast, it is close to my heart, and it will stop pumping.' This is years of story. Can this story be finished in 15 minutes? You need good listening skills. You need to be patient. When she tells me the story, she hasn't gone to medical school. She is not going to be able to tell me the history, how it started, when it started, or how it presented itself. She is going to talk about the pain.

To successfully fill a gap in society, incorporating the beneficiaries' context into the solution will garner implementation support.

Margareth Chacha operates the bank on the principle that if they can't understand the customers, why bother trying to offer a solution to empower them?

> When we first started [the bank], we had meetings with women, and we asked them what makes them think that they can't have access to banking facilities. They said they didn't understand the papers. The first enemy is education. Many of the banks have their documents in English. Soon as the women get the papers, they run away because they are intimidated because of their lack of understanding of the English language.

Tanzanian Women's Bank became creative. They provided a one-page document that was simple to understand, both in English and Swahili, the official languages. Illiterate women were allowed to sign with their thumb. Knowing women were reliable voters, they accepted voter ID to open an account. Most women are in the informal sector, so they allowed informal groups to open an account and assist them with taxpaying documents before they gave them loans. They even provided microfinancing for the small businesses. These microloans account for

35 percent of the bank's income, more than any other product. The Tanzanian Women's bank opened an average of 50 accounts a day.

Cultural norms manifest in everything we do: what we eat, how we work, how we treat the environment, interact with animals, raise children, and respect elders. Learning another's perspective is the best way to add value to beneficiaries' circumstances. Without due diligence it's like aimlessly walking in the forest hoping to find your way out.

Supporter analysis

Supporter analysis is paramount when launching an initiative, whether you *create, lead* or *influence*. When considering prospective supporters of your contribution, assess what is in it for them, their family, and their society. If a contributor is unable to understand the opportunity and impact of their contribution, they probably won't participate.

Prospective benefactors' decisions are influenced by many factors including their experiences, objectives, and values, all of which are more static choices. However, benefactors are also influenced by dynamic choices — circumstances, feelings, and relevance. Therefore, supporters can be swayed by the situation created in the moment.

Learning how stakeholders make choices will provide tremendous insight into their conditioning, beliefs, and mindset. However, to create a complete picture of how decisions are made, elicit prospective supports' priorities. This level of importance is often overlooked and may be the barrier to receiving early buy-in to a contribution idea.

An individual may be part of a decision-making team. A good strategy is to first learn about her perspective, and then ask what she perceives will be essential criteria to gain buy-in from each of the other stakeholders. Speaking with each stakeholder, however, while listening to cues to indicate how an individual makes decisions will provide you with a more accurate assessment, rather than relying on someone else's interpretation.

Ask stakeholders questions that expose their personal perspectives and values e.g., what are your experiences, objectives, and vision? Exploring an individual's views and experiences allow for a more meaningful understanding of their interests and motivations.

Incorporating each stakeholder's concerns, objectives, priorities, and values into a compelling proposal will increase the likelihood of gaining the support of a conscious-contribution. Understanding their cultural norms will guide your delivery.

Lead a contribution from within — obtain organization support

When trying to gain consensus, you want to align with the organization's purpose, vision, mission, and values. The more aligned your message and conscious-contributions are, the more likely you will gain leadership's support.

Bience Gawanas witnessed firsthand the importance of reminding leaders of the organization's vision and the necessary next steps, mainly when it came to gender equality. Although in the 54 nations of the AU there is a general acceptance of the principle of gender equality, this is not a reality. Bience continued to emphasize the importance of federal parity. They discussed issues including HIV/AIDS and malaria, which affect both genders. To shine a light on the gender disparity, she brought forward an ignored female atrocity.

> I started a Campaign for Accelerated Reduction of Maternal Mortality Africa (CARMMA). I put it in the face of people that there is no reason that women on this continent should die of childbirth. It challenges our culture; children are so important in the African family, but the question is, does Africa care about those who are producing those children?
>
> This created a good entry point to discussions about gender equality, women's health, and include cultural elements. The reason for the campaign was we have all these wonderful policies and instruments that we have adopted at the continental level, how do we translate that to action on the ground? CARMMA was a campaign to try and bridge that gap. I tell them, 'Don't be politically correct while doing this, put yourself on notice to the women and the children in your country that you care.'

As of August 2019, 46 African nations had launched CARMMA and six were preparing to launch — a huge shift in gender disparity on the continent.[81]

Influence a contribution — gaining donor support

Understanding a philanthropist is no different from understanding anyone else. Similarly, persuading a philanthropist is no different from persuading anyone else. A face-to-face conversation will drastically increase your influence. According to Chuck English and Mo Lidsky, the authors of *The Philanthropic Mind: Surprising Discoveries from Canada's Top Philanthropist*, for donors connecting live is their muse.[82] Therefore, *dynamic choices* become much more prevalent. A fundraiser's passion can lure donors, but it is often not enough.

With any attempt to gather support, people need to know you are authentically interested in them. You have done your research as to what causes they traditionally support. Understanding the motivation for their chosen causes is worthwhile. This insight will help frame your initiative. Philanthropists want to give, however, not necessarily only to causes that are in line with their philanthropic mandate.

Donor participation in a cause can vary drastically. Some want a position on the board, others an opportunity to volunteer in the trenches, and yet others just want to give their money. Younger donors who are stewards of philanthropic dollars tend to want to be more involved. Those who earned the wealth may have a more hands-off mentality. Therefore, to influence support, learn the philanthropist's desire for participation, and then incorporate that information in your proposal and execution plan.

It is one thing to influence a donor with a message, and another to implement an efficient process. If you are hosting a fundraising event, and you receive *no* to further donations at the event, the response may mean *not now*. After any fundraising event, follow-up with delegates, as this is the optimal time to leverage your event's emotional appeal and seek participation in a cause or open the purse strings wider.

Philanthropists want to make a change. Draw them in by focusing on the results their support will have for a cause. Sharing *social return on investment* would be well utilized here. People want to be conduits to solving a problem, making a difference, making tomorrow better than today. Show a philanthropist that with their help you move closer to that reality. However, be realistic and forthcoming to encourage a donor's trust in you.

Collect relevant information

In addition to the beneficiary and supporter analysis, collecting information about your cause's history, circumstances, progression, and impact will help to frame a compelling case.

Regardless of whether you *create*, *lead*, or *influence* a community contribution, acquiring a deep understanding of issues and opportunities will assist you in tailoring information to various stakeholders. You will find cultivating your contribution capacity will come from a variety of sources, such as researching documents, books, government reports, charity marketing materials, and social media.

TSiBA Education was established to meet the realities of South Africa. Gia Whitehead explains.

> In South Africa, there is something called Black Economic Empowerment (BEE), and there is a scorecard. Companies are required to spend a certain amount of money on corporate social investment and enterprise development. They are also required to spend in other areas such as management and employment equity. We are addressing a need for these companies, not just a tick box exercise. Our students can move into the business, and they can add value, and that is incredibly important.

The BEE was implemented by the African National Congress party as a direct intervention in the redistribution of assets and opportunities. The intent was to resolve the economic disparities for black people created by apartheid. In 2007, there was the introduction of a modified program, Broad-Based Black Economic Empowerment (B-BEE), to include all disadvantaged people. TSiBA meets the mandate by educating disadvantaged peoples of diverse races, making it easier to gain support.

By volunteering for a cause that fills a social or environmental gap you will escalate your insight and expertise. Read news from the country or community you are researching or use Google alerts to flag any articles that may be relevant to your area of interest.

To contextualize your conscious-contributions, you need to ask the right questions to gain support. The more insight you can provide, the more persuasive you start to become. Gain first-hand experience of the environment, conduct research, connect with the beneficiaries and benefactors, and learn the laws and cultural priorities. The insight will offer a solid foundation to gain commitment.

Set your objectives

Before a meeting, or making a presentation, it is essential to know what you want to accomplish.

Think of your objectives:

1. What do you want to happen because of your conversation / presentation?
2. How do you want your stakeholders / audience to feel about you, your initiative, and organization?

When you have decided on the objective, write it out in one sentence. It should be clear, concise and compelling, without any negative words. Keeping the specific purpose in mind will ensure your interaction is relevant, to the point, and will help you select meaningful supporting materials.

For my first presentation in Kenya to a group of 70, my objective was to assist these individuals in how to develop a persuasive presentation; I wanted them to feel I was approachable, and my organization was an expert in influence. I needed to find a way to connect to over a dozen cultures, predominantly male, all Evangelic Christians — none of which I am.

It was time to morph myself in an attempt to connect. As a five-foot-ten woman, I made myself smaller. I rounded my shoulders, and although it felt fine at the time, the video evidence was less than flattering. Being an expressive personality, I also wanted to minimize my energy and soften my tone. I became a smiley, friendly person that would work alongside you, rather than my usual high-energy self that will challenge you to be better than you thought you could be.

I used words, examples, and energy in an attempt to connect. Thankfully, it worked.

After the presentation, an American woman who had lived in Kenya for years came up to me and said, "You did an outstanding job, except for the one example about rehearsing your presentation in the shower. The water is too cold here, and no one takes long showers."

She was right. The overall delivery is what gets the audience engaged, but the nuances are what ingratiate you.

When planning communications, clear objectives will dictate what you say and how you say it. If you aim to get an immediate decision on a proposal, be specific about how you would like them to address your cause. However, if your objective is only to receive a favorable response to a project that does not call for immediate implementation, you may elect to save that discussion on methods of execution for another meeting or solicit the stakeholders' thoughts on how they would like to proceed.

Each item in your interaction should be there only because it helps to put your proposal across more convincingly to the stakeholders who are present and to the decision-makers to who will eventually receive your recommendation. Keeping your objective and your decision-makers' motivators in mind will help you to keep your presentation lean and purposeful.

Structure your interaction so that it is understood

Misunderstanding is common in communication, for reasons varying from language barriers to cultural nuances to misuse of words to an inappropriate tone or incongruent body language. To help reduce misunderstanding, use a well-structured message, which includes repeating critical ideas in different ways.

Communications should have a beginning, middle, and end. After 20 years of training leaders, business professionals, including sales teams, I can assure you this is uncommon sense. We need to grab the attention of our audience and instantly engage them. Many people jump right into the middle, where the substance resides. Moreover, most ignore the importance of stating the next steps and gaining agreement on the way forward.

If you are interacting with a community leader to gain buy-in to your idea or trying to influence your colleagues or a donor, then prepare the listener, deliver the message, and make sure the message is understood. In other words, have a subject, agenda, body, summary, and conclusion.

This simple structure can be used conversationally one-to-one, or in a more formal presentation to a group. Throughout the presentation explicitly stating the agenda, summary, and the next steps will make it easy for the audience to follow. Well-organized content helps you to command attention and interest while inspiring confidence of the listeners. Also, your ideas will be easy to understand. They will flow naturally and logically while building to a powerful climax. You may choose to use visuals to drive retention while bringing your message to life.

Whether it is an informal conversation or formal presentation, a structure will increase understanding, retention, and action.

Influence through persuasion and perseverance

Conducting all the necessary stakeholder analyses to tailor your proposal can still lead to a rejection. Providing the right information at the right time in a conversation will increase your ability to influence a desired outcome.

One of the most persuasive techniques to compel someone to your perspective is the use of evidence. Sharing proof is more paramount now than ever since differentiating between fact and fiction is becoming more difficult. Tailored details coupled with evidence will make your message more persuasive. Saying it is so doesn't make it true. Evidence directly related to your prospective stakeholders' interests can be a convincing factor in building confidence in your ability to execute a conscious-contribution that will meet their personal and organizational objectives.

There are many forms of evidence you may want to include, such as what other supporters have done and why. Incorporate relevant facts, data, figures, and statistics about what you are proposing and its impact. Also, include what might happen in the future if an issue is ignored. Fear, regret, and consequences are all motivators. A case study or anecdote that addresses not only the result achieved, but also pulls on the emotional heartstrings, will be hard to ignore. The more specific the story, case study, or anecdote is, and the more relevant to the stakeholder's experience and values, the more persuasive is your message.

Take it one step further by connecting your cause to a beneficiary's story and share his or her transformation. Deliver the story in a manner that shows the stakeholder how their participation will provide a positive future outcome.

Unfortunately, persuasion although effective, may not be enough to garner support. That is where perseverance steps in.

Nouzha Chekrouni realized that she had all the skills, ambition, and vision in the world, but the Moroccan patriarchal social paradigm would not allow her to succeed. Regardless, her determination and continued confidence in her pursuit to be an elected official did not waver. Society may not have been ready for her to be part of the government, but she was. That was enough to continue her political pursuits until society's viewpoint evolved.

> I was a candidate three times before I won the elections. Two times, I was a candidate at the municipal level. The first time was 1987. When I was doing my election campaign, I remember the first door I knocked on. It was a man who opened the door. He asked, 'Who are you?' I said, 'I am a candidate. I want to represent you in your municipality.' He said, 'Two men couldn't do what we need them to do, how can a young woman like you do it?' Thanked me, then he closed the door.
>
> The second time, people were more open to dialogue, but they were still not ready for a woman's participation.
>
> The third time, I was a candidate for the parliament. I was mature; my speech was strong; my message went everywhere. I was in dialogue with women and men in rural areas and cities, young and old. There were 36 candidates, and I was ranked third. Although I didn't win, I felt very accomplished. I never lost confidence. The reality is only one person can win. So, even though I lost, my reaction was the same every time. I will run again. I will win it next time.

This sort of confidence and perseverance intrigued me. I had to ask the ambassador where it came from. And she responded:

> Life is not easy. It challenges you. When life is too easy, you can't go very far. It is hard, but you must learn from your failures. It makes you stronger. The first time you fail, it is hard. It is harder, however, to say, 'I will continue, but I will do it differently.'

Make your contribution count

Regardless of who you are appealing to, learn their values, objectives, culture, language, and connect your message and demeanor to them. This will start you down the right path to gain commitment.

Communicating from the perspective of the person you are trying to influence in line with their priorities, will expedite a decision in your favor — now. However, if that doesn't work, try, try, and try again.

I admire my three friends' impact. They put Joytown and Bethany Kids Children's Center's needs and wants ahead of their own. They asked questions and set a clear objective. They minimized religious differences, optimized sharing expertise, and did not overshadow the medical team. They checked their egos and worked alongside the physicians and staff. They added to the sustainability of the institutions while providing a better life for children who are often forgotten.

Reflect on how to make your conscious-contributions™

1. What cultural norms do you need to consider? Would your communication style have to change to connect with the chosen beneficiary?
2. What skills, abilities, and resources do you want your supporters to possess to help sustain your contribution?
3. What does your prospective supporter value? In what priority?
4. What evidence do you have that your contribution will have the desired impact?

Chapter 21
Commit through communications

Words of Wisdom

Make a promise, communicate it, keep it, and strengthen it by expanding it.

Eva Muraya, president and founder BSD Ltd, Kenya
Pioneer: co-founded the Kenya Association of Women Business Owners (KAWBO)

Mike and I were in downtown Dar es Salaam, Tanzania, working in an itty-bitty room, side by side. As we were making plans for the next interview, a disagreement erupted. But as fast as the fury emerged, it terminated with a slam of his hand on the table. He glared into my eyes communicating I was about to get an earful. With all the vigor he could voice, he barked, "My contribution counts ... and besides, I have nowhere to go."

We both broke out into laughter. That was our reality. All we had was each other. So, you suck it up and start to appreciate that you're trapped — together. An option, that more often than not, brought us joy.

Most people will say, "I couldn't work with my spouse." It is not an easy path. As with any business, there is the merging of different personalities, experiences, and abilities. When you are married, there is a healthy dose of romantic tension (if you're lucky) combined with a familiarity that can turn into making assumptions and having unhealthy expectations. The challenge multiplies when two leaders have to adapt to assume the position of follower. You both are continuously learning how to manage each other, communicate together, and get stuff done out of the eye of the storm. The other difficulty is identifying when the working partnership ends, and the life partnership begins. Lines become blurred.

When we returned home after the bulk of our interviews, in response to my question of whether he wanted to do something else, Mike replied, "No. We are partners, for better or worse. I believe in our vision." I have asked Mike this question several times over the last six years and every time, his answer is the same.

Our vision for our marriage and our social enterprise is what has bound us. Without it, and the mission and values that accompany it, no doubt Mike would be pursuing an alternative course of employment. No work environment is perfect. Recommitting to the vision, mission, purpose, and values will assist in navigating any storm about to happen.

An overarching organizational focus provides an anchor from which all communications should emanate.

The organization's mission is the difference it wants to make in the world. Its vision is what it aspires to achieve. Its purpose is why the organization exists. The impact statement incorporates what you will achieve (outcomes), for whom (beneficiary), by when (timeframe). Strategies are the broad methods to achieve the vision. Theory of transformation is a gauge to measure the progress between strategies implemented, the performance expected, and results realized.

Lastly, consider the values, which are the behaviors for delivering the plan. Without core values clearly articulated to achieve *we* actions, the contribution and your ability to lead it will be sabotaged.

Once you incorporate all the elements into the strategic plan, you have a basis for making all decisions. All your stakeholder communications and daily dialogs are anchored in these components, allowing for consistent decision-making and messaging.

Engaging stakeholders in learning the value proposition will amplify the message and ensure consistent communications. A value proposition is a statement that highlights what you do, for whom, how you do it, and why it is needed. Make sure you emphasize what makes your contribution distinctive and valuable to your contributors, and why it is required now. At the onset of a relationship, differentiate your organization by including how you address a social problem in a financially sustainable way.

Vision, mission, values as the communication catalysts

The more stakeholders that are aligned with the vision, the easier it is to execute. Make the aspiration the catalyst for intradepartmental and stakeholder communications. To influence actions that will help achieve the vision, communicate it based on the relevancy to each stakeholder group.

The vision of Gita Goven's firm is a collection of the team's passions and purposes.

> There are moments in growing the organization when you stretch yourself, and you have to think about how you will stay connected to your team. You can't assume your team is following you.
>
> What we have done as partners is communicate what we want as our vision for our lives as individuals and the firm. By getting each team member in our practice to think about what they are committed to and what they are passionate about identifies a common purpose. And to drive that common purpose, we look at the skills that we need.

Once a vision is created and committed to, the challenge is to ensure it remains as the beacon. With the continual ebb and flow of stakeholders, the aspiration must remain the guide to execute strategies; however, an organization can go off course. In over 20 years of working with organizations, I have observed three catalysts for the vision disconnect:

1. Stakeholders don't align with the vision.

2. Stakeholders don't understand how the aspiration is relevant to them.

3. The vision, mission, and values are not repeated in multiple media to promote clarity and recall.

The most engaged stakeholders are those who believe in an organization's direction, approach, and behaviors and feel their contributions are adding to its overall success. It is important for millennials to feel they are affecting the growth of the organization. Knowing what they do every day in the context of the overall vision will give them a sense of purpose. Without that communication, their efforts and engagement will probably fall flat.

To keep the vision front and center, Gita Goven's firm has multiple touchpoints to connect the team to organizational drivers.

> Every Monday, we have a team leader meeting which is themed. The first Monday of every month, we do a three-hour session with the entire staff, and we do something inspiring to share the values of some of the projects we are working on. Even the juniors gain insight into what we are dealing with. Now we have started a formal tea session where we come down to the social space every day for fifteen minutes. We use that time to share what's going on, what hasn't worked, and what has worked.

Jane Wathome is very conscious of hiring employees on their values and ensuring they align with the organization's mission: to empower and equip women with and affected by HIV/AIDS within poor communities to meet their spiritual, physical, emotional and economic needs. Jane uses annual staff retreats and interdepartmental monthly presentations to promote organizational alignment to the vision: To be a model of excellence in wholesome community transformation globally.[83]

> Once a month, the entire staff comes together to hear presentations. No matter what your role — cook, gardener, nurse, or head of the clinic — you are in these presentations so each person can understand one another, and no one is left behind. It inspires people to own the vision, and own the organization, as they are part of it. After these presentations, we pray together.

Transparency and accountability through communications is the glue that sticks the employees to a worthy cause.

Ultimately when an organization and its stakeholders conscious-contributions align, the biggest beneficiaries are those whom the initiative was created to serve. The primary segments served by Tanzania Women's Bank Ltd. are women in micro and small businesses who are considered high risk. Margareth Chacha shares how they communicate to align every employee down to their bank chauffeur to know what the bank does and how it differentiates itself in the market.

> Some organizations promote hierarchy. People will challenge why you have done their work, so people don't cross over to someone else's territory or assignment. I discourage this approach.
>
> When we train, we have a value for the bank; you have to be efficient, do it the right the first time. This is a one-stop service. You, as a customer come to me, I listen to your problem. If I can't solve it, I make an appointment or a promise. The most important thing is to remember the problem and deliver a solution.
>
> We spend a lot of time on how to retain customers. You don't always have to look for new customers, but it is important to retain customers.

A strategy recommended to re-engage a stakeholder who has gone rogue is to remind them of their goals and how they align with the vision and mission of the organization. You will also find communicating a specific company core value is an effective way to bond someone to an organization, particularly when his or her values align.

Communicating a vision, mission or values through story can also be an effective way to inspire stakeholder collaboration.

Commitment through story

Stories are a compelling way to inspire emotion, as they capture the imagination of an audience or a prospective supporter. They can profile a cause, provoke collaborators, and gain support for conscious-contribution. If you are trying to raise funds or increase sales, or gain buy-in to an idea, your stories can capture attention, move emotion, create an alternative vision, and leave your audience wanting more — or better yet, wanting to support your efforts.

Gia Whitehead relied on storytelling to secure funding that has provided 4,000 student scholarships. She shares her secret:

> It is creating a story that you are passionate about. Then you need a tangible project that is doing some real grassroots empowerment. What better investment than education, where you are giving people the skills to go out and be self-sustaining? You need to know it is working and it is needed.
>
> Regarding funders, they not only need to believe in the project but believe in the individual. They need to know you can do what is required. They need to have confidence in you.

Stories can help build confidence in others, but that is just a launching pad to garner support. I was coaching a director for international charity whose mandate was to raise funds for starving children. In each of his examples, he would share a photo of the child, the name, and diameter of the child's arm. Then he would compare a healthy child to the malnourished child — visually gripping. He emotionally connected his audience to the child and the problem. The audience was confident in his expertise and the need.

Although the director had a worthy cause and was a proficient presenter who connected people to stories, the audience left without donating. They didn't know how to go from connecting with the presentation to solving the problem. Ideally, a presentation needs to move people to the desired action. Your ask needs to be precise, incorporating the difference someone's involvement will make, the ease of supporting the cause, and when you want their support.

No matter whether you are trying to raise funds, gain support, or ignite passion in others, using stories is a compelling way to provide people with a lens to experience a circumstance they have never encountered. The more grassroots view you provide, the more emotionally charged the receiver will be. The ebb and flow of the emotional details will keep a stakeholder, philanthropist, or entire audience engaged while your story unfolds.

Donors and conscious-consumers want to know their contributions will count. Janet Nkubana harnesses that need by sharing a story with the company's international buyers to show their support is transforming an individual's life.

> If they bought from a particular group of weavers, I would update them on how that group is performing, especially what they have earned from them. I always share stories of the impact of their business on Rwandan communities, which motivates them that they are changing lives.

> We share success stories in the communities. For example, Linda may have been able to put electricity in her house because they have sold baskets. We would share that story with Macy's. Or if Teresa was able to buy a cow, we share that story.

Janet Nkubana doesn't say, "The community is uplifted," but rather, "Teresa is able to buy a cow." Incorporating some detail is what makes a good story and what people will remember as it connects them emotionally to a faraway place. Buyers feel they know Theresa and her progress. Specifics conjure gratification and participation.

One of the most potent story techniques is through the first person. If a contribution altered Theresa's situation, capture the experiences in her words, preferably on video. There are many story formats; one is to describe the situation, then the action taken, followed by what result achieved. Using statistical changes in the result will assist with its persuasiveness to stakeholders. An alternative format is to describe the situation, why it's important, and the relevance to the audience.

A *helper's high* can also motivate contributors. Harnessing the *high* by communicating a contributor's story of support will provoke others to participate. As Ralph Waldo Emerson once said, "It is one of the most beautiful compensations of life that no man can sincerely try to help another without helping himself."[84]

Emotionally connecting people to your social, economic or environmental contribution will create momentum for your mission.

Amplify your message

Doo Aphane always found the informal face-to-face conversation in the least expected places garnered the most support for her women's

Commit through communications

rights initiatives. If she was shopping, at a funeral, or at a gathering anywhere in eSwatini, she would take the opportunity to connect and educate. Doo describes the success of her guerrilla marketing approach: "When I see women are able to access funding from those community members because I have had conversations with them, I have created awareness for them that they are entitled." Doo also believes success is about not giving up, which means communicating her firm beliefs of equality until everyone is listening.

There are few approaches with more power to influence commitment than face-to-face communications; however, when you are seeking to tell your story far and wide, other forms of communication will have a broader reach. Doo says what she would have done differently to gain momentum quicker: "Using media [is] the way of amplifying one's voice. I think I could have fine-tuned the strategy and started bottom-up, rather than top-down."

There are several communication methods for spreading our message. To control the interpretation of your perspective use email, newsletters, organizational intranet, articles, blogs, vlogs and your website. To optimize the understanding and retention, using a combination of media to communicate, and being authentic will pack a punch.

The author has less control in social media, but when used by the beneficiary or a stakeholder not at the helm, such as volunteer or professional-contributor, it can carry extra clout. The more produced your story, the lower its sense of veracity. It feels more authentic when a message that is not perfectly crafted hits the market. Use the tools where your target audience resides, such as YouTube, Instagram, Facebook, Twitter, LinkedIn, and other social media. Encourage stakeholders to share their experience of either contributing to your initiative or benefiting from it. If your contribution is in the developing world, you will in all likelihood be able to connect with a beneficiary via mobile phone.[85]

Angela Dick uses email to reinforce commitment from her team. Her secret sauce is reaching out with an authentic daily email that provides her staff a glimpse into the woman who founded the Transman recruitment company. This raised-curtain philosophy grants staff the confidence to share ideas with Angela directly, and Angela the opportunity to listen to insights that influence how she retains and inspires her team. She shares:

> I think [my team] all know me pretty well, and they realize I accept them as part of my family. I send them an email every single day. I call it *my thought for the day*. It is something that I have been thinking about, a concern of an employee, or something that is happening in the country. It is just a positive thought that I am thinking about this and you perhaps should think about this too. I get wonderful feedback from all corners. It is amazing when you stretch out to people and touch their hearts and minds; you just never know what is going to come back. It is just incredible.

Connecting to the hearts and minds of all stakeholders is an effective strategy to maintain a commitment to a conscious-contribution. By implementing systems to allow for simple ongoing communications, an organization can keep their values and mission at the forefront of supporters' mind. Creating an email campaign, along with other innovative touchpoints to let contributors know why they *count*, will elevate your message and their recall. To distinguish your message, connect without an ask for time, a donation, or support. To strengthen the message, tailor your communications by reaching out when it matters most to the recipient — an achievement, a health issue, or a note of appreciation. Connecting at a personal level will promote commitment and recall.

In the words of Eva Muraya, a Kenyan brand expert: "Make a promise, communicate it, keep it, and strengthen it by expanding it." All communication mechanisms that get the right message to the masses have benefit, but perhaps most compelling is having one day a year dedicated to reminding the society in question of the importance of an issue. Lydia Muso has lobbied with other citizens of Lesotho to create an annual day that focuses on the importance of the prevention of child abuse. That day is November 19.

We work hand in hand with other organizations to promote community awareness. We also apply for sponsorships. November 19 is the day put aside to make people aware of the prevention of child abuse. We are really focusing on human trafficking because it is one hidden crime. Reported cases are so few, but it is happening so often. Many people do not even think it is a crime. People think that they are so poor, and they can't feed their child. If someone comes with money, parents don't stop to ask where you got the money, they are too hungry, and they take the money to buy food to eat.

If you are in Lesotho on November 19, share your experience. Better yet, ask a Mosotho person, a citizen of Lesotho, her thoughts about the day. With her permission, take a video and share it with your network. The message will gain momentum, possibly catapulting a life-saving movement.

Make your contribution count

Consistent, concise, persuasive, and repetitive communication is vital to gain momentum of any conscious-contribution. Stories are a launching pad to engage, however, it is essential to clearly tell prospective benefactors what to do to support your contribution. Using multi-media to disseminate the message will attract listeners. The key is to make it as easy as possible to help others spread your message. What is amplified is heard, and what someone connects to, will be amplified.

Reflect on how to make your conscious-contributions™

1. Which media do your prospective contributors utilize?
2. How will you communicate your vision/mission through various media to connect with stakeholder groups?
3. What stories can you share to engage people emotionally?
4. Which beneficiary would be a good spokesperson for your mission?

Chapter 22
Create a conscious culture

Words of Wisdom

Integrity is the most expensive currency that we should carry. Always keep your promise and work on your promise. If you keep your word, die keeping your word, you will always be trusted — there will always be success.

Tereza Mbire, serial entrepreneur, Uganda
Pioneer: UWEAL founder, co-founder of Uganda Women Financial Trust

When we interviewed Angela Dick, her power and passion were oozing, and her humility was ever-present. I was curious to know how she was able to change the recruitment industry in South Africa. At the time she had employed over 10,000 people and still moves the business forward with such focus and humanity. Her secret weapon is converging a clear vision for the organization, empowering her employees, embracing the cultural circumstances, while maintaining a positive attitude.

> I think it comes back to the perspective, and the view I have always had is that I am not important. I am just a little speck in this huge universe. It is my responsibility to look after people, and I must do whatever it takes, even if I find myself in a traumatic situation. I have to be there, be seen to lead and be stable; you have to do that for your team. It's not for me.

Angela believes the secret to her success is leading *with her people*:

> If you look at my senior executive team, which there are eight, I believe very much in participatory management, and I accept that I do not know everything. They have been developed over the years. I am perfectly happy to accept advice or recommendations from any level. Some of the best ideas in this company have come from a housekeeper. I think it is important they

know I take the advice, format it, and implement it as something positive for all of us.

One of the most critical assets of any organization is its people. Regardless if an organization is a socially conscious enterprise focusing on profitable social good, or a not-for-profit embracing conscious leadership techniques, a critical metric of its success is stakeholder well-being. Emphasis is placed on engaging each member of the team by creating a culture that will attract, retain, and inspire colleagues. A conscious culture empowers the team and sets the foundation for high-trust, high-performance, and high-happiness. Angela counts on it. She hopes that when she retires that she will leave behind something most important to her:

> I hope to leave behind a happy company; a company motivated to help other people, which is very much the culture I have created. I hope to leave a company that is sustainable that will continue to make a contribution; not just in this country but also in the continent.

With millennials increasingly wanting to contribute to the community, but not necessarily having the time to pursue opportunities outside work, volunteer programs are quickly becoming one of the most engaging ways for businesses to retain their most valued assets. If employees find more meaning at work, they are more engaged and stay loyal to the company longer. Result? Less employee turnover, less employee onboarding cost, more productivity. In companies that provide opportunities for employees to volunteer their time in their area of expertise, those employees find a higher level of job satisfaction because their talents are having a positive impact on the community. This approach holds true with different generations and organizations. If members feel connected to the mission and use their gifts for the greater good, they will also be inspired.

Another way to engage a team is to encourage them to use their full personality to achieve desirable results. Gita Goven of ARG Design, shares the importance of tapping into masculine and feminine energy and knowing when to tap into which to inspire the best from your team.

I work with a lot of men who bring great feminine energy into the work we do — looking for opportunities to connect with people at an individual level and bring more nurturing, love, courage, and wisdom to what we do.

It is not only about the money; it is about appreciating those qualities of human beings, those softer qualities of society, those softer qualities of spaces and places that really allow people to experience the joy of being alive every day and engaging with each other and having fun doing what we do. That is the kind of stuff that women can bring. It's knowing when you draw on that feminine energy and when you draw on that masculine energy.

When I need to be straight and forthright, I can be a real dictator when necessary. Most of the time, we achieve a lot with love and courage.

To establish a conscious culture, you must be trustworthy, stay humble, and be assertive toward the change you want to make. Being *humbly assertive* is emphasizing the message, not the messenger. Ela Gandhi explains:

> If a leader does not have integrity, then the leader will not be followed, nor will what they say be accepted. Your message must be very clear and distinct. At the same time, you must have the humility to discuss it.

To create a conscious culture, start with being transparent, accountable, collaborative, and communicate how each employee's contribution impacts the mission. Conscious cultures are interdependent, and if one part of the ecosystem is compromised, it affects the performance of the whole. Angela Dick ensures each member of the team realizes their role.

> My team knows we are all dependent on each other because that is the culture I have built over time. They also know that we are all responsible for our own actions, but they know there is a ripple effect if things haven't been done.

Angela's approach to business creates a high degree of trust and loyalty from her team and the citizens she recruits. Every day she demonstrates conscious leadership, and the reward is a socially conscious enterprise that spawns a conscious culture. Angela, and many pioneering African women, are able to create a positive ripple effect due to establishing a culture where everyone's voice matters.

Applying characteristics of a conscious culture will increase employee, member, and other stakeholder engagement; however, to manifest them into an organization, one needs to lead for longevity.

Lead for longevity

One crucial element to being followed is making the team aware of where you are going. Employees don't aimlessly walk behind you without a clear direction, which is why an organization forges a mission. Self-vetted allies become enticed by the road you are traveling.

It is a leader's responsibility not to waver while leading the team to a common goal. Eva Muraya believes:

> Leadership is an opportunity to serve people on a journey that is clearly defined and has an end in mind. It is a service that is focused, persuasive, and will transform people from one level to the next. Each one of us has the opportunity to lead. You don't need to be at the forefront to be defined as a leader. If you raise children, run a home, or are an elder aunt, you are a leader. Leadership is service, not *rulership*. It needs to be purposeful.

Tereza Mbire, a Ugandan serial entrepreneur, describes what it means to be focused. "Know the line you are following. A blind man cannot lead other blind men. You need to have one eye open. You need to be focused, know what you want to do, and be able to reach the goal you are aiming at."

Mission leaders practice conscious leadership: they care, respect, cultivate, empower, engage, inspire, appreciate, and promote their teams. Each one of these behaviors, in and of itself, is motivating; however, when implementing one, another will emerge.

Care

Janet Nkubana of Gahaya Links shares that caring about her team results in committed producers.

> I relate to them easily. I crack jokes with them. I compliment them. I tell them my story. I share what went wrong in my life. Women were hesitant to share after the genocide. I tell them I am a single mother, that I have no husband. I eat with them, I share a drink with them, I hold their children,

and I visit with them in their homes. I am one of them. I ask them about their family. I open my home to them.

Caring about a team member is intensified when you demonstrate interest in their family. Leah Ngini keeps the focus on her school's greater cause by incorporating an employee benefit that infuses the mission of the school where the students come first.

> I give my teachers' children scholarships to the school, so their minds are in the school and not in another school where their children attend. Their children take the school buses, are given lunches, they have the same service as all the other students. My teachers stay a long time, which brings continuity to the school.

Care is reciprocal in a conscious culture. A leader needs to create open communication so that their employees know they can demonstrate authentic care and not be perceived as jockeying for a promotion. Jennifer Riria embraces the practice of mutual care that creates a harmonized environment. "I start taking care of people so they can take care of me. I need to help them grow, so they will help me grow. You have to see your success in their success."

Although a business needs performance to progress, care is feeling that if for reasons beyond an employee's control, they can no longer contribute to an organization's success, they are not going to be discarded but encircled.

One of the most compelling demonstrations of care is to actively listen with all your senses to a colleague's perspective, interests, and issues. Demonstrating intent in all communications will foster respect and a loyalty.

Respect

Sara Abera, the founder of Muya Ethiopia, is transparent with her employees. She ensures the artisans are part of every element of the business as it evolves and grows.

> For our employees, this is a family business of seven or eight generations. When we start a new collection, I bring them in and make them part of the idea. They feel pride, and they see what they are producing. I want them

to understand the product, where it is going. They are contributing to the success of the organization.

Many of the conscious-contributors interviewed show respect for their artisans work by placing their names on a tag that accompanies the handcraft. This creates a real sense of ownership. Sara takes the recognition a step further by sharing their story. Because pottery producers invest so much of their time in creating a masterpiece, Sara places the producer's given name and information about her children, family, and how many generations have made pottery on a tag that accompanies each unique design. It often takes eight hours a day, seven days a week to make a well-crafted piece of pottery, an acknowledgment also imparted to the buyer.

Amani ya Juu products also bear the woman's name on handcrafts and in return, the producer feels they are taking control of their family's future. Amani ya Juu meaning *peace from above*, is a compound in Nairobi, Kenya, that houses a restaurant, store, workshop, and a meeting place. It was founded to provide a haven for women broken and devastated by the horrors of civil conflict. They use Fair Trade practices and flexibility to promote respect and inclusion of their team of women refugees. Joyce Muraya explains, "We give the women a just wage, higher than minimum wage. We also allow women to bring their children to work or work from home so they can attend to their families."

Joyce respects that everyone has something to contribute and ensures all the Amani team has the opportunity to lead. For women who are predominantly refugees, encouraging them to take control of their destiny is welcome.

> Leadership development is a priority — we start with little tasks that draw our team into leadership. We ask newer individuals to lead initiatives. They take ownership. They see their worth as they contribute. We have women in different departments that have grown into leadership. We partner with organizations that want us to train a group of children or women. This provides leadership opportunities.

As a leader, it is not about me; therefore, I don't have to be at the forefront. My role is to help other women to walk strong. Amani needs a leader who walks with women.

Through respecting the ability of refugees, Joyce is able to cultivate their skills and their influence.

Cultivate

Joanne Mwangi advises: "You need to move with the group and not be too far ahead of them. If you are too far ahead, all you are doing is taking a walk. There needs to be a succession of leaders."

People have a thirst to grow. An environment that builds skills will quench stakeholders' desires and keep them engaged as the innate need for growth is satisfied.

Margareth Chacha embraces the need for development by challenging her team to resolve their issues.

> I don't like micromanaging people. I give them a challenge, and I want to see the potential in them. I encourage people to come to me with problems and solutions. I don't like giving solutions, even when I have one.

One strategy to cultivating one's abilities is to provide ongoing scheduled dialogue. This embeds learning into the culture and if authentically implemented can induce an open communication where feedback is embraced from all sources.

As much as it is essential to cultivate your team, if committed to cultivate a culture of learning, Katherine Ichoya suggests, "Ask people to critique you. This keeps you grounded, so you don't live a lie." In addition, continued self-assessment will keep a leader humble and authentic.

Different cultures have to work through social norms and practices to create space for predisposition that may exist. Yetnebersh Nigussie has actively gathered youth to become involved to be successors, but first, they need to address the ageism bias.

> In Ethiopia, there is a deep-rooted mentality that young people should not be involved in big decision-making. Many people who are good leaders

don't think that someone else can do things better. They don't leave their positions. One of the characteristics of a good leader is someone who has people who can sustain things while he or she is not in place.

Perhaps Yetnebersh's disinclination toward hierarchy is why at her school she cultivates children to have a voice at a young age.

> We get the children involved. When we talk about polluted water, not only do the kids have to write an essay about it, but they also will visit polluted water in the community. They then can bring the issue up to government officials. We choose different issues every month together. This approach gets the kids highly involved in the community. You don't expect a young child to get involved and challenge the issues, so as an adult, we feel embarrassed by it, so they listen.

> We read about it, write about it, experience it, and then do something about it. It is good to make children think about their future and participate in their community. Because once they do, they feel a sense of belonging and therefore are less likely to want to leave.

Cultivating people is the single best investment any organization can make. It communicates a person is valued and therefore empowers them to create a ripple effect.

Empower

As a young leader Modesta Lilian Mahiga recalculated how she approached leadership. Instead of leading her vision from the front, she moved to the middle where she could allow others to tap into their strength and amplify it in the processes of advancing the mission. On reflection, she recognizes what her role is and what she would change:

> I would have groomed my team for leadership a lot sooner. I started leading from upfront and had capable, competent followers, but I wasn't grooming leaders from the onset. I believe I have been called to groom leaders. There are giants that are meant to step over me to lead. I am more deliberate about it now.

> Now I get to know what motivates [my team]. How is this place serving their vision? If it is not, it is just another job. By getting to know their interests, I am very deliberate about giving opportunities. Because I am loud and visible, invitations will come to me, but I have giants on my team who aren't known of because they are in my shadow. People on my

team are on their own journey; it may align with mine or not. I don't want anyone to ever say they fed my vision. I want to feed their vision.

Mwamvita Makamba echoes the importance of empowering the messenger and the message.

> I also think women should be inspired by other women who have done it already. I look at other women such as Asha-Rose Migiro, from Tanzania, who was the deputy secretary general of the United Nations. We all could see what was done because she made sure that she was delivering a cause. She is not talking about herself, 'I am good, I am excellent,' she is doing something to impact and bring change, and people will see it. When you are bringing change, you have to talk about it. You inspire other people to speak up.
>
> I make sure women working for me are seen; they sing their song. They present to management, so they are seen to have achieved success.

The most energizing way to become empowered is to grasp the opportunities. Norah Odwesso, of Coca-Cola Central East and West Africa, encourages us to embrace our power.

> We shouldn't wait for permission to make things happen. We need to stop thinking, who will give me a promotion? Many of us don't understand that we can lead without titles. As a woman, it is in your right to make a difference, to take charge of your world. It is in your right to add value to whatever it is you are doing. Then opportunities open up for you.

To create a conscious culture, an environment that promotes stepping into your light needs to exist. It starts with how a leader engages their team.

Engage

Norah Odwesso highlights the importance of engaging teams in decision-making. "I am a firm believer that when there is a will, there is a way. And when there is a team, there must be more than one way."

Norah isn't suggesting using everyone's ideas. Collecting perspectives for collaborative decision-making is critical. If board members, teams, or advisors feel heard, and their insights are considered, they will be more inclined to accept and implement a solution, since they had a part in its formulation.

Audrey Kahara-Kawuki, the pioneer of MUBS Enterprise Centre Uganda, encourages leaders to engage their teams outside work.

> To succeed as a leader, you need to allow others to work with you. You need to know how to build a team. It is good to go out with your staff. Remove yourself from the work environment. People open up outside work and you will learn how to relate with them better.

Samrawit Beyene would agree about reducing barriers to connect with her team. She has a horizontal leadership philosophy so she can connect and support her team from a position of equals. Samrawit manifests this philosophy by providing opportunities for open, honest dialogue in and outside the office.

> We have retreats. There is no hierarchy. They address me with my first name. More like a friendship relationship. We pay for education. I accept constructive criticism. We have a weekly meeting where we discuss improvement, but also rewarding people. If they have any personal problems, we are always there.

Engagement is such a critical practice to produce a conscious culture. From here leaders can inspire possibilities.

Inspire

Leaders can't build a successful organization or execute a conscious-contribution for sustainability unless they do what they say. Demonstration is essential to inspire people to follow your lead. Yetnebersh shares how to inspire supporters and expand reach:

> Don't tell others how to do things. Do it and let them learn from that. You need to be a risk-taker. Make sure you are taking the maximum risk so others can learn from you. Make sure you have other successors that can maintain the change you have started, to maintain the processes that you have developed.

When you think of some of the most impactful leaders throughout history, like Mother Teresa, Dr. Martin Luther King Jr., or Mahatma Gandhi, they inspired, rather than told others what to do.

Modeling behavior can be lonely as there is often no one ready to emulate. Doo Aphane recalls tirelessly trying to get eSwatini to ratify the 1995 Beijing Women's Conference, which created the blueprint for women's equality:

> In 2007, the movement was quiet. Land ownership remained an individual thing. I realized it was a clear opportunity; I did not need to stress about organizing and mobilizing, just that others should follow. There is a time to lead, and others will follow.

Inspiring co-conspirators creates a swell but mobilizing beneficiaries can generate a tsunami. Organizations or institutions can provide inspiration by instilling strong values in the culture. TSiBA Education encourages scholarship students to pay-it-forward. There isn't a written contract, but rather an implied cultural norm. Each student makes up his or her mind whether they choose to contribute to society based on receiving a scholarship. Gia Whitehead shares:

> As part of their leadership curriculum, they do have to be involved on campus and in their communities. They get what we call leadership hours. They are part of a program that hours are recognized. It is one way to demonstrate the expectation, but it does become part of the culture. You find students are hungry for the opportunity to learn and grow. They see the value of other people giving back, mentoring, and showing them what it is like to be supported. It is something that is instilled and engrained in our students from day one.

Transformation occurs when colleagues are inspired to embrace a conscious-contribution as their own. To sustain it, they need to feel meaning in the work, and appreciation for the work.

Appreciate

A stakeholder will reconfirm their commitment to the mission with every demonstration of authentic gratitude. Saying *thank you* can provide a contributor with a sense of purpose.

Appreciation is recognizing someone for their behavior, actions, or impact. It is a vital element of optimizing a contributor's performance and needs to be a line item in every organization's budget.

We can't ignore the influence of external acknowledgment. We all have egos, and appreciation at some level may be the motivation to stay the course for greater things to come. Yetnebersh Nigussie shares her reality of what keeps her motivated to be a trailblazer.

> I am being recognized for every single thing I am doing. The more I am recognized, the more I feel I need to do better to be recognized for something even more impactful.

Incorporating appreciation as part of your conscious-contribution philosophy will inspire those alongside you. Different things motivate different people. Combining reward (a gift for a goal achieved) and recognition (an unexpected acknowledgment) is a compelling way to attract, retain, and inspire stakeholders.

Recognition appeals to the receiver at a more fundamental level. It stirs emotions of pride, dignity, and acceptance, which also satisfy the ego. According to a study done by Interact, the number one complaint of 63 percent of employees is a lack of appreciation from managers.[86]

Colleagues want their contributions to be noticed, acknowledged, and appreciated. Millennials, especially, crave being part of a solution and want to know they've had an impact.

Appreciate with C.A.R.R.E: Communicate it, be authentic, make it relevant and respectful, and be explicit about the behavior you are acknowledging.

Acknowledgment can create a domino effect of positive actions. Recognition can be expressed in person, in a written note, through a gift, or publicly at a meeting or a ceremony. Making it relevant to the receiver will pack the biggest punch. For example, if saying thank you with a donation, make it to the receiver's charity of choice. Appreciation doesn't need to be complicated; it just needs to happen.

Thank often, praise many, appreciate the unexpected, compliment in detail, celebrate collaborators, and recognize your team at every opportunity. Learn what they care about and appreciate and promote them accordingly.

Promote

Leading for longevity is about caring enough, cultivating, inspiring, and appreciating an individual to promote them to their potential — whether that is working with you, or encouraging them to spread their wings.

A conscious leader's job is to select who in the organization's talent pool could be groomed and earmarked for an essential leadership position. These individuals are then nurtured and developed in preparation for any foreseen or unforeseen vacancy. Invite the candidate to lead who has the desire, acumen, and capacity while offering continuity. With any conscious-contribution, its ripple effect is only as powerful as the next wave. Without succession planning, the water that sustained an organization's growth can evaporate. Having a network to pull from will provide a life raft if the unexpected occurs.

Nigest Haile helps women build their businesses through long-term oriented business practices. No matter whether you are leading a business, social enterprise, an organization, or a conscious-contribution, the principles are the same.

> When they do grow and start making money, they don't need to do everything anymore, yet they still want to do everything. Entrepreneurs cannot find their replica, but women want that. They have to employ someone they can train to succeed them. They need to learn to delegate. The more people employed, the more an entrepreneur can delegate, and the more resources they need, but the more profits they can make.

Philippa Reiss Thorne was a successor at Gone Rural whose passion and natural capacity to lead helped elevate the craft company and its social contribution. She changed her approach to helping her team to lead sooner:

> [I would have believed] more in the capabilities of the staff and invested in them. We are offering the women shares in the business and had a two-day leadership session where we present a new corporate model. They said they were afraid to take responsibility. That is why I suggested getting people more involved sooner. For me, the biggest challenge has been letting go of responsibility.

As tempting as it is to groom a successor and make them your clone, this strategy won't produce the best business growth or community impact. We need to dig into our feminine energy and curtail our ego to seek the successor that will serve the whole. The successor should have aligned vision, mission, and values, and the necessary skills. That is where the similarities can end. Your successor can be someone with different strengths, personality, and experiences, as the successor may see the blind spots of the organization or conscious-contribution. Some of the best partnerships, personal or professional, have aligned values, but contrasting personalities.

Part of the leadership obligation is to ensure someone can continue to live the leader's legacy. Gladys Ogallo feels that each leader must pull someone up.

> Many women who make it to the top have a desire to mentor other women. I often will say to women it is important to succeed, but you don't want to get there alone; you will be lonely. Let's get there, but also carry our sisters along with us.

Olive Luena takes that advice to heart. She was very thoughtful in putting a plan together so that Tanzania Gatsby Trust will continue upon her retirement.

> As a leader, I believe in succession planning. When I retire in two years, this organization continues and is even better than when I was here. I believe in mentoring my staff. I believe in coaching, training, and motivating them. I had to stand firm about my career so I can pull others up.

Make your contribution count

Incorporating *lead for longevity* practices will establish a conscious culture whereby the team is inspired, and their talents are retained to benefit the organization and the community it serves. No matter whether you are leading an organization or a conscious-contribution, whether you are colleague, volunteer, or professional-contributor, using principles that promote conscious leadership will elicit diverse opinions, creative thinking, and innovative execution.

Reflect on how to make your conscious-contributions™

1. How transparent are you with the people you want to engage with? Why is that?
2. To create a conscious culture where you solicit diverse perspectives, would you have to change anything about yourself?
3. Are you aware of your actions and the messages they portray to the people around you?
4. What leadership practices do you utilize? Which ones need attention?
5. How can you prepare youth to feel empowered to contribute to an initiative?
6. How can you recognize your stakeholders to let them know they are appreciated?
7. Can you identify a successor for your contribution, or would you like to be a successor for an initiative? What next step can you take to make it a reality?

Chapter 23
All we need is love

Words of Wisdom

Be yourself. Know your strengths and develop those strengths. Focus on the positive and let the negative wash by. Love will guide you.

Sheila Freemantle, founder, Tintsaba Master Weavers, the Kingdom of eSwatini
Pioneer: founder of first social enterprise in eSwatini, co-founder Swaziland Fair Trade organization

Dedicated in loving memory of Sheila Freemantle

On June 3, 2012, we arrived at Sheila Fremantle's homestead, surrounded by mountains, gardens, and powerful spiritual energy. To learn about the organization Sheila envisioned coming to fruition in eSwatini, and how it provided a livelihood for more than 900 handcrafters, was beyond inspiring. Sheila opened her home and heart to us.

Piggs Peak is on the North Western border of eSwatini, which meant we had a few hours to drive. Sheila generously invited us to stay overnight in her cozy home before the interview. We enjoyed the evening with Sheila and her 28-year-old daughter, Tengetile, whom Sheila and Richard adopted when she was seven. Richard being in forestry unfortunately meant he was working at a remote location and unable to join us. I had hoped to meet the partner of this tiny but mighty woman.

As we sat in Sheila's living room, she shared her passion for astrology, the power of her meditation, and the love for Swazi women. We enjoyed a vegetarian meal prepared by Tengetile.

When we awoke early the next morning, Sheila had breakfast on the table. She had been up since 4:00 a.m., already connected with the universe through her meditation, a practice that grounded her and prepare her for the day.

Following breakfast, Mike and I were swept up into the Tintsaba rituals. With the workshop at the homestead, we didn't need to go far to meet the leadership team and watch them prepare for the day. We all gathered in a circle surrounded by mountain peaks, the early morning dew on the ground, and positive energy engulfing us. Sheila started with a welcome and a prayer of hope and collaboration. Brain gym continued the ritual; exercises focusing on cross-pollinating analytical skills with creativity.

After we were all aligned for the day, Sheila encouraged each of the 10 women to share words of gratitude. One said she was grateful for family, another mentioned the opportunity to work at Tintsaba, and to my surprise, many said they were grateful for Mike's and my visit. I was overwhelmed. Tears flowed down my face as my gratitude was becoming apparent. When they asked me to share, I wiped my eyes. "I'm grateful for these tears because they are from the warm welcome I'm experiencing. I'm also grateful that one day I'll have the opportunity to share your collective success with so many."

I could no longer compose myself, overcome by the powerful energy of this circle of women who had been suppressed and now have a market for their talents.

As the group dispersed, the work of the day began. Mike and I went on a tour of the process of what makes a master weaver, and how the silversmiths refine jewelry. After admiring their skills, we set up in a garden to dive into the mind and soul of Sheila Freemantle. We didn't know this would be the last time we would speak with her.

Lead with love

During our interview Sheila shared a story about attending an International Folk Art Alliance Market in Santa Fe California with the annual master weaver winner.

> At the event attendees remarked that they could feel the love radiate from the baskets and one of our master weavers replied: 'Do you know we cannot weave a basket if we are in a bad mood?'

Love is the energy we feel when an offering is infused with deep affection. That was Sheila. She imbued everything she did, and everyone she touched with love. Sheila dedicated her entire life and business to the universe and the love it provides.

> I believe putting love into our products creates excellence. Putting love into our work means the staff enjoy themselves. Putting love into themselves, they are happy to be here. The more we can put love and joy into everything we do, into all the training, to have a holistic approach where we care about the health, the brain development, provide a mobile clinic, organic garden, it becomes a pride to become part of Tintsaba.

Sheila's approach to leadership was to recognize and learn about each woman as an individual. She hired an organizational therapist to learn her team's personality traits and to guide her on how to engage each individual. She did strength and weakness assessments and harnessed her team's talents to get the best out of them, less to benefit the organization than to advance their well-being. By starting each meeting with brain gym, Sheila describes:

> It is important for me and the full-time staff to develop our creative side, as we are often doing left-brain activities. It gives us a point of stillness, calmness. If there are outside problems, it gives us time to clear that energy so we can focus on work.

> We want women to respect the earth, to be grateful. We believe that gratitude is the beginning of development. We have a philosophy where we say, 'Well done, myself.'

> We build each person and positivity spreads quite rapidly. The more we push positivity, the more we change the balance between the positivity and negativity in each person, the more they are happy inside.

Because Tintsaba is far-reaching, many women are in rural communities and will never visit the workshop. Sheila's business structure insured the love reached them wherever they weave their masterpieces. Each artisan group has a leader who created a ripple effect by replicating the model of gratitude and love.

> We do skills training with each rural group, three to five different programs. We also do motivational training. We start any meeting or buying day, any group leaders meeting with brain gym. We include prayer and God. During the process, we start laying the foundation of working with love.

> I think this is one of Tintsaba's strengths that we recognize each woman as an individual, and we want to build her economically, mentally, psychologically at every opportunity. Those who show promise, they start at a different level and then grow into roles.

> We create a culture of not hiding but communicating our mistakes. We all need to develop communication skills. Fair Trade instills this philosophy of having the groups come to a conclusion. We practice ubuntu, collectively coming to a decision rather than feeling it is being imposed.

> There is a lot of structure involved in Tintsaba — first the structure, then the love, then altogether.

The birth of a social enterprise

Sheila and her husband arrived in eSwatini in 1982. As Richard continued his career in forestry, Sheila was seeking more meaning and craved to contribute to her local community.

> Because I came from South Africa and grew up with that legacy of apartheid, we wanted to correct that. We wanted to live in a country where color and race were not an issue. We thought we could make a difference here. I thought people were willing to organize themselves here to make life better.

> My education is in development and African languages, and I wanted to make a difference, particularly with rural women in Africa. I also have a passion for quality, and I appreciate the fine textures of traditional craft and use that as a motivator to create products of excellence and uniqueness.

Sheila and Richard found a small, dilapidated craft market in the town of Piggs Peak. Richard describes:

> The tiny structure had burned down and no one seemed to notice its absence. Sheila and I discussed the possibility of starting a market. A friend overheard us and said he was interested and would put up the capital, US$530 in today's money. We found a small room at the local hotel and opened in April 1985. Sheila was there seven days a week. A government field officer introduced Sheila to a group of six women who were making traditional baskets, and together they refined the craft of the fine work one sees today.[87]

As Tintsaba grew, a network of crafting companies aligned by embracing the Fair Trade practices. Sheila formed Swaziland Fair Trade (SWIFT), with four others, one of which was Gone Rural, with the support of their primary funder a UK organization, Comic Relief.

Sheila's desire to improve the craft industry and the lives of the women meant she was continuously educating herself so she could teach others. With 50 percent of her team being semi-literate and 25 percent being illiterate, Sheila implemented an accelerated literacy program, funded mainly by the Sahee Foundation from Switzerland and to a lesser extent, Tintsaba. This two-year course had terrific results, both practically for the students' self-esteem and Tintsaba's business.

Education didn't stop. Richard shares:

> Sheila enrolled in a homeopathic course and with a friend founded a roving clinic that visits our groups on the same days as we do field runs. In its sixth year now, it is the only course in her life that she couldn't finish.

When Sheila returned from the International Folk Art Alliance Market in Santa Fe, she arrived in a wheelchair, with stage four cancer.

Sheila passed away on October 29, 2012, six months after our interview.

Being of the Jewish faith, Sheila was buried within two days of her death, leaving many of the rural weavers unable to say good-bye. Richard responded by having a memorial a month later so the Tintsaba family could attend, and 200 people came to say goodbye to Sheila.

At significant expense, one weaver attended. She had to say goodbye to Sheila. She told Richard, "I'm forever indebted to Tintsaba for educating my children."

Richard responded, "It was your hard work that educated your children."

That is what the social enterprise provided: A living that empowered women to own their future.

The Tintsaba management, weavers, and their families felt the tremendous loss. Every weaver is estimated to provide for eight family members, therefore over 7000 Swazis questioned their future.

With no successor, the outlook for Tintsaba was in question.

Two decisions changed what could have been the demise of Tintsaba. Sheila's decision to collaborate with competitors through SWIFT meant that other handcraft companies assisted when the social enterprise was in distress. Sheila's husband who decided, *you led, and now I will follow*, sold his forestry company to continue Sheila's legacy.

Richard now faced the reality of leading a social enterprise.

> With 30 years of running errands for Tintsaba, I was surprised and embarrassed at how little I knew. We then came to realize how much Sheila had been doing. We'd overlooked the marketing aspect a bit, expecting regular customers to continue to place orders. I had never done any marketing in my life, so I concentrated on production as usual. Soon we had a storeroom full of stock and no money in the bank.

A neighbor's daughter had a marketing background and taught them the basics. A year later, it paid off.

Richard's partner in life and love awed and inspired him:

> Sheila worked with such passion in all she did. This can only be driven by love. This then becomes infectious. The staff is so proud to work for Tintsaba, working for very little for so long. My single goal is to correct this. Friends and associates are always interested in Tintsaba and willing to help, people want to be associated with us, and that too is driven by love.

When asked, 'What it's like to be swimming in someone's wake?' Well, actually it feels like surfing. Sometimes you fall off, but it's exhilarating.

YouMeWe is a customer of the exclusive uniquely designed, colorful, high quality, renewable sisal baskets. It can take up to 50 hours to make a small basket, and with every stitch, it is woven with love to create a masterpiece. *You, me,* and *we* can use more love.

Sheila attributed her business longevity to:

> Having discipline and structure in your business helps create boundaries. Persevere knowing if you do something from the heart, it will work out. If doing it for a higher ideal, the end will be successful.

For the love of humanity

Ela Gandhi profoundly describes the need for peace in the world.

> We need to acknowledge that we need to be humble and to acknowledge that we don't have the answers to everything on the earth. Despite the fact that we have scriptures, we cannot say that those scriptures give you an answer which is acceptable to everyone. It may be acceptable to me; another answer will be acceptable to you. We need to grant that space to people. So, diversity is an important aspect of life. We love different colors in flowers, in drawings, in paintings — why can't we embrace that diversity in human beings? If we were all the same and thought the same things, how dull would life be?

> We should appreciate our diversity, embrace it, respect it and then learn to live with it. Killing diversity, which is what we are doing presently, we don't like it, we kill it. I think it is the worst thing that humankind has done in the last few centuries. They have just decided that diversity is bad.

Ela shares what Gandhi said, "All religions have certain basic shared values. The rituals and the beliefs are somewhat different, but the values are the same." Embedded in those values is love.

Although we are diverse, at our core we need the same essentials to survive: food, water, shelter, safety and health. We also need the same conditions to flourish: education, growth, connection, confidence, meaning, and love.

Make your contribution count

My philosophy is to treat people equally while at the same time, differently. Meaning don't treat people the way you want to be treated, but rather the way they want to be treated. We are all unique and bring value to society. Respecting our diversity will allow love to flourish. Our uniqueness will assist in self-actualizing ourselves and guide us in how we transcend, where we will live our most meaningful life, where love is at the core.

Reflect on how to make your conscious-contributions™

1. Under what circumstance could you alter your course, en route to living your most meaningful life?
2. How do you embrace diversity?
3. How are you bringing the principle of love into your leadership, life, and legacy?

Chapter 24
The time is now

A social shift is prevailing. Pioneering African women inspire us to *make our contribution count*. Consumers are scrutinizing the supply chain, dialoguing about our responsibility to citizens and the environment, and taking action. Millennials are demanding to work for mission-driven organizations. Corporations are utilizing strategies to attract, retain, and inspire workforces through volunteerism. There is a measure to assess social and environmental corporate contributions focusing on an inclusive and sustainable economy. Not-for-profits are tracking the social return on investment. There is a surge of creating, assisting, and promoting social enterprises. Organizations are rallying around to achieve the United Nations 2030 Sustainable Development Goals. There is a rise in recognizing feminine energy's power, potential, and impact. Diversity is a conversation happening in board rooms. More people are seeking purpose and crave meaning. Our mental health craves to know what is right with the world. There is an appetite for a global movement to raise human consciousness and contribution. All these indicators lead to an ethos, a movement, and a social enterprise whose time has come — YouMeWe.

LOVE AND CARE ARE values not traditionally associated with the work environment. Being a caring organization is rarely linked with being competitive, but it is essential in creating a conscious culture, where care is a cornerstone.

More organizations are becoming conscious of how and with whom they do business. As you embark on this journey of conscious-contributions, and are either evaluating or creating your operational values, consider the foundation on which you want to build your organization's practices. What guiding principles do you want stakeholders to have? Communicate them; promote people who embody them; celebrate those who emulate them.

YouMeWe embeds love into our core values. Each value has context and meaning behind the words. The words themselves, although compelling, don't tell the entire story or echo the intended philosophy. The combination of values are guidelines to live your most meaningful life. When the values are connected, the overarching ethos of YouMeWe emerges — WE ARE ONE.

Contribution – Contribute to the betterment of society in line with your purpose and mission.

Consciousness – Adhere to ethical practices while considering the impact of your decisions on the greater community.

Consistency – Implement sustainable solutions that rely on steady income generation that produces a long-term social impact.

Inclusivity – Promote the social, economic, and political inclusion of all in the execution of your contribution.

Care – Encourage an attitude of care and mutual respect for all stakeholders, people, and the planet.

Empowerment – Implement contributions to empower the people executing the initiative and the recipients of it.

Collaboration – Encourage open dialogue, consider all stakeholders' perspectives, and seek partners to optimize impact.

Courage – To seek innovative solutions to optimize positive social, economic, or environmental impact.

YouMeWe Manifesto

By embracing these values, we invite you to uphold the YouMeWe manifesto where you care for fellow global citizens through consistent conscious-contributions. You have the courage to be inclusive and empower members of society through collaboration because WE ARE ONE.

I leave you here to contemplate your role in the social, economic, and environmental evolution.

Through our journey
of mining wisdom from 70 African women
in 17 countries, there appeared to be
a message in our midst,
a message for the world,
a message that had a mission attached
so formidable that it could not be squandered.
It was the message of ubuntu:
I am because we are.

Anyone who has traveled to Sub-Saharan Africa
has been bitten by its power
and consumed by its energy.
Pioneering women seemed to believe that each of us has a duty
to serve humanity for the greater good.

As we absorb this message,
we become obligated to share their guidance,
to research it, to understand it, to organize it,
and ultimately communicate it
to people who crave to suppress the negative
and reverberate the positive.

By embracing the YouMeWe manifesto,
you care for fellow global citizens
through consistent, conscious-contributions.
You have the courage to be inclusive
and empower members of society through collaboration
because WE ARE ONE.

We realize many won't be able to hear the message
through the chatter of the media
where every day we are bombarded with negative,

Part 3: we — make your contribution count — sustainably

destructive, and corruptive noise,
where every tragedy is instantly in our hands.

The reality is,
avoiding many of the people-made incidents
is also in our hands.
Using technology for good,
to empower, to cultivate,
and to celebrate our conscious-contributions
can turn the negative preoccupation
into positive life affirmation.

This force of energy can create
a powerful wave.
People all over the world have implemented
innovative ideas for the love of humanity.
These ideas celebrate our difference
and galvanize our sameness.
They promote inclusion and kindness.
This is a wave we all can surf,
as it leads to the shores of unity
and creates a ripple effect of connecting all people to each other
and ensures all living things matter.

Now, that is the world we can live in!
Collectively we have an enormous opportunity to create a profound movement,

It just starts with one – YOU.

ONE person. ONE decision. ONE consistent conscious-contribution.

We have the power to weave the world together.

What choice will you make?

To stay the course or to *make your contribution count*?

Now, imagine, what if we all made the same choice.

#YourContributionCounts

Acknowledgments

Thank you for entrusting your time with me on this journey. I know it is precious, and for you to share it reading this book, I'm grateful.

Africans say it takes a village, and no more authentic sentiment applies to this book. The journey wouldn't have started without the love, support, and willingness of my business partner, best friend, and husband. In 2010 when Michael Gingerich said, "you lead, and I will follow," neither of us knew how far we would travel. He has taken a leadership role in so many elements of our journey. Mike was the videographer and photographer and captured each pioneer's essence. His wisdom and recall of the details rounded out the manuscript. And his assistance with the design and the execution were instrumental. Most importantly, I appreciate his love and being my cornerstone on route to bringing our mission to the world.

This book and the wisdom in it would have never been possible without the seventy pioneering African women we interviewed. Their spirit, generosity, and perspectives engulfed me with every word I wrote. To receive a glimpse into strangers' lives was such an extraordinary gift. I will be forever grateful for the willingness to open their doors and hearts to Mike and me. Their insights have forever changed my perspective on how to consciously contribute, lead, and live a life of *we*.

Forever grateful to: Sara Abera, Hellen Acham, Doo Aphane, Meaza Ashenafi, Christine Asiko, Rusia Orikiriza Bariho, Dorothy Baziwe, Hilina Belete, Samrawit Beyene, Margareth Chacha, Nouzha Chekrouni, Florence Zano Chideya, Nelisiwe Zanele DeSousa, Angela Dick, Dudu Dlamini, Thandiwe Stella Dlamini, Sheila Freemantle, Marsha Gabriel, Ela Gandhi, Bience Gawanas, Gita Goven, Tisha Greyling, Nigest Haile, Hanne Howard, Katherine Ichoya, Regina Ingabire, Mulumebet Iori, Audrey Kahara-Kawuki, Immy Kamarade, Beti Olive Kamya, Rehmah Kasule, Irene Kiwia, Olive Luena, Lerato Majara, Modesta Lilian Mahiga, Mwamvita Makamba, Thandeka Mazibuko, Tereza Mbire, Happiness Mchomvu, Gcina Mhlophe, Xolile Mkhwanazi, Gladys Muhunyo, Susan Muhwezi, Zulfat Mukarubega, Mbabazi Mulinda Grace, Eva Muraya, Joyce Muraya, Christine Murebwayire, Lydia Muso, Antonia Mutoro, Joanne Mwangi, Benedicta N. Nanyonga, Leah Ngini, Yetnebersh Nigussie, Fikile Nkosi, Janet Nkubana, Norah Odwesso, Gladys Ogallo, Sylvia Owori, Philippa Reiss Thorne, Jennifer Riria, Sibongile Sambo, Maria Sarungi Tsehai, Teryl Schroenn, Hajjat

Acknowledgments

Aphwa Sebyala, Lois Shaw, Elizabeth Thande, Jane Trembath, Jane Wathome, Gia Whitehead, and Lydia Zingoni.

In a village, some neighbors encourage you from afar, and others help with the heavy lifting. I was fortunate to have dear friends assist in the book editing process to ensure the readers' journey was going to be a pleasant experience. Nicki Agnew took her editing brilliance and insightful perspective and shared it freely. Susan Kawa guided issues close to both of our hearts. She ensured inclusivity was coming through in the writing as she combed through to proofread the manuscript.

After a significant re-edit, the first person I entrusted with a labor of love was Helen Wilkie. I appreciate her holding my words gently and editing this vital message. Grateful to Tiffany Maxwell, who provided invaluable feedback in the first draft. I appreciate the creative flair of Carla Wynn Foster and Jushua Mancil in creating a cover that honors the women who inspired this book.

Thank you to Ruth Douglas for inviting me to join the first WOW African adventure in 2007. Ruth has offered an ear and been an advocate for all my initiatives supporting women. She has never faltered, and for that, I'm genuinely grateful. To Lois Shaw, for being the instigator to gather a group of Western women to visit with, learn from, and contribute to her neighbors in Kenya. Our in-depth conversations about contribution and the realities of helping or hurting were the catalyst for deep reflection and the window that opened the door to my role. You are a wonderful host and ambassador for Kenya. Mark and Lois continuously inspired me and always offered warm hospitality in their home away from home. Thank you to my fellow travelers on that first African adventure: Karen Anning, Gail Pennington, Pat McNamara, Kathy Sutton, Lynn Shinn, Susan Rutherford Dianne Finn-Kelcey, Katherine Haine, Linda Taylor, Louise and Michael Berube, Barbara Heney, Megan Douglas, Jeanne Bryceland, Patricia Manson, Lisa Hyde, and Ruth Douglas, Nicki Agnew, and Susan Kawa. Through their eyes, I started to see how to offer value to the developing world.

A village isn't complete without caring neighbors. Friends, authors, creative thinkers, and supporters encircled me. Without the moral support of Deri Latimer, I don't know if this book would have seen the light. I'm grateful for her check-ins, willingness to listen, and for her words of encouragement. Both Deri and Jennifer Spear were generous with their insights into YouMeWe Social Impact Group's direction, and the nuances of this book. Their availability to offer perspective, while ensuring I was inflated to carry on the journey was invaluable. Thank you to my other mastermind members: Cate Collins, for your love, openness, and insight; Meg Soper for your humor; and Peri Shawn for your book publishing guidance over the years and encouraging this path.

I appreciated the friends we made during this journey. Many welcomed us into their homes or offered friendship during our travels. Mary and George Ogalo, who challenged and inspired me. I'm proud to call them friends. Fortuna Tioya, for being my first Kenyan friend. Watching Mary and Fortuna turn into influential women emphasized why investing in higher education is the gateway to women's potential and impact. Thanks to Samuel Mwangi for igniting me to share my knowledge with Kenyans. It was his passion and contribution to help the vulnerable that opened my mind to contribute my expertise. I appreciate the generosity of the entire Thorne family in eSwatini for making their home ours for an extended period. Daniella Mastracci, a fellow Canadian based in eSwatini, for being gracious with her time and hospitality. Zoe Dean-Smith for welcoming us strangers to stay with her while we were interviewing in Johannesburg and Claire Newton for being our guide in Durban. Mark Berger and his family welcoming us to their home in Cape Town and the entire Professional Speakers Association of Southern Africa, who were our first South Africa guides. We appreciate the special time spent with interviewees Zulfat Mukarubega over dinners, with Tereza Mbire and her son over lunch; and Leah Ngini and daughters on several occasions. I reflect fondly on my gal time with the pioneering women of Ethiopia that truly opened their homes and social networks to us. Samrawit Beyene, Mulu Iori, and their gracious husbands, Thomas Mattanovich and Carlo Iori, along with Genet Kebede; thank you for being connectors and enhancing our Ethiopian experience.

Thank you to Africa International University and its students, residents, and faculty for always making us feel welcome. We appreciated Kamal Maggie for organizing some of our travels, and for Richard for escorting us on some adventures. Thanks to Harrison, our Kenyan driver, who not only got us to many interviews and sites but provided thought-provoking insights into leadership, business, family, and Kenya's future. No home is complete without a Mama. Linnet Otieno continually welcomed us back to Kijiji Guesthouse where she always offered a warm hug when we arrived from a long journey.

I appreciate Kathleen Holland for connecting us to some interviews and locals in Africa and who was a constant connection to home. The International Alliance of Women's yearly awards made finding pioneers less challenging and many other local publications and people

Acknowledgments

who brought accomplished women to our attention.

The village is never complete without those who arrive just in time to offer a helping hand. There are several people in my professional association (Canadian Association of Professional Speakers) that provided me with the contacts or insights needed to make educated publishing choices. Thank you to Janet Rouss, Lea Brovedani, Dana Pharant, Sarah McVanel, Stephanie Staples, Sylvia Plester-Silk, Rhonda Scharf, Paula Morand, Dan Poynter, and Peter Chapman.

A heartfelt thank you to the book reviewers who instantly said they would be happy to read. It is in these moments when respected individuals say yes, you feel your village has become more extensive. Thank you to Aaron Hurst, Roxanne Joyal, Modesta Mahiga-Mbughuni, Susan Kawa, Jennifer Spear, Cate Collins, Jen Scholte, Joanne Mwangi, Diane Tompson, Shelby Taylor and Vicki Saunders.

The journey and depth of insight were possible because of the institutions, researchers, government websites, and authors that have traveled before and alongside me. I am grateful for experiencing the shift in consciousness coming from businesses, institutions, not-for-profits, and consumers.

Appreciative to Rotarian, Frank Tilley, and friend George Jeril, both who bought my first and second book months before it was published. Your faith and encouragement moved me. Thank you to my local bar staff for asking about the book's progression every time I was a patron. I appreciate my mother-in-law, Barbara Gingerich, who would text to ask, "When can I buy Suzanne's book?" This interest encouraged me when it felt like I would never finish.

Lastly, thank you to my family for the dinner debates that taught me to ask insightful questions. Thanks to my parents, Virginia and Robert Stevens, for treating me as an equal to my three older brothers. You instilled in me the curiosity to travel, the courage to be uncomfortable, the appreciation for taking the scenic route, and the wisdom to know when it's time to come home. Your support of all my adventures gives me the will to have more.

To each and everyone one of you — Your Contribution Counts!

About the author

Suzanne F. Stevens, Conscious-Contribution™ Cultivator and amplifier of social contributors' voices. She is a social entrepreneur, volunteer, and philanthropist. She provides keynotes, training, facilitation, panel moderation, interviews, and a women's social impact leadership community.

Suzanne has worked with fortune 500 companies on five continents since 2000 and has interviewed leaders and entrepreneurs in 21 countries. She now brings her business-building insights and YouMeWe ethos to small businesses and organizations internationally.

Suzanne is a Certified Speaking Professional (CSP-one of 70 in Canada, among 15% of professional speakers globally), past national president of The Canadian Association of Professional Speakers (CAPS), and multi-service award recipient. She has received the TIAW World of Difference Award for women economic empowerment. In 2019 she received the Peter Legge Philanthropic Award, and the Sovereign's Medal for Volunteers, Canada's highest volunteer honor. She is the co-founder of YouMeWe Social Impact Group: WisdomExchangeTv, YouMeWe Amplified, YouMeWe Media, YouMeWe Foundation Fund, and YouMeWe Movement.

In every speaking engagement, Suzanne brings her audiences to the front row by using a customized approach, her entrepreneurial and leadership experience, her many international adventures, human observations, slice of humor, and interactive process to get the audience to explore how to *make their contribution count.*

Suzanne is an "interactive, thought-provoking, dynamic speaker" who shares strategies on how to implement conscious-contributions consistently for you, your company, in the community, and beyond. She transforms perspectives on how to maximize personal meaning, while attracting, engaging, and retaining colleagues, customers, and collaborators - profitably.

Utilizing the YouMeWe ethos, Suzanne ignites a culture where **your contribution counts • for you • your company • your community.**

YouMeWe resources

Subscribe to **weWednesdays** — a short weekly video infusion on how to make your contribution count · for you · your company · your community. https://youmewe.ca/wewednesdays/

Join the **YouMeWe community: Women leaders driving social impact** — Join a one-of-a-kind community. If you are a leader who wishes to maximize your meaning, grow your business while having a social, economic, or environmental impact...this community is for you! https://youmeme.ca/women-entrepreneurs-community/

Subscribe to receive **WisdomExchangeTv interviews** — Suzanne is the host of a web platform Tv show and podcast, where socially conscious contributors internationally are highlighted. These leaders have consciously contributed to their community, country or beyond. Learn how you can apply their strategies to your contributions and business. https://wisdomexchangetv.com/

Learn more about **YouMeWe Foundation Fund** – Donate to provide higher education scholarships to women in Africa. Investing in the future leaders of a continent. Real change now. https://www.youmewefoundation.org/

Participate in #**YourContributionCounts Campaign** — Share your or celebrate someone's conscious-contributions™. For every listing, YouMeWe will invest US$1 in a woman's business or education. Investing to turn poverty into prosperity. https://youmewe.ca/your-contribution-counts/

Visit the **YouMeWe blog** – to gain insight how to make your contribution count — sustainably. https://youmewe.ca/youmewe-blog/

Visit the **book community for additional resources** for your journey on how to *make your contribution count*, at https://youmewe.ca and use **MyContributionCounts** promotion code to gain access.

To **order books** please visit
https://youmewe.ca/make-your-contribution-count-book/
(Special pricing for book clubs and conscious-contribution™ circles.)

To **purchase books** in bulk, email us at: we@youmewe.ca

Glossary to guide your journey

Cause: any charitable undertaking, such as civil rights, education, or disease

Compassion-connection™: a group of people or issue that a person has a profound concern or care for and acts upon

Conscious-contributions™: understanding the needs of those you would like to contribute to while being conscious of the implications of fulfilling those needs

Conscious-contribution circle: a gathering of a group of like-minded individuals who collaborate to consciously contribute to society

Contribution continuum: indicates different degrees of contribution from passive to active and money drive to mission motivated: a range of time, energy, and focus is indicated

Contributing vs. giving: giving is handing something over that you may or may not want; often a short transaction. Contributing has more emphasis on helping to achieve the desired outcome

Edgeness™: describes an enhanced version of oneself discovered while pushing the edge of one's comfort zone

Feminine energy: reflects qualities that embrace willpower, nurture, courage, humility, intuition, compassion, collaboration, integrity, and authenticity

Impact statement: a clearly defined goal that focuses on the desired impact; incorporates outcomes, beneficiary, and time frame, typically less than 5 years

Key performance indicators: specific metrics that demonstrate if a mandate is being achieved within specified time

Meaning: is a soulful feeling when one's authentic self serves something greater than the individual

Meaning vs. mission vs. purpose: a purpose is lived; a mission is pursued; meaning is realized. You maximize your meaning when you live your purpose, pursue a mission, and progress society

Measure: a value that can be summed or averaged

Micro-enterprise: usually a business that has less than five employees; in Canada, defined as having 1 – 4 employees[88]

Metric: one or more measures that are used to track and assess a specific process

Mission: a strongly felt aim, ambition, or calling that transcends self-interests and exists to benefit the whole

Movement: informal groupings that focus on specific political or social issues to carry out, resist, or undo a social change

Not-for-profit (NFP) is used as a universal term throughout this book to include *non-profits, foundations, registered charities,* **and** *non-government organizations*

> **Registered charities**: are charitable organizations, public or private foundations that are created and reside in country of residence. They must use their resources for charitable activities such as: the relief of poverty, the advancement of education or religion, and other purposes that benefit the community.[89]
>
> **Non-profit organizations (NPO):** are associations, clubs, or societies that are not charities and are organized and operated exclusively for social welfare, civic improvement, pleasure, recreation, or any other purpose except profit. NPO, contrary to their name can make a profit, however, can't be designed primarily for profit making.[90]
>
> **Non-governmental organization (NGO):** is any non-profit, voluntary citizens' group, which is organized on a local, national, or international level. Task-oriented and driven by people with a common social (often including human rights or health) or environmental purpose. NGOs perform a variety of service and humanitarian functions: bring citizen concerns to Governments, advocate and monitor policies and encourage political participation through provision of information. NGO's are not limited by short-term financial objectives, and therefore tend to engage in long-term pursuits.[91]

Professional-contributor™: is a person who provides expertise, accountability, and professional attitude in an unpaid role to advance the organization's mandate

Purpose: the reason we / an organization exists

Self-actualize: the fulfillment of one's talents and potential, especially considered as a drive or need present in everyone

Self-transcendence: rising above the self and relating to something greater[92]

Social collateral: a form of insurance on a microfinancing loan where in a group, if someone can't pay the loan, the group takes on the responsibility

Social enterprise: uses commercial practices to have a social, economic, or environmental impact and measures both *social return on investment* and profitability

Socially conscious enterprise: a business that aims to have a positive social, economic, or environmental impact

Social return on investment (SROI): is a method of measuring the social, economic, and environmental impact calculated by evaluating the ratio of every dollar spent to how many dollars' worth of social value is created

Stakeholder: person with an interest or concern in an organization (i.e., customers, clients, colleagues, collaborators, employees, beneficiaries, benefactors, suppliers)

Strategy: broad methods to achieve a vision

Symbiotic partnership: a sustainable long-term partnership where collaborators benefit from an ongoing relationship and refer to each other for strategic insight and synergies

Theory of transformation: a social gauge to measure the progress between strategies implemented, the performance expected, and results realized

Values: the behavior required to deliver on all aspirations

Vision: what you or an organization aspires to achieve; a vivid, imaginative conception or view, of how the world will look once your mission is largely realized

Pioneering African women listing and links

Abera, Sara: founder of the first Ethiopian company to obtain highly-coveted International Fair Trade Association membership https://wisdomexchangetv.com/sara-abera/

Acham, Hellen: founder of North Chilli Association that promotes production and peace in Northern Uganda https://wisdomexchangetv.com/hellen-acham/

Aphane, Doo: first female land-owner and women's activist in eSwatini https://wisdomexchangetv.com/doo-aphane/

Ashenafi, Meaza: established the most successful national women's rights advocacy organization: the Ethiopian Women Lawyers Association. Co-founder of the first Ethiopia women's bank. https://wisdomexchangetv.com/meaza-ashenafi/

Asiko, Christine: advocate for dyslexia throughout Africa, Kenya/UK https://wisdomexchangetv.com/christine-asiko/

Bariho, Rusia Orikiriza: under 25 award-winning entrepreneur, environmentalist, Uganda https://wisdomexchangetv.com/rusia-bariho/

Belete, Hilina: part of the leadership team of an Ethiopian life-saving food manufacturer https://wisdomexchangetv.com/hilina-belete/

Beyene, Samrawit: first travel company in Ethiopia that has permanent female guides https://wisdomexchangetv.com/samrawit-moges-beyene/

Chacha, Margareth: first woman to establish a new bank in Tanzania https://wisdomexchangetv.com/margareth-chacha/

Chekrouni, Nouzha: first female Moroccan Minister https://wisdomexchangetv.com/nouzha-chekrouni/

Chideya, Florence Zano: first female and first Zimbabwean Senior diplomat (Dean) in Canada https://www.wisdomexchangetv.com/florence-zano-chideya/

Dick, Angela: formalized temporary employment in South Africa https://www.wisdomexchangetv.com/angela-dick/

Freemantle, Sheila (deceased): co-founder of a Fair Trade organization, SWIFT, and established the first social enterprise in eSwatini https://wisdomexchangetv.com/sheila-freemantle/

Gabriel, Marsha: a social entrepreneur that consults with non-profits in South Africa https://wisdomexchangetv.com/marsha-gabriel/

Gandhi, Ela: honorary international president of the World Conference on Religions for Peace. Carrying Mahatma Gandhi's legacy in South Africa
https://wisdomexchangetv.com/ela-gandhi/

Gawanas, Bience: launched the African Union's Campaign on Accelerated Reduction of Maternal Mortality in Africa (CARMMA)
https://wisdomexchangetv.com/bience-gawanas/

Goven, Gita: second black woman in South Africa to qualify as an architect. The only black women to head an interdisciplinary architectural and urban design practice
https://wisdomexchangetv.com/gita-goven/

Greyling, Tisha: founder of the first public participation company in South Africa
https://wisdomexchangetv.com/tisha-greyling/

Haile, Nigest: founder of the first NGO in Ethiopia. Co-founder of the first Ethiopian women's bank https://wisdomexchangetv.com/nigest-haile/

Howard, Hanne: co-founder of a foundation supporting children in Lenana slum, Kenya/Canada https://wisdomexchangetv.com/hanne-howard/

Ichoya, Katherine: co-creator of COMESA (Common Market for Eastern and Southern Africa) gender policy, co-founder of Maasai market, Kenya
https://wisdomexchangetv.com/katherine-ichoya/

Ingabire, Regina: co-founded a forum for Rwandan youth to exchange ideas about the future of their country post genocide
https://wisdomexchangetv.com/regina-ingabire/

Iori, Mulumebet: established the beauty care industry in Ethiopia
https://wisdomexchangetv.com/mulumebet-iori/

Kahara-Kawuki, Audrey: established the Entrepreneurship Centre at Makerere University, Uganda focusing on SMEs development with special attention to women
https://wisdomexchangetv.com/andre-kahara-kawuki/

Kamarade, Immy: founder of Benishyaka Association, focusing on care and support for widows and orphans in Rwanda
https://wisdomexchangetv.com/immy-kamarade/

Kamya, Beti Olive: first woman to form a political party in Uganda
https://wisdomexchangetv.com/beti-olive-kamya/

Kasule, Rehmah: advocates for women empowerment in Uganda https://wisdomexchangetv.com/rehmah-kasule/

Luena, Olive: founding secretary-general of the Tanzania Association of NGOs
https://wisdomexchangetv.com/olive-luena/

Mahiga, Modesta Lilian: using national media to empower Tanzanian youth. Internationally recognized as one of Africa's Young Leaders
https://wisdomexchangetv.com/modesta-lilian-mahiga/

Makamba, Mwamvita: instrumental in mobilizing maternal health in Tanzania through Vodafone Foundation https://wisdomexchangetv.com/mwamvita-makamba/

Mazibuko, Thandeka: first black student accepted to specialize in radiation oncology in KwaZulu-Natal, South Africa. Brought cancer screening to rural townships https://wisdomexchangetv.com/thandeka-mazibuko/

Mbire, Tereza: co-founder of Uganda Women Finance Trust, a microfinance institution. Founder of Uganda Women Entrepreneurs Association Limited https://wisdomexchangetv.com/tereza-mbire/

Mhlophe, Gcina: internationally renowned storyteller, one of the few woman storytellers in South Africa. Founder of Gcinamasiko Arts and Heritage Trust https://wisdomexchangetv.com/gcina-mhlophe/

Mkhwanazi, Xolile: financial manager in the energy sector in eSwatini. WisdomExchangeTv.com interview not available

Muhunyo, Gladys: first woman to head Information Communication Technology Network in Africa, Kenya https://wisdomexchangetv.com/gladys-muhunyo/

Muhwezi, Susan: chairperson Uganda Women's Effort to Save Orphans https://wisdomexchangetv.com/susan-muhwezi/

Mukarubega, Zulfat: founder of the first Rwanda Tourism University College https://wisdomexchangetv.com/zulfat-mukarubega/

Muraya, Eva: co-founded the Kenya Association of Women Business Owners (KAWBO). Entrepreneurial success in building an award winning regional branding business https://www.wisdomexchangetv.com/eva-muraya/

Muraya, Joyce: led a social enterprise that provides women refugees a safe haven and employment opportunity https://wisdomexchangetv.com/joyce-muraya/

Muso, Lydia: creator of the first Children's Voice online newspaper in Lesotho. Founder of Lesotho Child Counseling Unit, which provides a temporary and safe home for the rehabilitative care of sexually, physically, and emotionally abused children https://wisdomexchangetv.com/lydia-muso/

Mutoro, Antonia: first female executive director at the Institute of Policy Analysis and Research (IPAR), Rwanda https://wisdomexchangetv.com/antonia-mutoro/

Mwangi, Joanne: founder and chair of Federation of Women Entrepreneur Associations. First woman to be awarded an MSK Warrior Award https://wisdomexchangetv.com/joanne-mwangi/

Ngini, Leah: first woman director at Africa International University https://wisdomexchangetv.com/leah-ngini/

Nigussie, Yetnebersh: founder of the first school for abled and differently abled children in Ethiopia. Recognized as one of the most influential advocates for people with disabilities internationally https://wisdomexchangetv.com/yetnebersh-nigussi/

Pioneering African women listing and links

Nkosi, Fikile: first woman in Swaziland to hold a managing director post for an international bank https://wisdomexchangetv.com/fikile-nkosi/

Nkubana, Janet: co-founder of the social enterprise that produces the internationally renowned peace baskets https://wisdomexchangetv.com/janet-nkubana/

Odwesso, Norah: leads reputation management of the Coca-Cola business and its brands across 39 countries in Sub-Saharan Africa https://wisdomexchangetv.com/norah-odwesso/

Ogallo, Gladys: recognized as top 40 under 40. Pioneer of Put Your Best Foot Forward program, a mentoring program for teenage girls in Kenya https://wisdomexchangetv.com/gladys-ogallo/

Owori, Sylvia: one of the leading figures in East Africa's fashion, media, and modeling industries https://www.wisdomexchangetv.com/sylvia-owori/

Reiss Thorne, Philippa: led one of the largest social enterprises in eSwatini https://wisdomexchangetv.com/philippa-reiss-thorne/

Riria, Jennifer: led and transformed the largest women's financial trust spread throughout Kenya https://wisdomexchangetv.com/dr-jennifer-riria/

Sambo, Sibongile: owns the first 100% black female aviation company https://wisdomexchangetv.com/sibongile-sambo/

Sarungi Tsehai, Maria: first recipient in East Africa of the prestigious Commonwealth Vision Awards (UK) for excellence in TV production https://wisdomexchangetv.com/maria-sarungi-tsehai/

Shaw, Lois: creator of Africa by Design, a unique and authentic experience connecting Western women to African realities https://wisdomexchangetv.com/loisshaw/

Trembath, Jane: first female pilot in South Africa qualified to fly the Boeing 747 - 400. First commander of an all-female Boeing crew in South Africa https://wisdomexchangetv.com/jane-trembath/

Wathome, Jane: empowering women with HIV/AIDS within poor communities with spiritual, physical, emotion and economic needs https://wisdomexchangetv.com/jane-wathome/

Whitehead, Gia: recognized as one of South Africa's 100 Brightest Young Minds awarded Top Women Entrepreneur of the Year. Co-founder of a revolutionary business school https://wisdomexchangetv.com/gia-whitehead/

Zingoni, Lydia: first organization that focuses entrepreneurship for teenagers in South Africa https://wisdomexchangetv.com/lydia-zingoni/

Endnotes and references

Chapter 1: Make your contribution conscious

1   Douglas Carew. "Welcome remarks." Africa International University. January 21, 2007.

2   Dambisa Moyo, *Dead Aid: Why Aid is not Working and How There is a Better Way for Africa* (Farrar, Straus and Giroux, New York, 2009, distributed in Canada by Douglas & McIntry Ltd.), 43-44.

3   "Definitions of NGOs." Global NGO community, organization associated with United Nations Department of Public Information. http://www.ngo.org/ngoinfo/define.html (accessed February 1, 2019).

4   The Global Journal. http://www.theglobaljournal.net/ (accessed January 13, 2019).

5   Shelagh Gastrow. "State Security and Civil Society in South Africa." Sangonet. http://www.ngopulse.org/article/2016/05/19/state-security-and-civil-society-south-africa (accessed June 17, 2018).

6   Martin Turcotte. "Donations totalled about $10.6 billion in 2010." Statistics Canada. https://www150.statcan.gc.ca/n1/pub/11-008-x/2012001/article/11637-eng.htm (accessed October 27, 2017).

Chapter 2: Infuse the social gap with feminine energy

7   "Girls Education." The World Bank. https://www.worldbank.org/en/topic/girlseducation#1 (accessed Jan 21, 2019).

8   Phil Borges. *Women Empowered: Inspiring Change in the Emerging World*, (New York: Rizzoli, 2007), 13.

9   "What is Fistula." Fistula Foundation. https://www.fistulafoundation.org/what-is-fistula/ (accessed February 10, 2019).

10   "Mobilizing maternal health in Tanzania." Vodafone and Vodafone Foundation. https://www.vodafone.com/about/vodafone-foundation/our-projects/mobilising-maternal-health (accessed February 15, 2019).

11   Risenga Maluleke, "Quarterly Labour Force Survey Q3: 2018" (Labour Statics, Statics South Africa, 2018), 1.

12   "Impact." TSiBA Future Business Leaders. https://www.tsiba.ac.za/about/our-impact/ (accessed February 10, 2019).

13   Elizabeth Asiedu, Claire Branstette, Neepa Gaekwad-Babulal, Nanivazo Malokele, "The Effect of Women's Representation in Parliament and the Passing of Gender Sensitive Policies." https://www.aeaweb.org/conference/2018/preliminary/paper/an5yEb5h (accessed February 20, 2019).

14   "UN Women calculation based on information provided by Permanent Missions to the United Nations. Some leaders hold positions of both head of government and head of state. Only elected Heads of State have been taken into account." https://www.unwomen.org/en/what-we-do/leadership-and-political-participation/facts-and-figures#notes (accessed September 25, 2019).

15 "Percentage of Women in National Parliament." Inter-Parliamentary Union ranking. https://data.ipu.org/women-ranking?month=9&year=2019 (accessed September 25, 2019).

Chapter 3: Amplify the social impact

16 "Our Impact." Gone Rural. http://www.goneruralswazi.com/bomake-our-impact (accessed January 20, 2019).

Chapter 4: Take small actions to cause big reactions

17 "Fall 2012 Report: Revealing Key Practices for Effective Recognition." *Workforce MOODTracker* 2012, (Globoforce: fall 2012), 4.

Chapter 5: Consider the contribution consequences

18 Patricia Illingworth, Thomas Pogge, and Leif Wenar. *Giving Well: The Ethics of Philanthropy* (Oxford University Press, 2011), 3.

19 Yomi Kazeem. "Getting Schooled: Only ten of the world's top 1,000 universities are in Africa, according to one list." Quartz Africa. https://qz.com/africa/731712/only-ten-of-the-worlds-top-1000-universities-are-in-africa-according-to-one-list/ (accessed January 19, 2019).

Chapter 6: Choose a channel of contribution to induce consciousness

20 Blumberg Segal LLP. "FAQs." Canadian Charity Law. https://www.canadiancharitylaw.ca/faq (accessed February 1, 2019).

21 Imagine Canada. "Sector Impact: What is the Charitable and Nonprofit Sector?" Sector Source. http://sectorsource.ca/research-and-impact/sector-impact (accessed March 10, 2019).

22 Lions Clubs International. "Making History Every day." https://lionsclubs.org/en/discover-our-clubs/interactive-timeline (accessed September 8, 2019).

23 Soroptimist International of the Americas, Inc. "About Us." Soroptimist. https://www.soroptimist.org/about-us/index.html (accessed August 9, 2019).

24 Rotary International. "Who We Are." Rotary. https://www.rotary.org/en/about-rotary (accessed August 15, 2019).

25 International Federation of Red Cross and Red Crescent Societies. "Who We Are." International Red Cross. https://www.ifrc.org/en/who-we-are/ (accessed July 4, 2019).

26 The Global Disaster Preparedness Center. "Kenyans for Kenya (K4K) Initiative." PrepareCenter.org. https://www.preparecenter.org/content/kenyans-kenya-k4k-initiative (accessed June 10, 2019).

27 100 Who Care Alliance. "About Us." http://www.100whocarealliance.org/about-us/list-of-chapters/ (accessed June 10, 2019).

Chapter 7: Measure what matters

28 Mary T. Ogalo. "Home." County Girls Caucus. http://www.countygirlscaucus.com/ (accessed Jan 5, 2019).

29 Mary T. Ogalo. "Country Girls Caucus: Home Bay County Report." Global Bag Project, (Presentation: November 2015).

Endnotes and references

30 "Lake Turkana fish processing plant, Kenya." Infinity 2017. http://busociety.com/lake-turkana-fish-processing-plant-kenya/ (accessed April 15, 2016).

31 Chepkemoi, Joyce. "Countries with the Highest Rates of HIV/AIDs." World Atlas. https://www.worldatlas.com/articles/countries-with-the-highest-rates-of-hiv-aids.html (accessed September 26, 2019).

32 Moyo, *Dead Aid*, 27-28.

33 "The Millennium Development Goals Report 2015." (New York: United Nations, 2015), 3.

34 United Nations. "The Millennium Development Goals Report 2015." 3.

35 United Nations. "The Millennium Development Goals Report 2015." 7.

36 United Nations. "The Millennium Development Goals Report 2015." 11.

37 United Nations. "Social Development for Sustainable Development." Department of Economic and Social Affairs: Social Inclusions. https://www.un.org/development/desa/dspd/2030agenda-sdgs.html (accessed December 20, 2018).

38 SheEO. "Home." http://sheeo.ca/ (accessed January 22, 2019).

39 United Nations. "Transforming our world: the 2030 Agenda for Sustainable Development: Preamble." Sustainable Development Goals: Knowledge Platform. https://sustainabledevelopment.un.org/post2015/transformingourworld (accessed February 20, 2019).

40 United Nations. "Your Human Rights." United Nations Human Rights: Office of the High Commissioner. https://www.ohchr.org/EN/Issues/Pages/WhatareHumanRights.aspx (accessed February 16, 2019).

41 Amnesty International Canada. "International Human rights Principles." https://www.amnesty.ca/our-work/issues/international-human-rights-principles?gclid=CjwKCAjwyqTqBRAyEiwA8K_4O4XhaYnjuC5MwOGBlxnJQ-2pxw2BbLsb2uCkjoehwXwpyrfhuD85kxoCqeMQAvD_BwE_ (accessed February 20, 2019).

42 United Nations. "What we do." https://peacekeeping.un.org/en/what-we-do (accessed October 22, 2019).

43 The HR Council. http://techreport.ngo/previous/2017/facts-and-stats-about-ngos-worldwide.html (accessed September 4, 2017).

44 Ryan Lenora Brown. "From women's rights activist to Supreme Court chief: meet Meaza Ashenafi." Christian Science Monitor. https://www.csmonitor.com/World/Africa/2019/0520/targetText=Meaza%20Ashenafi,%20president%20of%20the%20Federal%20Supreme%20Court%20of%20Ethiopia. (accessed May 30, 2019).

45 Anne Kingston, "We are the dead." Maclean's. https://www.macleans.ca/news/canada/we-are-the-dead/ (accessed November 25, 2019).

Chapter 8: Embrace your community responsibility

46 António Guterres. "International Women's Day March 8." United Nations. http://www.un.org/en/events/womensday/ (accessed March 10, 2018).

47 Martin Luther King Jr. "Address on Courage" at Brown Chapel in Selma, Alabama. (March 8, 1965). https://www.youtube.com/watch?v=0On19DRA2fU (accessed March 10, 2018).

Endnotes and references

48 David Bornstein and Susan Davis, *Social Entrepreneurship: What Everyone Needs to know* (New York: Oxford University Press Inc., 2010) Kindle edition 752.

49 Cone Communications. "Millennial Employee Engagement Study." (Boston: Cone Communications, 2016), 1.

50 Neilson Research. "Press Room: Global consumers are willing to put their money where their heart is when it comes to goods and services from companies committed to social responsibility." The Nielsen Company (US) LLC. https://www.nielsen.com/us/en/press-releases/2014/global-consumers-are-willing-to-put-their-money-where-their-heart-is/ (accessed October 29, 2017).

Chapter 9: Explore your purpose

51 Aaron Hurst, *Purpose Economy: How Your Desire for Impact, Personal Growth and Community Is Changing the World* (Idaho: Elevate, 2014) Kindle Edition 149.

52 Hurst, *Purpose Economy: How Your Desire for Impact, Personal Growth and Community Is Changing the World*, Kindle Edition 237.

Chapter 10: Discover your purpose

53 Samuel Muraguri "Mission & Goals" Pipes International. https://www.pipesinternational.org/mission-and-values.html (accessed March 22, 2017).

54 Kathleen Elkins. "Nearly a third of the world's billionaires didn't graduate college." CNBC Make It. https://www.cnbc.com/2016/08/11/nearly-a-third-of-the-worlds-billionaires-didnt-graduate-college.html (accessed April 10, 2019).

Chapter 12: Enhance your essence

55 Leah Eichler. "Yes, Stress Can be Good." The Globe and Mail. https://www.theglobeandmail.com/report-on-business/careers/career-advice/life-at-work/yes-stress-can-be-good/article18044876/ (accessed May 12, 2018).

Chapter 14: Volunteerism, the good, the bad, and the opportunity

56 Hurst, Purpose Economy. How Your Desire for Impact, Personal Growth and Community Is Changing the World. Kindle Edition 218.

Chapter 15: Move from messenger to the mission

57 Wikipedia. "Social Movement." https://en.wikipedia.org/wiki/Social_movement (accessed November 20, 2018) and Shannon Deric. *Political sociology: oppression, resistance, and the state*. (Pine Forge Press, (2011-01-01), 150.

58 Erica Chenowet. "The success of nonviolent civil resistance: Erica Chenowet at TEDxBoulder." YouTube. https://www.youtube.com/watch?v=YJSehRlU34w Erica Chenoweth TEDxBoulder (accessed August 25, 2019).

59 Women Deliver and The Population Council. "Having a Child Before Becoming an Adult: Exploring the Economic Impact in a Multi-Country Analysis."(New York: Women Deliver, 2019.), 5.

60 American Charities. "Snapshot 2015: The New Corporate DNA: Where Employee Engagement and Social Impact Converge." (Virginia: American Charities, 2015).

61 Impact2030. "Activate employees for the Global Goals." https://www.impact2030.com/viewpage?id=activate_vms (accessed Oct 19, 2019).

Endnotes and references

62 Neilson Research. "Press Room: Global consumers are willing to put their money where their heart is when it comes to goods and services from companies committed to social responsibility." https://www.nielsen.com/us/en/press-releases/2014/global-consumers-are-willing-to-put-their-money-where-their-heart-is/ (accessed April 22, 2019).

63 Bell Canada. "Bell Let's Talk Day is January 30: National awareness campaign begins with Canadians from around the country sharing their stories about mental illness." Bell Let's Talk. https://letstalk.bell.ca/en/news/1176/bell-lets-talk-day-is-january-30-national-awareness-campaign-begins-with-canadians-from-around-the-country-sharing-their-stories-about-mental-illness (accessed April 22, 2019).

64 Bell Canada. "Growing the global conversation and supporting Canada's mental health." Bell Let's Talk. https://letstalk.bell.ca/en/results-impact/ (accessed April 22, 2019).

65 YouMeWe Social Impact Group. "Your contribution Counts." https://YouMeWe.ca/your-contribution-counts/ (accessed October 29, 2019).

Chapter 16: Generate a ripple effect

66 Quotes.net, STANDS4 LLC, 2019. *"The Power of One Quotes."* https://www.quotes.net/mquote/1111505 (accessed September 21, 2019).

67 Computer Aid. "About Us: Mission and Story." https://www.computeraid.org/about-us/mission-and-story (accessed March 3, 2019).

68 Global Health Policy. "The Global HIV/AIDS Epidemic." KFF. https://www.kff.org/global-health-policy/fact-sheet/the-global-hivaids-epidemic/ (accessed Sept 12, 2019).

Chapter 17: Make your conscious-contributions™ sustainable

69 SWIFT Swaziland Fair Trade. "About SWIFT." http://www.swazifairtrade.org/about-swift/ (accessed January 3, 2019).

70 Home of Fair Trade Enterprises. "10 Principles of Fair Trade." World Fair Trade Organization. https://wfto.com/fair-trade/10-principles-fair-trade (accessed January 3, 2019).

71 SWIFT Swaziland Fair Trade. "Key Facts and Figures." http://www.swazifairtrade.org/key-facts-figures/ (accessed January 3, 2019).

72 North East Chilli Producers Association. http://www.necpaug.org. (accessed October 3, 2016).

73 KhoKho. https://khokhocollection.com (accessed October 10, 2017).

74 SheEO. "What is SheEO?" https://sheeo.world/about-us/ (accessed April 11, 2019).

Chapter 19: Develop symbiotic partnerships

75 WEConnect International. "About Us." https://weconnectinternational.org/en/about-us/who-we-are (accessed July 10, 2019).

76 American Charities. "Snapshot 2015: The New Corporate DNA: Where Employee Engagement and Social Impact Converge." 18.

77 David LePage. "A Guide to Social Procurement." (Buy Social Canada CCC Ltd., 2018), 15.

Endnotes and references

78 David LePage. "A Guide to Social Procurement." 15.

79 John Mackay and Raj Sisodia, *Conscious Capitalism: Liberating the Heroic Spirit of Business* (Boston: Harvard Business Review Press) Kindle edition 1900. Mohanbir Sawhney, presentation at "Does Marketing Need Reform?" conference, Bentley University, Boston, 2004).

80 David Gouthro, Meeting Facilitator, Keynote Speaker, Event Emcee. Vancouver, BC. https://www.davidgouthro.com/

Chapter 20: Cultivate your capacity to influence support

81 CARMMA/African Union. "Countries Scorecards." Campaign on Accelerated Reduction of Maternal, Newborn and Child Mortality in Africa. http://carmma.org/scorecards (accessed August 6, 2019).

82 Chuck English and Mo Lidsky, *The philanthropic mind: Surprising Discoveries from Canada's Top philanthropists* (Indianapolis: Dog Ear Publishing, 2015), 115.

Chapter 21: Commit through communications

83 Beacon of Hope. "About Us." http://www.beaconafrica.org/about-us (accessed Oct 29, 2019).

84 Ralph Waldo Emerson. "Thoughts on the Business of Life." Forbes Quotes. https://www.forbes.com/quotes/7810/ (accessed Sept 30, 2019).

85 Grace Dobush. "How Mobile Phones Are Changing the Developing World" (July 27, 2015) Consumer Technology Association. https://www.cta.tech/News/Blog/Articles/2015/July/How-Mobile-Phones-Are-Changing-the-Developing-Worl.aspx (accessed August 10, 2019).

Chapter 22: Create a conscious culture

86 Lou Solomon CEO of Interact. "The Top Complaints from Employees (June 24, 2015)." Harvard Business Review. https://hbr.org/2015/06/the-top-complaints-from-employees-about-their-leaders (accessed December 15, 2018)

Chapter 23: All we need is love

87 Richard Freemantle, email. June 29, 2016.

Terms

88 Government of Canada. "Glossary: Employment size category" https://www.ic.gc.ca/eic/site/cis-sic.nsf/eng/h_00005.html#employment_size_category (accessed April 15, 2019).

89 Government of Canada. "What is the difference between a registered charity and a non-profit organization?" https://www.canada.ca/en/revenue-agency/services/charities-giving/giving-charity-information-donors/about-registered-charities/what-difference-between-a-registered-charity-a-non-profit-organization.html (accessed January 6, 2019).

90 Government of Canada. https://www.canada.ca/en/revenue-agency/services/charities-giving/giving-charity-information-donors/about-registered-charities/what-difference-between-a-registered-charity-a-non-profit-organization.html (accessed January 6, 2019).

91 Definition of NGO. "NGO Special Interest Area." http://www.ngo.org/ngoinfo/define.html (accessed January 5, 2019).

92 Courtney Ackerman. "What is Self-transcendence?" PositivePsychology.com. https://positivepsychologyprogram.com/self-transcendence/ (accessed March 10, 2019)

Index

A

Abera, Sara. *See* Social entrepreneurs
Acham, Hellen. *See* Social entrepreneurs
Activists
   Aphane, Doo *81, 82, 109, 130, 131, 148, 152, 196, 252, 266, 283*
   Ashenafi, Meaza *68, 80, 112, 128, 141, 151, 190, 283, 299*
   Gandhi, Ela *33, 90, 258, 277, 283*
   Nigussie, Yetnebersh *4, 110, 129, 137, 262, 267, 283*
Africa International University *i, ii, 28, 34, 40, 46, 48, 70, 74, 106, 145, 195, 285, 295, 297*
African culture *25, 62*
   Chief *82*
   Healer *62*
African Growth and Opportunity Act *159, 224*
Aphane, Doo. *See* Activists
Appreciation *44, 124, 168, 207, 254, 266*
   Recognition *267*
   Reward *267*
Ashenafi, Meaza. *See* Activists
Asiko, Christine. *See* Educators
Associations *159, 165, 204, 205, 207, 290, 295*
   Canadian Association of Professional Speakers *287*
   Professional Speakers Association of Southern Africa *285*
   Women's
     Federation of Women Entrepreneur Association *21, 106*
     FEMCOM *11, 49*
     Kenya Association of Women Business Owners *21*
     Uganda Women Entrepreneurs Association *22*

B

Bariho, Rusia Orikiriza. *See* Social entrepreneurs
Belete, Hilina. *See* Social entrepreneurs
Beyene, Samrawit Moges. *See* Entrepreneurs

Business leaders
   Chacha, Margareth *89, 224, 235, 250, 262, 283*
   Greyling, Tisha *60, 119, 220, 283*
   Haile, Nigest *42, 88, 128, 140, 156, 220, 223, 224, 268, 283*
   Makamba, Mwamvita *18, 264, 283*
   Mkhwanazi, Xolile *49, 283*
   Mutoro, Antonia *140, 183, 283*
   Nkosi, Fikile *41, 42, 125, 283*
   Odwesso, Norah *111, 180, 264, 283*
   Riria, Jennifer *24, 50, 151, 199, 207, 209, 210, 260, 283*
   Trembath, Jane *52, 112, 183, 284*

C

Canada *10, 64, 65, 91, 95, 96, 162, 228*
Care *110, 187, 279, 280*
   Care about *67, 68, 94, 96, 97, 102, 114, 115, 171, 177, 196, 201, 237, 260, 267, 281*
   Self care *116*
   Take care of *25, 35, 52, 111, 145, 146, 153, 188, 232, 233*
CARMMA *237*
Chacha, Margareth. *See* Business leaders
Chekrouni, Nouzha. *See* Civil servants
Chideya, Florence Zano. *See* Civil servants
Child pregnancy *17, 71, 73*
Children *35, 232, 233, 245, 295*
   Boys *32, 50, 51, 145, 150*
   Girls *16, 17, 18, 19, 38, 40, 41, 50, 51, 52, 53, 63, 65, 71, 73, 77, 91, 111, 117, 145, 149, 150, 296*
   Orphans *159*
Circumcision *31*
Civil servants
   Chekrouni, Nouzha *57, 63, 92, 148, 155, 186, 191, 209, 216, 243, 283*
   Chideya, Florence Zano *132*
   Gawanas, Bience *25, 41, 70, 79, 150, 237, 283*
   Ichoya, Katherine *2, 11, 15, 48, 150, 262, 283*

Index

Collaboration *vii*, 17, 24, 94, 115, 211, 229, 281
   Client collaborator 213
   Colleague collaboration 226
   Community collaboration 225
   Company collaboration 222
   Competition mentor 211
   Competitors collaborator 213
   Employee-aligned collaboration 216
   Government collaboration 71, 224
   Leaders collaborate 11, 63, 219, 220
   Mission-aligned collaboration 216
   Not-for-profit collaboration 221
   Social collateral 11
   Supplier collaboration 228
   Symbiotic partnerships 173, 174
   Tribal collaboration 190
Communications 57, 71, 160, 163, 165, 220, 227, 239, 244, 255, 260, 262, 274
   Amplify message 255
   Using stories 252
   Vision 250
Compassion-connection 110, 160, 171, 196, 227
Conscious-contribution circle *vii*, 219, 220, 227, 289
Conscious culture 259, 260, 264, 265, 279
Contribution continuum 169, 172, 289
Corporate social responsibility 12, 75, 172, 227, 230
Courage *iv*, *vii*, 17, 25, 89, 115, 116, 124, 140, 187, 196, 258, 280, 281, 286, 289
Criticism 116, 125
   Constructive criticism 265

D

Democratic Republic of the Congo *ii*, 106, 221
Dick, Angela. *See* Entrepreneurs
Dignity 19, 23, 24, 27, 79, 80, 82, 171, 173, 190, 267
Donations 5, 17, 47, 65, 66, 95, 170, 172, 197, 198, 201, 238
Dr. Martin Luther King Jr. 92, 96, 265

E

Education *ii*, 12, 52, 100, 108, 150, 184, 190, 235, 277, 289
   Children's education 30, 35, 50, 51, 59, 73, 147
   Higher education *ii*, *vii*, 16, 17, 21, 35, 47, 48, 59, 64, 128, 138, 149, 175, 191, 195, 200, 231, 239, 265, 266, 274, 275, 288
Educators
   Asiko, Christine 102
   Ngini, Leah 34, 50, 145, 147, 149, 195, 260, 283, 285
Empowerment 25, 50, 65, 115, 141, 171, 194, 251, 287, 294
   Black Economic Empowerment 239
Entrepreneur *i*, *vi*, *vii*, 6, 7, 12, 19, 43, 48, 49, 88, 94, 103, 130, 135, 173, 176, 194, 195, 206, 209, 211, 212, 218, 220, 268, 287. *See* Associations
   Social entrepreneur 3, 12, 22
Entrepreneurs
   Beyene, Samrawit Moges 31, 265
   Dick, Angela 23, 32, 33, 143, 219, 254, 256, 258, 283
   Goven, Gita 43, 127, 136, 248, 249, 257, 283
   Iori, Mulumebet 212
   Kahara-Kawuki, Audrey 265
   Kamarade, Immy 164
   Mahiga, Modesta Lilian 35, 98, 139, 157, 222, 263, 283, 286
   Mbire, Tereza 6, 21, 191, 256, 259, 283, 285
   Mhlophe, Gcina 167, 177, 183, 283
   Muhwezi, Susan 159, 283
   Mukarubega, Zulfat 126, 138, 283, 285
   Muraya, Eva 21, 216, 217, 246, 254, 259, 283
   Mwangi, Joanne 21, 106, 122, 221, 262, 283, 286
   Ogallo, Gladys 269
   Owori, Sylvia 125
   Sambo, Sibongile 130, 198, 224, 283
   Tsehai, Maria Sarungi 128, 283
Equality 24, 25, 26, 33, 49, 50, 52, 63, 70, 79, 80, 81, 82, 91, 130, 152, 171, 190, 194, 206, 209, 216, 226, 237, 253, 266

Index

eSwatini 14, 29, 30, 41, 49, 51, 75, 81, 82, 109, 127, 130, 152, 180, 181, 188, 189, 193, 194, 213, 223, 228, 229, 253, 266, 271, 274, 285, 293, 295, 296
Ethiopia 4, 8, 25, 31, 32, 42, 62, 68, 81, 88, 89, 92, 112, 129, 141, 190, 191, 212, 220, 260, 262, 285, 293, 294, 295

F

Fair Trade 180, 193, 194, 228, 229, 261, 271, 275, 293, 301
  SWIFT 193, 194, 204, 275, 276, 293, 301
Faith 99, 101, 152, 154, 185
  Christian 58, 145, 240
  Jewish 275
  Muslim 64, 103, 148, 234
Famine 66
Feminine energy v, vi, ix, 17, 25, 27, 69, 84, 97, 121, 149, 169, 177, 210, 219, 257, 258, 269, 279, 297
Fistula 18, 19
Freemantle, Sheila. *See* Social entrepreneurs

G

Gabriel, Marsha. *See* Social entrepreneurs
Gandhi, Ela. *See* Activists
Gawanas, Bience. *See* Civil servants
Goven, Gita. *See* Entrepreneurs
Greyling, Tisha. *See* Business leaders
Guilt 9, 14, 50, 123, 131, 162

H

Haile, Nigest. *See* Business leaders
Health care 61, 101, 232, 273
Health care providers
  Mazibuko, Thandeka 61, 142, 151, 235, 283
Howard, Hanne. *See* Not-for-profit leaders
Human rights iv, 7, 17, 32, 36, 71, 79, 81, 84, 89, 91, 96, 130, 152, 171, 190, 290

I

Ichoya, Katherine. *See* Civil servants
Impact statement 203, 204, 208, 247
Inclusivity 115, 173, 177, 185, 284

Ingabire, Regina. *See* Not-for-profit leaders
Inner strengths 113, 114, 116, 160
  Strength thread 112, 117
Integrity ii, iii, 16, 17, 27, 33, 68, 69, 90, 148, 185, 186, 210, 217, 224, 258, 289
Iori, Mulumebet. *See* Entrepreneurs

K

Kahara-Kawuki, Audrey. *See* Entrepreneurs
Kamarade, Immy. *See* Entrepreneurs
Kasule, Rehmah. *See* Social entrepreneurs
Kenya i, ii, 2, 8, 11, 16, 21, 24, 29, 34, 38, 39, 46, 58, 66, 70, 71, 75, 100, 101, 102, 106, 108, 111, 115, 123, 125, 132, 145, 180, 193, 199, 209, 231, 240, 241, 246, 261, 284, 285, 293, 294, 295, 296, 298, 299
Kenyans 4 Kenya 66
Kindness 40

L

Leadership ii, vii, 16, 21, 27, 94, 117, 138, 190, 209
  Conscious leadership techniques vi, 42, 257, 269
  Horizontal leadership 187, 265
  Leadership development ii, 17, 20, 24, 48, 50, 71, 165, 206, 273
  Lead within an organization 234, 238, 239
  Mission leadership 187
  Women leadership 29, 80, 112, 121, 155, 189, 207, 214, 272
Lesotho 32, 114, 226, 254, 255, 295
Love 112, 116, 168, 177, 186, 203, 231, 258, 274, 276, 277, 279
Loyalty 22, 68, 148, 172, 174, 176, 186, 187, 198, 208, 257, 258
Luena, Olive. *See* Not-for-profit leaders

M

Mahatma Gandhi iv, 18, 33, 90, 210, 265, 294
Mahiga, Modesta Lilian. *See* Entrepreneurs

Index

Makamba, Mwamvita. *See* Business leaders
Malawi 2
Malnutrition 62
Mazibuko, Thandeka. *See* Health care providers
Mbire, Tereza. *See* Entrepreneurs
Meaning. *See* Part 2: maximize your meaning
Measure impact
  Key performance indicators 74, 78, 81, 289
  Measurement 6, 68, 85, 165, 203, 204, 210, 247, 279, 290, 291
  Metrics 74, 76, 77, 78, 84, 94, 257, 289, 290
  Social return on investment (SROI) 12, 75, 203, 239, 279, 291
Mental health 34, 78, 175, 279, 301
Mhlophe, Gcina. *See* Entrepreneurs
Microfinance 12, 195, 211, 212, 221, 295
  Microloans 11, 12, 235
Millennials 95, 158, 197, 249, 257, 267, 279
Millennium Development Goals (MDGs) 77
Mission 85, 147, 185, 250
Missionary i, 46, 115
Mkhwanazi, Xolile. *See* Business leaders
Models
  Conscious-contribution™ model 54
  Contribution continuum individual participation 169
  Contribution continuum organization participation 172
Morocco 57, 63, 92, 155, 186, 191, 209, 216
Mother Teresa 181, 265
Movements v, 14, 50, 77, 91, 93, 94, 101, 117, 141, 169, 186, 210, 255, 266, 279, 282, 287
Mozambique 56
Muhunyo, Gladys. *See* Not-for-profit leaders
Muhwezi, Susan. *See* Entrepreneurs
Mukarubega, Zulfat. *See* Entrepreneurs
Muraya, Eva. *See* Entrepreneurs
Muraya, Joyce. *See* Not-for-profit leaders
Muso, Lydia. *See* Not-for-profit leaders
Mutoro, Antonia. *See* Business leaders
Mwamvita Makamba,. *See* Business Leaders
Mwangi, Joanne. *See* Entrepreneurs

N

Namibia 79
Nelson Mandela 210
Networks 21, 56, 64, 65, 66, 68, 160, 161, 167, 193, 196, 207, 221, 255, 268, 275
Ngini, Leah. *See* Educators
Nigussie, Yetnebersh. *See* Activists
Nkosi, Fikile. *See* Business leaders
Nkubana, Janet. *See* Social entrepreneurs
Not-for-profit leaders
  Howard, Hanne 101, 102, 171, 283
  Ingabire, Regina 161
  Luena, Olive 214, 269, 283
  Muhunyo, Gladys 112, 184, 186, 193, 204, 283
  Muraya, Joyce 102, 261, 283
  Muso, Lydia 32, 113, 149, 254, 283
  Shaw, Lois i, 284
  Wathome, Jane 100, 108, 125, 151, 171, 216, 249, 284
  Zingoni, Lydia 296

O

Odwesso, Norah. *See* Business leaders
Ogallo, Gladys. *See* Entrepreneurs
Olive Kamya, Beti. *See* Politicians
Oscar Muriu 74, 216
Owori, Sylvia. *See* Entrepreneurs

P

Patriarchal society 149
Paul Kagame 77
Pay-it-forward 47, 48, 266
Peace vii, 13, 36, 37, 52, 72, 78, 80, 90, 190, 223, 261, 277, 293, 296
Persuasive presentations 28, 108, 117, 240
Philanthropy 74, 84
  Philanthropist vi, 74, 238, 239, 251, 287
Politicians
  Kamya, Beti Olive 90, 207
Poverty ii, vii, 6, 7, 11, 23, 29, 31, 32, 59, 71, 76, 77, 78, 175, 181, 184, 194, 211, 226, 288, 290
Purpose. *See* Part 2 maximize your meaning
Pushing the edge 144

Index

R

Resource
  Download from YouMeWe.ca *68, 160, 161, 164, 217*
Riria, Jennifer. *See* Business leaders
Rwanda *2, 13, 26, 37, 51, 106, 108, 140, 152, 161, 184, 294, 295*

S

Sambo, Sibongile. *See* Business leaders
Self-actualize *99, 142, 291*
Self-transcendence *135, 144, 168, 291*
Service club *65, 157, 162, 171, 173, 206*
  Lions Club *65*
  Rotary *157*
  Soroptimist *65*
Shaw, Lois. *See* Not-for-profits leaders
Small and mid-size enterprise *128, 221*
  Co-operative *190, 222*
  Small business *viii, 108, 172, 173, 205, 211, 212, 221, 235, 250, 287*
    Micro-enterprise *211, 290*
    Social enterprise *iv, vii, viii, 12, 13, 14, 20, 22, 30, 44, 59, 70, 72, 75, 95, 104, 117, 158, 171, 175, 176, 181, 182, 188, 190, 198, 204, 220, 228, 247, 268, 274, 276, 279, 291*
Social entrepreneurs
  Abera, Sara *260*
  Acham, Hellen *52, 82, 189, 191, 199, 222, 283*
  Bariho, Rusia Orikiriza *21, 56, 68, 283*
  Belete, Hilina *62*
  Freemantle, Sheila *14, 127, 189, 198, 228, 271, 272, 283*
  Gabriel, Marsha *59, 74, 129, 201, 233, 283*
  Kasule, Rehmah *103, 234, 283*
  Nkubana, Janet *13, 52, 152, 153, 223, 251, 252, 259, 283*
  Thorne, Philippa Reiss *30, 52, 76, 181, 194, 212, 213, 268, 283*
  Whitehead, Gia *19, 20, 48, 195, 200, 231, 239, 251, 266, 284*
Social procurement *228*
  Conscious-consumers *251*

South Africa *ii, 8, 10, 19, 23, 33, 43, 48, 52, 59, 60, 61, 72, 74, 90, 112, 119, 127, 129, 130, 132, 142, 143, 167, 182, 183, 200, 201, 202, 219, 220, 221, 224, 231, 239, 256, 274, 285, 293, 294, 295, 296, 297*
Survival of the fittest *209*
Sustainable Development Goals 2030 *ix, 78, 95, 173, 279, 299*
  The World's To-do List *84, 97, 176*
Switzerland *275*
Symbiotic partnerships *176, 187, 230*

T

Tanzania *8, 18, 19, 35, 36, 89, 90, 161, 214, 222, 223, 224, 235, 236, 246, 250, 264, 269, 293, 294, 295, 297*
Theory of transformation *204, 247, 291*
Thorne, Philippa Reiss. *See* Social entrepreneurs
Training *ii, iii, v, 23, 24, 28, 29, 31, 51, 71, 107, 108, 117, 189, 193, 211, 226, 234, 242, 273, 274*
Trembath, Jane. *See* Business leaders
Trust *12, 68, 69, 84, 123, 153, 163, 174, 187, 219, 220, 221, 227, 239, 257, 258*
Tsehai, Maria Sarungi. *See* Entrepreneurs

U

Ubuntu *8, 26, 274, 281*
Uganda *4, 5, 6, 13, 21, 22, 51, 56, 82, 83, 90, 103, 125, 126, 152, 159, 189, 190, 199, 200, 207, 256, 265, 293, 294, 295*
United Kingdom *29, 102, 185, 194, 275*
United Nations *viii, 17, 65, 77, 78, 79, 150, 264, 279*
United States *36, 48, 74, 161, 162*

V

Values *vi, 20, 26, 33, 50, 64, 66, 79, 83, 90, 92, 95, 97, 115, 141, 145, 150, 154, 162, 164, 170, 173, 174, 203, 216, 217, 220, 228, 234, 237, 250, 269, 277, 279, 280*
Vision. *See* Communication:Vision

Index

Volunteer *vi, viii,* 65, 66, 67, 83, 93, 100, 110, 166, 173, 202, 205, 227, 238, 240, 253, 257, 279, 287
  Professional-contributor 166, 253, 269, 290

W

Wathome, Jane. *See* Not-for-profit leaders
WEConnect International 223
Whitehead, Gia. *See* Social entrepreneurs
Women's rights 80, 91, 112, 130, 148, 150, 190, 191, 223, 253
WOW-Africa by Design adventures 38, 39, 40, 41, 58, 74, 231, 284

Y

YouMeWe Social Impact Group *v,* 284, 287
WisdomExchangeTv *iv, viii,* 3, 17, 29, 42, 46, 67, 70, 99, 111, 117, 119, 135, 153, 167, 168, 287
YouMeWe Foundation Fund *ii,* 17, 28, 44, 59, 64, 70, 71, 117, 195, 197, 287
YouMeWe Movement *v,* 14, 287

Z

Zimbabwe 132
Zingoni, Lydia. *See* Not-for-profit leaders